"The rooms at Pueblo Bonito where "wa[r] arrows are near other late habitation r[ooms] violently have been found in group bur[ials] dates to the 1100s. But the core of Chac[o] been irreparably shattered by the time t[o] to contain the violence and reduce cha[os]. North America had come undone, a vic[tim] of the drought of the 1090s. In a stunning but final building frenzy, the Chacoan elites then erected their grandest buildings in an effort to "pump up the economy." Apparently they failed to realize that without the small farmers to produce corn, they were already finished. That point was cruelly, forcefully, and finally driven home by a second drought beginning in 1130—the coup de grace.

"To me, the citadel of Bis sa'ani on the Great North Road says it all. That fortified house, atop its formidable shale ridge, was clearly built for defense. Erected during the 1130s, it contains the latest roof beam datable to the great-house elites in the Chaco heartland—A.D. 1139. It was the last gasp of the Chaco phenomenon, probably built to protect the northern approaches to the canyon when the second drought hit in 1130."

David Stuart, 'The Fall of Chacoan Society'
Anasazi America, 2000.

BLACK AND GREEN REVIEW
NO 4 | WINTER 2016

BLACK AND GREEN REVIEW NO 4
WINTER 2016

CONTENTS

1. Opening Editorial: Kevin Tucker

ESSAYS
8. Fear Factor: Sky Hiatt
14. Maps: Natasha Alvarez
15. Towards a Feral Future: Four Legged Human
53. Modernity Takes Over: John Zerzan
64. Society Without Strangers: Kevin Tucker

DISCUSSION
136. Response
139. Frequently Made Assertions: Kevin Tucker
145. Offshore Wind: Ian Smith
148. Means and Ends: Kevin Tucker
157. Meaning in the Age of Nihilism: John Zerzan
160. Without Adoration: Sine Cultus
164. Moralism: A Technological Problem?: Kevin Tucker

FIELD NOTES FROM THE PRIMAL WAR
168. True Crime Case Files: Shutting Down the Tar Sands Pipelines
172. Shutting Down the Dakota Access Pipeline
174. Stemming the Tide: Cliff Hayes
188. Ecology of a Bubble: Kevin Tucker
205. The Hidden Ones: from *Ishi in Two Worlds*

REVIEWS
208. *Becoming Nature* review
210. Two European Thinkers to the Rescue: John Zerzan
212. *Children of the New World* review

Printed in Canada on recycled paper.

OPENING EDITORIAL
KEVIN TUCKER

Unrelenting heat.

That feels like the summation of the world right now: like being in a boiling cauldron and the temperature just keeps escalating.

I'm talking about the climate. I'm talking about society. I'm talking about politics. I'm talking about the economy. I'm talking about ecology. Every facet of the world we face feels like it is on fire. This is literally the case as record-setting wildfires overtake chunks of the map and as constant bombing campaigns continue to devastate others. 2015 was the hottest year on record and 2016 is on track to surpass it.

This is the future unfolding before us: the consequences of industrialized growth and technologized expansion extrapolating the caustic downfall of a globalized civilization. And that is the overwhelming feeling you get every day when you wake up and open your computer or turn on your devices, opening yourself to the flood of seething anger and impotence.

But we do it.

We carry on. We get lost in the sea of reactionary reiterations. We fall into the crushing waves of the mutual assured destruction of our own empathy. We are willing to accept the destruction so long as we are right.

Why? How are we able to do this?

How do we simultaneously bask in the endless cycles of perpetual call-and-response of social media and ignore the world as it becomes only further engulfed in catastrophic and systemic destruction?

We do this because we shut off. The atrocities of civilization are simply too much for our regionally based hunter-gatherer minds to comprehend. This is existence with implications that we were never psychologically prepared for because neither we nor any other being is physically capable of causing them. Not without technology.

This is beyond our realm as empathetic beings, so we stop our minds from going there. This is our mind in survival mode: solely able to address the immediate fight-or-flight impulse, redirected through technological intrusion. We double down. We embody the ethos of accepting reality as it is and fragmenting our experience of life into individual issues. We plant ourselves and we defend that position until the next thing comes along.

We define ourselves by our own acts of active defeatism. We immerse ourselves in the immediacy of technology so we no longer have to keep the totality in our minds. We are just reacting.

Meanwhile, the predictions for the earth are dire. The potential for human extinction looms heavily underneath a perpetual loss of ecosystems and species. The thresholds once considered tipping points for endemic climate shifts are being surpassed.

If we start to unplug, we can see it, but it is no less overwhelming. The *New York Times* recently released a site that charts the high and low temperatures of 2015 by city against what has been considered the baseline temperatures for each place based on 160-year-old data.[1] It has to be seen to be believed, but, as with nearly every climate change scenario, the worst-case scenario predictions for 2100 are being passed already. Places like Fort Chipeyan in Canada have already had an average temperature increase of 5.8° Celsius.

Methane sinkholes become the new norm. Exaggerated cycles of drought and flooding become the new norm. Increased temperatures have resulted in concentrations of nitrates, hydrogen cyanide, and mycotoxins in cash crops.[2] And have resulted in the thawing of long frozen reindeer carcasses in Russia unleashing anthrax.[3]

Social and political tension is impossible to ignore.

We see in Donald Trump social media personified: exaggerated blasts of reactionary conspiracy, the billionaire acting as the underdog. We see the ignition of the xenophobic and racist underpinnings of civilization come back to the forefront. We see in Hillary Clinton the smiling voracious face of Neoliberal surgical strikes and expansive systemic subjugation sold as policy reform. We see a fanning of flames on liberal blindness to the iron fist of a society built upon violent subjugation of Others. We see people buying into the mythos of democracy: of the notion that any State is sustainable.

We see the blow back as the climate refugees of one nation are corralled in camps, forced back by nations under their own economic and political duress. We see the need for scapegoats and watch as the Westernized identity of the Sacred Individual feels attacked and becomes militarized: as the frustrated and afraid are given access to hyper-technological weaponry and psychological justifications to kill en masse.

Salvation, martyrdom, the elated subjects of a hero's return, capturing headlines: the suicide bomber, the religious zealot, the soldier, and the mass murderer all share in the flaccid rage of living in a boiling world and feeling as though the promises of civilization have let them down. We are all boiling. And given direction, we will seek revenge on whoever is possible. Be it the ex-military cop gunning down unarmed black people in the streets or the suicide bomber seeking vilification beyond this world by killing as many within it as possible.

When we open ourselves to the depth of this reality, it becomes impossible. It is beyond comprehension, beyond our threshold for pain and empathy. It is easy to opt back in: to get lost on social media, to bury ourselves in our Self.

It is easy to become lost in distraction.

As sad as that option is, it makes sense. Against the reality that we surely face, any bit of hope stands against the most uphill battle imaginable.

The problem we face is that distraction remains an option.

We have no choice here. The reality that is unfolding before us is real. It is our home, this earth, being destroyed. It is those that we love, those we hate, those we wish we could not love being lost in an unrepentant mirage of distraction. It is our own fate intertwined with the fate of all life on this planet.

We started *Black and Green Review* not because it would be the catalyst to save the world, but because we need to start somewhere. We need to stake our ground and attack from that position. It isn't enough to continually react and respond while staying prepped for the next round of continual arguments on the same subjects forever through every cycle of the News Feed.

As John Zerzan stated in the Opening Editorial of *BAGR 3*, we wanted to carry on the debates and discussions that *Green Anarchy*, *Green Anarchist*, and *Species Traitor* had taken part in. Those were discussions that spilled far beyond the microcosm of anarchist debate and circles. They had grown and found their way to filter into society at large.

And in their absence, that trajectory atrophied. Through sites like Anarchist News, it became insular. The cheerleaders for insurrection-for-insurrection's sake faded as the attention shifted towards the comfort afforded the critics. Anarchism has never been absent of the philosophical hollowness of eternal dissection of lingo, nor strayed far from the politics of negation. But these are the aspects that the internet and social media amplified.

And they grew.

This trajectory has led anarchists into the cul-de-sac of nihilistic terrorism and egoist soul searching. In that trajectory, anarcho-primitivism is a lightning rod for having the audacity to stand for something: to have staked our claim on seeing a world that is worth fighting for and defending. To want to build communities of resistance, support those that are and have been resisting civilization's advances and to refuse the domestication process as it seeks to tear us from the wildness that runs through all life.

We began *BAGR* in part to expand and challenge those discussions alongside others. There is merit among them, but the problem is that there is no end point, nothing worth acting upon. The politics of negation are discussion for the sake of discussion. They are about carving out the perfect anti-ideological ideology. To set out the perfect anti-moralistic moralism and to carry out the pure will of the Individual.

Dedicated to finding and chasing out the boogey-men of impure thought, there are only two options: to celebrate in discussion as praxis, as stated by one of its advocates, "to laugh at the futility of it all", or to embrace the absurdity of unthinking acts of terror under the guise of "eco-extremism" while leaning further and further towards eco-fascism.

If we are to accept that there is no hope, that there isn't even a sliver of chance that we can divert or lessen the catastrophic conclusion of civilization's collapse, then we have nothing to offer but another noun to justify our particular brand of online voraciousness.

I have no time for those discussions.

I have two daughters. I have two daughters that I will, above all else, do anything to protect and to provide for. I have two daughters whose fates are intertwined with the fate of all wildness. I have two daughters who have no future on a dead planet.

I have no false assumptions or heroic ambition to save the world, but if I'm not even fucking trying to do anything about all of this, then what am I worth? What am I worth to the world to just waste away finding new ways to demonize the grounds that I am standing upon, the grounds I have placed my stake in: the grounds that I will always fight for?

All of the editors and contributors of this project have poured themselves into this. And we have gotten untold support from others who resonate with our simple call to action: for a wild resistance, for a passionate resistance.

We are not, nor have we ever been, satisfied with vilifying ourselves for a spot within anarchist history. We are driven by a hatred of civilization. Driven by a vile contempt for the consequences of domestication. We are motivated by the nomadic hunter-gatherer within our bodies and minds that yearns to embrace the wildness.

We see that within generations of communities, that there is hope. That there is that sliver of chance that this world will not be destroyed and that life may continue on. We take solace in the world our grandchildren's grandchildren may one day inhabit where our lives and our struggles are forgotten memories.

This resistance, like wildness, exists far beyond us. We aren't leading the call: we have just seen the cracks and have sought to continue pursuing them.

It would be easy to look at what we have done and to remain cynical: to continue the negation of critics and to wonder what any exploration based in ecology, anthropology, history or questions of technology could possibly have upon the world civilization has created. In the end, it may not matter at all.

But that is where we split.

We want discussion, but if it serves no end, then it serves nothing. With civilization, we have had everything taken from us. We are left with reflections and mirrors of its history. We are left with the scars of our elder's own subjugation to the false future of empire building. We are left with their emptiness.

But these are tools. They are a part of piecing together and deepening our understanding of how domestication begins, how it functions which, paired with building relationships beyond reification and beyond abstraction, we find the cracks. We find the pressure points, the bottlenecks.

It is through this search that we find what has been taken from us and we take it back.

Without question.

Without hesitation.

For us, there is no other option. There is no appeal to endless discussions that have long ago dismissed the idea of purpose. There is nothing to be gained from that.

This discussion speaks to the soul of every domesticated being. And that is whom we are speaking to. We know our enemy. We have found its weaknesses and we will continue to search for more vulnerabilities.

We aren't interested in distractions and cycles: for discussions without end.

We seek to do everything within our power to further push civilization beyond the brink. We seek to protect and fight for the world that we love.

And we remain absolutely unapologetic to that end.

We are in one of the most unique moments in history: to be at the end of this dying civilization. We face a world of uncertainty and we have the knowledge of how our ancestors had adapted for that. When distraction no longer remains an option, will you look back and wonder why you didn't do everything in your power to make the most of it?

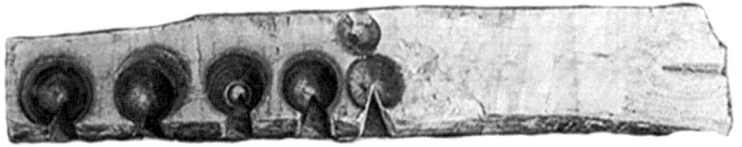

It's time to start our own fires.

Endnotes

1 http://www.nytimes.com/interactive/2016/02/19/us/2015-year-in-weather-temperature-precipitation.html
2 http://www.csmonitor.com/Science/2016/0602/Climate-change-could-trigger-toxic-corn-what-can-be-done
3 http://www.cnn.com/2016/07/28/health/anthrax-thawed-reindeer-siberia/

Black and Green Review is a bi-annual journal of anarcho-primitivist critique, discussion and praxis, published by Black and Green Press. Editors: Kevin Tucker, Four Legged Human, Cliff Hayes, John Zerzan, Yank, Lilia, and Evan Cestari.

For information on current deadlines, please check out website: blackandgreenreview.org.

All submissions, letters, and responses can be sent to the addresses below. More information on submission guidelines, subscription info and distribution are on the website.

Black and Green Review
PO Box 402
Salem, MO 65560
blackandgreenreview@gmail.com
blackandgreenreview.org

ESSAYS

Speckled Kingsnake. Photo by Yank.

Fear Factor

Sky Hiatt

Green snake. Photo by Yank.

The advanced civilization of the present is marketed as a stronghold of fortified security where citizens can confidently live out their lives free from the dangers posed by uncivilized life. Life spans advance, health improves, and we are protected from the threat of wildlife attacks, attacks from nation states or terrorist invasions. Considering this popular narrative on its own terms, it would seem that those fortunate enough to be living in such societies would be typified by fearlessness and living fearless lives. But, ironically, though securities have advanced and proliferated, our fears have not receded. To the contrary, they have evolved in step and thus are ever-escalating. So far at least, our fears are always one step ahead of our security technologies.

When European settlers landed in North America facing a primal paradise unknown even in their fantasies, reaction was mixed. Some, perhaps only a few, embraced it. Many, if not most, feared the untamed, wild world and set forth to alter and destroy it. According to Brooks Atkinson in *This Bright Land,* many pilgrims despised the "hideous wilderness full of wild beasts and wild men."[1] At least one settler committed suicide rather than face life in the howling wasteland of the New World.

These were the vast primordial forests of the lost continent into which light could barely penetrate nor men pass through. Europe had already reconfigured most of its prehistoric woodlands into rolling farmlands, shrub-bound homes, lawns and formal gardens. From this subdued world the conquerors, entrepreneurs, freed-serfs, and adventurers set sail for a place where Nature reigned unrestrained. The newcomers, oppressed subjects of the Old World social order, were a fear-based people who often struck an antagonist approach to the New World. Fear was their untiring, constant companion. The settlers were un-wild and perhaps over-civilized, so it was difficult for them to see themselves as the future would see them—intolerant, misled, sickly, cruel, uprooted. To calm their fears, they pushed back the forest, cleared the land, killed the animals, exiled surviving tribes, and they prevailed. But this did little to assuage their fears. And hundreds of years later, that day is yet to come.

The uprooted, surging Old World masses, dislodged from inherited knowledge and fleeing the industrialized hubs of Europe, were at a historic disadvantage and poorly prepared to accept advanced philosophies of the native people to whom nature was a consoling confidant. Only a few took advantage of these ideas and the chance to be wild themselves. The rest picked up their saws and axes and bit into the empires of white pine, chestnut, red cedar, and other trees of the Eastern forests. They felt more secure in their solid log cabins with muskets by the door. But they would live and die in fear in that strange, unfamiliar New World, unaware the muskets fed the fear and helped set up an ill-fated model for the future.

Transplanted to the present day, the pilgrims might be astonished at how their tentative venture has prevailed and they might well yearn to live among us. But if they got that chance, they would soon notice, with the objectivity of time travelers, that we had suffered a series of unfortunate setbacks. The early hopes and ambitions carried unsuspected consequences. Surviving descendants still feared the forest, what was left of it. In the cities, some even feared the individual trees. They still feared the wolves, bears and bobcats, rarely seen but still terrifying. By now they'd come to fear almost anything wild: foxes, coyotes, opossums. Bats, spiders. Even bees.

And new fears evolved. The weather—wind, cold and rain, became increasingly difficult to tolerate. The Sun had become a hazard. There were increasing concerns about the purity of food, air and water. There was a growing distrust of other people. Community, family and extended families all depreciated. Tribes lingered as a faint mystic memory. Doors were locked, mace tucked into pockets. With wealth came fear of poverty, fear of the poor, fear of crime. In some areas, the modern vocabularies had trouble keeping pace. Neighborhoods were fortified by suburban version of the Great Wall—gated and patrolled communities. Such a monumental stronghold civilization had become, the size of it was also worrisome.

And so, in the cycle of cyclic times, the word *fear* became systematically outdated and the nomenclature advanced accordingly. The modern pilgrims suffered from clinical fears. Generalized anxiety. Chronic stress. Panic attacks. Post-traumatic stress disorder. Imaginary fears—hypochondria, paranoia. And phobias—lists too long to memorize. Fear of open spaces, fear of closed spaces, fear of heights, fear of the dark. Hydrophobia—fear of water. Phobophobia— the fear of fear itself. Obsessive compulsive disorder, personality disorder, multiple personality disorder. At a certain point, even the cracks in the sidewalk can get you down. By the twenty-first century, civilization and advanced technology, working together, had transformed fear into pathology. Against such fears as these the muskets didn't help much.

Self-help came to monopolize whole sections in the bookstore. *Stress Management. From Panic to Power. Plato Not Prozac. The Anxiety Disease. Panic Attacks. Don't Panic. 10 Simple Solutions to Panic. The Anxiety Answer Book. Anxieties, Phobias and Panic. Coping with Social Anxiety. Overcoming Anxiety. Feel the Fear and Beyond. Feel the Fear and do it Anyway.* And so many more.

To keep up with the neuroses, entire professions were carved out of the social bedrock to treat the teeming plague of fears. Fear therapy offered hope in coping with crippling real-life symptoms. Toward this end, pharmaceutical industries stepped up as a natural godsend manufacturing mood stabilizers, anti-depressants and anti-psychotics and soon became the most profitable industries of their time.

Microscopes revealed a universe of germs we never knew were there. Bacteria, virus, protozoa—extreme germs with unsettling resistant capacities. And the armaments intensified. Antibiotics, vaccines, hand sanitizers, placebos of medical nothingness. But, in the inevitable undertow of seething industrial antagonisms, the germs the scientists discovered, others yearned to weaponize. First there was fear, then terror, then terrorism, then bio-terrorism—a toxic epiphany of interdisciplinary cooperation synchronized by history. As innovation advanced, out-pacing human cunning, progress became the vehicle of perpetual promise that never quite materialized.

We built the walls, made the weapons, manufactured the drugs, designed the surveillance cameras, home-security systems, smoke alarms, house alarms, car alarms, bullet-proof glass, gated communities, peep-holes, missile systems, cudgels, nerve gas, razor wire. We refined basic tools into the tools of agriculture, refined the tools of agriculture into weapons, refined the weapons into an arsenal, refined the arsenal into a military industrial complex to appease the conquering mind. The result? Even thermonuclear warheads, the special weapon, were tainted with the promise of radioactive contamination that could make the planet unfit to live on.

An unlivable planet was just another uneasy compromise for the security-seeking mind. The bomb brought with it gamma rays, long-lived isotopes and radioactive-waste, assembled from a teeming sea of equations invented to stabilize our sanctuary and yet our worries easily outpaced them. In the end, the mushroom cloud was just another hollow victory eating away at the DNA.

Hunting blind. Photo by Yank.

These were the high-tech fears that neither Australopithecus nor Neanderthal ever knew of. Had there always been this nascent temptation in technology to disgrace us?

By the Twenty-first Century, as academia filled the pages of textbooks with secrets of heavy water and plutonium, we were born again, the ultimate suicide bombers: masters of potential self-immolation , self-termination. Lewis Mumford observed that we had given technology the authority to destroy us.[2]

Sheltered in our luxury fortresses, we've sharpened our enhanced perception of risk, and erected an advanced warning, global positioning radar of risk assessment. Yet, the wider the moats, the higher the walls, the more our security seems jeopardized. Where is the absolute equation of refuge? Is it asking too much to be invincibly protected in the error-prone wasteland of the melting pot? When carbon nano-fibers confirm the singularity and molecular machines become self-healing and self-replicating, what then? Acute fear? Totalitarian fear? Are we on a quest to distill fear into its deadliest form?

Outfitted with our accentuated perceptions of fear, we have navigated toward an aversion to discomfort of any kind. In an increasingly eccentric, sterile, but clearly still hazardous world, catering to the overly protected, overly troubled population inching their way toward a bondage to comfort, a mandatory aversion to being cold, hot, wet, thirsty, hungry or bored. By now, as our instincts and hardiness continue to fail us, we drift off course from original species strengths, practical achievements and intimate associated, primal joys.

The wild boy of Aveyron 'rescued' from the forest of France around the age of twelve in 1799, could sit exposed for hours in the cold rain. He could lift hot coals from the fire with his bare hands. On the inside, he spent his days by the window looking longingly at the moon and the forest.[3] He was wild. He wanted out. But his kindly captors trained him to crave comforts and he lost his feral vigor. We're a lot like him, implausibly altered versions of our former savage selves, domesticated into ghosts and apparitions.

As the present tightens its grip on urgency, we pass our days within a system of nesting shells, layers of security, walls within walls, each one more costly, forbidding and impregnable than the one before. But what happens when pressures from all other species, and the demands of the Earth's extremes, are removed? Diamonds fail to crystallize. Coal does not solidify. Species die out or unwind back into plasmids. Muscles atrophy. Inertia takes over. For us, species essence and genetic promise have corroded into a dependent lethargy. Crippled by machines and dependent on them, fluent in the jargon of compliance, how can we ever again comprehend our lost potential? How could a courageous, healthy future ever materialize among us?

Rachel Carson once wrote of "the irony of our accomplishments." Did she mean that living is a risk technology can never wholly minimize? Or, is there another New World out there waiting for us beyond this one? Is there a permanent demilitarized no-fire zone, a green zone, an archdiocese of absolute impregnable asylum? Or is it the human *race*, but with another meaning?

It's called the "revenge effect"—unanticipated negative

consequences of new technologies. Infinite fallibilities. Legacy defects. So much risk that the messages sent out in Voyager must have fallen out of date by now. Perhaps the gold, anodized disc should have suggested a declaration of technological wariness. By the time it reaches anyone we will have begun to suspect we're not immortal. Those that find it may already suffer from the blindness that afflicts us.

From vacuum tubes to solid state and digital dementia, we memorize the electronic hierarchies, sit back and wait for them to happen. From hostile take-over to hostile nations, to failed-state syndrome, we've seeded distressed signals of endangerment into the airspace of our exceptionally moribund version of paradise.

So much has happened since the pilgrims faced off with the forests and the wild men. Not even the prophets among them could have predicted it. The tentative pioneers thought the howling wilderness was dangerous. Now their fear has grown and endangers everything. Nature was subdued, the price alarmingly high. It's sad to win and realize you have won nothing. We've become the fragile cyberian wanderers who submitted to fear and built a world dependent on it. Daily life has become a kind of war we never counted on. The newest fear? That the wounds of our discontent now run too deep to ever heal.

Some say technology is innocent—it is the human mind that sins. But that's just linguistic mockery of real events. From the day that the first sword was raised, the sword has punished us. We've become the master criminals, but childlike, and incapacitated. Technology has generated an implausibly plundered planet, lifted us from the primordial past, tempted and tormented us. Ancient aptitudes have been bred out. Silhouettes of grandeur lie emulsified in doubt. Technology has created non-remedial, chronic fear where only natural fear existed before it. As Chilean social critic, Ariel Dorfman wrote in *The Empire's Old Clothes*, there's been "destruction of inner fears....survival of nightmares."[4]

Endnotes
1 Atkinson, Brooks. *This Bright Land*. Doubleday Natural History Press. 1972.
2 Mumford, Louis. *The Myth of the Machine: Pentagon of Power*. A Harvest/HBJ Book. 1970.
3 Lane, Harlan L. *The Wild Boy of Aveyron*. Harvard University Press. 1996.
4 Dorfman Ariel. *The Empire's Old Clothes: What the Lone Ranger, Babar, and other Innocent Heroes Do To Our Minds*. Duke University Press. 2010. Pg 180.

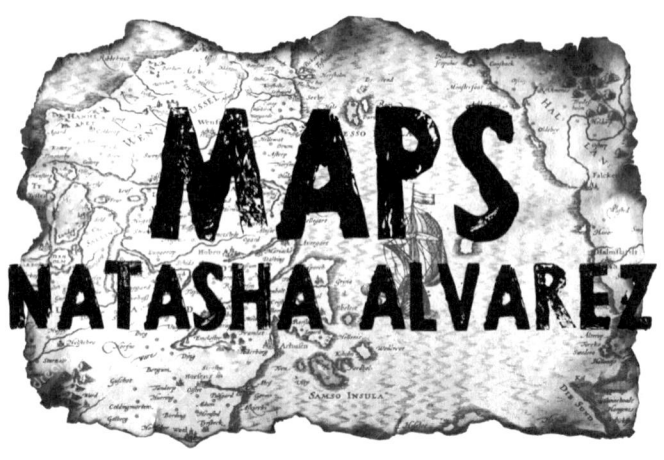

MAPS
NATASHA ALVAREZ

What a strange place this is,
   To wake with birdsong at dawn and sleep with the sound of sirens alarming through the night.
   Where whales fill their stomachs with plastic more often than food, and Polaris is drowned out by our own, more powerful lights.
   How are we to know which way is North?
   Things are changing and we have changed them. Roll up the maps and throw them away, burn them in fires that lick the sky. They are of no use to us here. This territory is unnavigated. We must find our own way now.
   There are creatures here so large their voices will explode your lungs; so powerful they'd crush you with a single blow.
   Seek their council, and bow in respect. Listen. Be humble, be still.
   We were taught wrong, and the ones who taught us were too. This is not a competition, but a dance.
   Our bodies hum with coming storms and still we wait, unmoved, as the clouds gather round our heads.
   Plant trees and water them. Fill the fields with wild plants, or none. It is not about us anymore.
   Some of us are sorry. Some of us are not. In the end it matters very little. The earth does not ask for atonement.
   That's what people do.
   And we?
   We are lost.

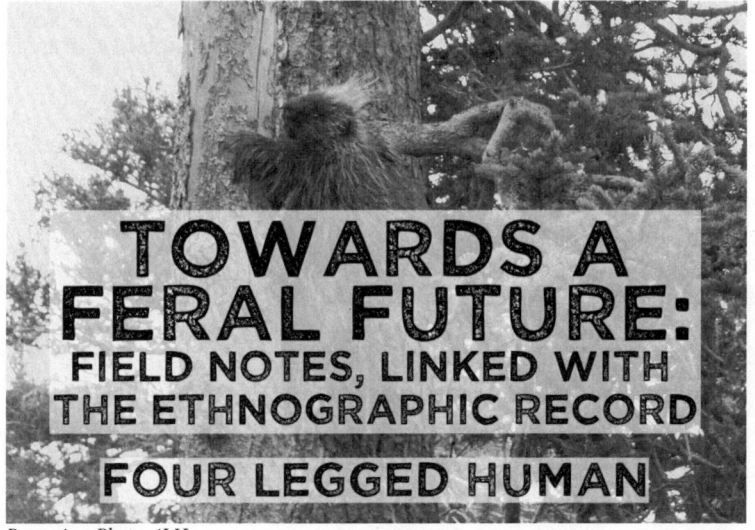

TOWARDS A FERAL FUTURE:
FIELD NOTES, LINKED WITH THE ETHNOGRAPHIC RECORD
FOUR LEGGED HUMAN

Porcupine. Photo: 4LH

This writing is a continuation of my previous article *The Wind Roars Ferociously: Feral Foundations and the Necessity of Wild Resistance* featured in Black and Green Review Issue #3,[1] which was an effort to establish a thorough foundation for the fundamental necessity of our feral return. In summary, not only is our domestication a condition of mass mental and physical alienation, an extreme distancing away from our animality and from our relationship with the natural world, our domestication IS dependency on power, hierarchy, authority, elites, social and technical programmers. As long as we remain its dependents the Leviathan feeds and thrives. As long as we direct our energies towards mediocre efforts such as pandering for better wages, government distribution, 'rights' within the system of various types, and insistence on access to cheap technology, we remain dependents, we feed the Leviathan, we maintain our relationship with it and by no means thwart its trajectory. Not only that, but even more direct confrontations with civilization and its infrastructure also require feral foundations if they are to endure and are to leave us with desirable traits and long-term results.

To counter our deeply embedded dependency we must now "make what was first and oldest in us new and immediate"[2] and take measures to undo "the effects of eight millennia of misdirected human ecology."[3] To that end, in the spirit of Marvin Harris' anti-ideological, pro-behavioral orientation to understanding social change, where "thought changes nothing outside of the head unless it is accompanied by the movements of the body or its parts"[4], I would like to share some of my personal experiences and field observations in the physical rewilding context and offer some on-the-ground considerations for moving forward with shedding our domestication.

This is by no means a complete list, as the diversity of tasks before us is immense. The undertaking is so immense that re-obtaining any of these elements to full capacity requires a multi-generational commitment. Therefore, child raising practices associated with, and the involvement of youth in, all of the activities listed here are mandatory for any serious forward effort.

These are observations and experiences that have been particularly relevant to my own pathway and have become baselines for me. I suggest that all of them are highly relevant components in a full-package of resistance against civilized modes of being[5]. I hope you find them useful.

Community Self-Reliance and Personal Integrity

> *We were…in the same situation that the Bushmen had been in for the past thirty-five thousand years. There was no 'rescue'. Our well-being was up to us.* – The Old Way[6]

> *The government says it is creating jobs for our people. Why do we need jobs? My father and grandfather did not have to ask the government for jobs. They were never unemployed. They lived from the land and forest. It was a good life. We were never hungry or in need.* - A Penan hunter speaking to the UN General Assembly[7]

> *There's something about those people who take into their own hands to relearn old skills, whether they be healers or hunters or something else – they are hard to control. Fear has little power over them. They celebrate the myth of industrial collapse while others cower. Just as the wound of civilization is not unreachably in the past, healing is present in what we do today with our bodies and hearts. As always, healing takes place at the level of food, not philosophy.* - Fire and Ice[8]

A reading of *Feral Foundations* (as well as other works citing countless ethnographic evidence for domestication's pathology) should make clear that begging those who control our food to change the circumstance is simply a ridiculous prospect and thus that dependency on power for our survival is an absolutely primary condition of domestication that we must confront. As such, any stirrings towards communal self-reliance represent mandatory steps away from domestication.

It is well known that hunter-gatherers place a high value on both personal and communal self-sufficiency.[9] For example, Daniel Everett, while living amongst the Piraha Indians of Brazil, noted that they were keenly aware that "each day's survival depends on…individual skills and hardiness" and thus each Piraha had developed a strong sense of personal responsibility for self and other.[10] While spending time with the Penan of Borneo, Wade Davis observed that "self-sufficiency was the norm, with everyone capable of doing every necessary task. So there was very little sense of hierarchy. [The Penan are] a society in which there are no specialists, in which everyone can make everything from raw materials readily found in the forest."[11]

Unlike Western views of self-reliance, however, the self-reliance of hunter-gatherers is *non-socially-segmented* and is based on trust and sharing among individuals who come "into being as a center of agency and awareness within an unbounded social environment which provides sustenance, care, company, and support."[12]

These attributes of hunter-gatherer sociality and personal character originate in childhood. The manner by which children are raised in many hunter-gatherer cultures facilitates a cultural expectation for self-sufficiency. The egalitarianism consistently noted as a driving ethos of many hunter-gatherer cultures applies not only to everyday interaction among adults but also applies to child raising practices. It has been noted that in many hunter-gatherer cultures children are not bossed and are expected to learn the ins-and-outs of personal survival and communal self-reliance under their own free-will through observation and trial and error.[13] Daniel Everett noted that "this style of parenting has the result of producing very tough and resilient adults who do not believe that anyone owes them anything."[14] Overall, researchers who have spent time with peoples living in traditional land-based lifeways have recurrently reported being:

> struck by the emotional security, self-confidence, curiosity, and autonomy of members of small-scale societies [who] spend far more time talking to each other than we do, and…spend no time at all on passive entertainment…such as television, video games, and books [a situation which provides for an upbringing that facilitates] the precocious development of social skills in children…The adolescent identity crises that plague American teen-agers aren't an issue for hunter-gatherer children …hunter-gatherer rearing practices don't

produce societies of sociopaths. Instead they produce individuals capable of coping with big challenges and dangers while still enjoying their lives."[15]

Food self-sufficiency is a vitally important component here, not only because people who control their own food are generally free from the tyranny of power over relationships, but because "food chains are fundamental connectors" between human communities and ecologies.[16] Among hunter-gatherers wild food subsistence practices maintain critical and inseparable connections with the wholeness of life.

Food self-sufficiency is a popular cause among many sustainability activists today, but we need to walk cautiously here being that the dominant pathways to this are centered on farming, liberal and bourgeois interpretations of 'permaculture', and a Great Forgetting that authority, stemming all the way back to the first indigenous chieftains, has a long history of being centered on the ability to control and distribute surplus foods.[17] Accordingly, 'food production', as both a process and an ideal, even in its most progressive formats, generally tends to reinforce our domestication and the exploitive control logic of civilization. Nonetheless, for multiple reasons, we cannot just instantaneously drop these garden-oriented pathways and successfully live on wild foods, so the urging here for now is simply to make any stride possible in learning what it might be like to nourish oneself from more direct efforts and relations with the land and particularly from the wild. Such an effort, even if sporadic for the time being, is critical to a desperately needed re-connectivity and a re-knowing of our human animal selves. Any attributes of non-domesticated life that we can apply in the here-and-now are an essential foundation, even if we remain primarily dependent on domesticated foods for the time being.

Like raven and coyote, I rarely miss the chance to pick up, process, and consume roadkill. This activity provides instant connectivity to the wildness within me. From scavenging we can learn a package of skills, connections, and liberatory emotions which go well beyond simply food. A next tier would be to develop a practice of your own hunting, fishing, and foraging. Ponderous life lessons regarding our humanity, our aptitude, and our possibility can be found here, even without actually killing. One critical lesson is to experience the spontaneity and oftentimes scarcity involved with depending directly on what wildness provides. Through this we often learn much about what it is to patiently and passionately struggle, to do without, to let go of our desire to control. Through various vision-quest oriented activities many hunter-gatherers trained themselves for this. For example, E. Lukas Bridges noted that, as a means of preparing them for living life not based on indulgence but on spirit of mind, young men from bands of Ona hunter-gatherers in Patagonia were sent by elders on solo explorations, "long tramps…during which he must either kill for himself or subsist on tree fungus and roots."[18] In the modern context, learning to get by in day-to-day life without dependence on high-density agricultural foods is important. This requires becoming familiar and comfortable with Paleolithic-based nutrition, ketosis, and caloric restriction. In contrast to this, focusing solely on high-density resources and production oriented strategies towards self-sufficiency, such as obsessing with gardening, will tend to reinforce our domesticated and civilized psychosis in multiple ways, and will affect the outcomes of our resistance efforts.

Within the horticultural and permacultural oriented efforts at food self-sufficiency that we do pursue, critical elements of enhanced domestication and enslavement throughout history can be avoided by approaching these endeavors purely at the subsistence level as opposed to incorporating a market orientation. By pursuing food self-sufficiency minus involvement with commodification, a large step is made towards resisting the dominant culture, not only as a means to our own liberation but also as a means of hitting the Leviathan where it hurts. The machine cannot expand or function without local and global markets and thus as a key resistance pathway we should strive to restrict markets and thus to increase desperation for those who cling to their domestication. An anti-commodification approach represents a solid threat to the bourgeois and elite classes, whose strategies for 'poverty alleviation' center around 'development', 'education', and 'micro-business'. But these simply reinforce our global crisis rather than alleviate it. Resistance and self-sufficiency means not doing 'business' with liberals or anyone else. History shows that the left, especially the bourgeois class, are absolutely not to be trusted. We would do ourselves and the planet well to cut their supply chains and let their domestication ruin them.

Self-reliance also means honor and integrity for oneself and one's community, which not only requires that we not get suckered into playing into the hands of the market any longer, but also that we maintain our physical and mental health, our clarity of mind, and an overall strong personal character. Even among the most 'savage' of tribes this was not an anomaly. Male Ona youth initiates, *klokten*, were "expected to be thoughtful and comparatively silent, listening attentively to words of wisdom from …elders…be industrious in carrying meat or fuel…be serious and earnest in all doings." It was a point of honor among African Bushman that when one went out alone in search of food for the group that they did not eat any food from dawn until dusk until all were eating together upon his return.[19] Among the Ona "for a hunter to begin the day with a heavy meal would not be approved of… carrying food away from an already hungry encampment was not only contemptible, but also an acknowledgement of defeat before starting."[20]

While personal integrity is inescapably linked to communal self-reliance, it does not mean annihilation of the individual – I cannot emphasize more that functioning community without power and authority requires strong, self-disciplined integrity for others and for otherness at the personal level.[21]

In this regard, it should be added that, at this stage in our struggle, addiction to alcohol and other substances are only another barrier to self-reliance. Intoxication is domestication's ally, not ours.[22]

When contemplating self-sufficiency, perhaps the most complex and difficult obstacle to overcome is taking responsibility for our own healthcare needs. Returning to my introductory story from *Feral Foundations*, we all need to learn the skills and the strength of mind to sew the fingers of our community members back together, and those of us who end up injured need to muster up the resolution to handle such misfortunes with the immense courage now required of us. A friend who is a health care professional recently wrote to me:

> *You talk about a broken link in a supply chain/system, if we were to see this in the health care supplies/basic public health care that we take for granted (like gloves, disposable syringes, antibiotics/vaccines – and we've already reduced their efficacy) we are not in any better position than some African communities (who might be better off since they've had to deal with limited supplies for so long) and this has been demonstrated in places like Russia (who I see is going to be taking another hit to health care soon). These are the things that worry me when you speak of any collapse in the system. Food, sure, but you can prepare yourself to some degree for food shortages (at the individual/community level) and develop strategies to cope for a period of time. But basic public health infrastructure, which is already largely overlooked and misunderstood, might not be so easy to manage. What's the adage? 'microbes know no borders' … or something like that. Now add food + microbes and that is an*

even larger problem.

This makes clear that attention to hygiene and healthcare self-sufficiency should not be disregarded by rewilding communities. Rewilders should make thorough investigation of traditional indigenous healing and medicinal knowledge and practice.

Much more can be discussed regarding efforts towards self-reliance and lessening our dependence on the Leviathan's matrix. Hopefully this brief overview will assist some of you in beginning your own conversations about it and, more importantly, provide some motivation for physical action in moving forward with attempts to liberate yourself and your community to the furthest extent possible from the shackles of dependency.

Experiential Knowledge

> *Knowledge of the environment, in this perspective, is not of a formal authorized kind, transmissible in contexts outside those of its practical application. On the contrary it is based in feeling, consisting in the skills, sensitivities and orientations that have developed through long-experience of conducting one's life in a particular environment.* - Tim Ingold[23]

The massive amounts of time spent philosophizing by anarchists and others has now run its course. It is time to act. Rather than simply read and theorize about the implications of life in wildness, we need to take on a relentless pursuit of first-hand-experiences in wild places, whether starting just with walks, observations, and meditations, or full-immersion attempts at the infinite number of practical life skills required for successful land-based lifeways.

Professed theoretical knowledge not based on direct experience is difficult to take seriously. In the logical world of hunter-gatherers, a person:
> must never accept what people tell you without first investigating the matter yourself...for the individual hunter, knowledge is only knowledge when he himself has tested and experienced it in practice... information [is not regarded] as real knowledge until a person has experienced the matter for himself. Firsthand knowledge is an absolute precondition to knowing anything at all.[24]

We have an extremely long way to travel here and every moment spent in on-the-ground experience is now critical. This is not only about material survival, it is necessary for undomesticating our minds.

Hunter-gatherers are known to teach their children to imitate other animals so that they are raised from early in life to see and experience the world through the eyes of wild otherness.[25] We don't teach children to make a bow-drill fire for the purposes of 'survival'. We teach them to create fire from scratch as a deep lesson in self-reliance, personal empowerment, human history, ecology, and wild essence all-in-one. This is the power and value of direct experience in wildness. The development of primitive skills, including tracking, stalking, animal mimicry, tool making, fire making, and shelter building, is a top-notch methodology for increasing self-awareness, self-confidence, community awareness, and building strong personal character.

Through intimate and direct moment-by-moment experience *within* the real world, without dependence on outside technology, land-based people are well-known for being highly aware, attuned, skilled, and competent. The Ona were said to have developed "incredible powers of memory and insight" as a result of lives spent tracking and in continuous intimate observation and relationship with wildness.[26] The people of the Old Way cultivated the ability to navigate and memorize landscapes and seascapes thousands of square kilometers in size. Captain James Cook told the story of the Tahitian, Tupaia who, using stones placed in beach sand, was able to accurately illustrate "a map from memory of every major island group in Polynesia."[27] None of this was possible without generations of people's direct and intimate experiences and observations living *within* the world of wildness. For us Tupaia's map would seem a massive feat but such earth navigation and geographic memory all accomplished without "logs, notebooks, or charts, no speedometers, watches, compasses" would be the normal day-to-day baseline for non-domesticated peoples.[28]

At surface level, large-scale effort placed towards wild experience might be seen as irrational and ineffective in terms of energy spent versus actual material gain and actual impacts against civilization. However, developing an intense interconnectedness with our local ecologies and an in-depth socioecological knowledgebase by means of an increasingly wild existence is mandatory for moving beyond domestication. So get out on the land and begin learning about yourself and your ecology!

Readers can follow up this brief discussion with immersion in the many published primitive skills field guides in existence and in seeking out people actually un-plugging and practicing these things, joining them whenever and wherever possible.

Running, Climbing, Land Travel, Water Travel, Swimming, Bushwhacking

> [For the Maniq] knowledge of the landscape and the ability to orient oneself within the forest is seen as one of the distinguishing markers between childhood and adulthood. - Being Maniq[29]

In *Feral Foundations*, I mentioned the overall legitimacy and necessity of training and physical fitness. Resistance and action now require optimizing physical health and well-being so we can begin to operate without the machines and the goods produced in the enslaving and desolate industrial landscapes of the planet. To become self-sufficient, adapted, feral humans, regaining the health of our bodies is mandatory, yet the effects should be holistic; healing for the mind, body, and spirit, and also ecologically binding. Whenever you walk, hike, run, climb, swim, and bushwhack within wild environs you are powerfully enacting your human animal, becoming animal, and becoming a part of the animal world, as "the human species emerged enacting, dreaming, and thinking animals and cannot be fully itself without them."[30]

Hunter-gatherers are not passive and lazy. In fact, they take their health and well-being seriously. Anthropologists have discovered that, rather than placing value on material wealth, what hunter-gatherers value above all else is *somatic wealth*, or fitness. This includes non-gender-specific grip strength, body weight, the ability to carry heavy loads long distances (including children), and the ability to maintain endurance during all-day foraging activities.[31] Ona hunters were known to walk 12 hours a day. !Kung Bushman were known to walk and run forty miles or more during a single hunt. The Tarahumara Indians of Mexico can run well over one hundred miles.[32] For the Ju/wasi !Kung "hunting was a test of character and strength as well as ability, as from start to finish a hunt could last a week or longer, sometimes much longer…During lengthy hunts the hunters might eat very little, if anything, and they often traveled very far, under extreme conditions."[33]

At every opportunity, I swim in wild waters, climb rocks, hills, and mountains, jump off rocks and over logs and stumps, and run. It's very likely that we were *born to run* and trail-running has been thoroughly beneficial to my overall rewilding practice.[34] More than a few anthropologists have come to the conclusion that we became human by chasing animals, with persistence hunting, running down game, beginning at least a million years ago. Elizabeth Marshall Thomas suggests we became human particularly by chasing elands on the African plain. "We became bipedal and more gracile, until we had long thighs, deep lungs, and well developed multipurpose feet that could carry us over everything from rocks to sand and mud."[35]

Ancient eland cave painting on the Mother Continent. Photo: 4LH

One of my greatest mental and physical health discoveries in a rewilding context has been a massive expanse of tidal mud flats by the sea. The surface is mostly clay-like, not too muddy, providing the most perfect padding for a barefoot runner. I strip down to only my shorts and run for miles barefoot across the clay. It is therapy for my feet, my mind, my entire body, like an *Homo erectus* running across the rift valley of Africa two million years ago, making perfect hominid tracks on the land.[36] Each place where a small creek drains from the land into the sea a ravine is formed and thus every few hundred meters I must jump over the ravines, some are big and some are small. The big ones require careful attention and technique so as not to fall in. So I am running and running and jumping and jumping, each time I jump and land on my bare feet the run becomes faster and more exhilarating, more wild. There are also many logs, pieces of large washed up driftwood. When I come to the logs I jump on them and use them as balance beams. I have developed an entire course through these logs, with different balancing acts and jumps; balance, jump, then continue running. Eagles fly above, flocks of sandhill cranes call out, and arctic terns dive at me from the sky, giving chase.

I only run on earthen trails and off-trail and never on paved surfaces. One should start slow and on mellow terrain and graduate to moving as quickly and stealthily as possible in trail-less wild landscapes; forests, mountains, deserts, sea shores. While running try to take in all of the information from the environment around you— every species of plant, insects, rocks, roots, all the textures, animal tracks, birds, squirrels, and elk, deer, antelope jumping from rock to rock, from log to log, snatching nibbles of wild greens and berries as you sprint by. A trail run can heal you from a destructive day in the confines of civilization and brings you deeply in tune with your animality. Graduate to running on ice and in the snow during the winter and barefoot in the summer. Run as if your life depended on it, enact your primal mind and body, pretend you are hunting. As you become stronger and develop endurance you too can run down deer to the point of exhaustion, I know because I have done it, fully entranced with going feral.

Developing the mindset and physique to travel off-trail on uneven ground, through water, and through thick brush is another important step. Make a conscious decision to bushwhack rather than stay on a trail simply to immerse yourself into a fuller wild state of being, to explore the depths of wildness. Soon enough you'll probably end up on a game trail, abundant with deer sign. As you scamper along try to integrate your movements with the flowing contours of the forest floor and the passageways through the trees, as the animal you are. Get comfortable getting wet and crossing water, whether fording or swimming.[37]

When you travel the land try to orient yourself away from the domesticated viewpoint of being in nature for the spectacle, for romantic observation, and instead for the purpose of spending time in a functioning relationship with your local land base. Hike not simply to hike, but to track and scout game. Bicycle not simply for exercise, but to reach distant lakes for fishing, to explore new areas for hunting, to discover the largest patch of wild strawberries one could ever dream. Climb mountains to further your awareness of the contours and feeling of the snow, ice, and rock, and to further awareness of your body and the ways in which your mind and body function in wild terrain, and to do so alongside mountain sheep, to forage for berries in an alpine meadow alongside a great bear.

Four Legged Human: Towards a Feral Future

Under mutual agreement, 4LH foraged for blueberries alongside this grizzly for over an hour, on hands and knees. Photo 4LH.

I am always boggled by people without a sense of direction who have no idea which way is north, south, east, or west; a product of our distant, alienated, domesticated lives which I have unfortunately encountered often. To overcome this, while traveling focus on maintaining your sense of direction and memorizing the features you encounter; a particular tree or rock for example. When the skyline is visible use it to mark where you are, try to memorize particular views and angles, keep track of the positions of the sun, the moon, and the stars. When darkness falls, operationalize your primal night vision by allowing your eyes time to adjust and practicing movement without artificial light. You will be amazed at how much you can actually see and feel if you just allow yourself. Through time you can be capable of travelling to any spot simply by memorizing landmarks and trajectories. The objective is for each of us to become Wayfinders – without need of compass or map (particularly the digital types) – just as your hunter-gatherer ancestors were.[38]

This brief overview of some of the physical aspects of rewilding should serve to get readers inspired, motivated, and active. The opportunities here are infinite. Get creative. Develop your own workouts which include stretching, weight training with natural objects, and self-defense methods. Absolutely do not discount the fact that all of the above are critical facets for effective and enduring resistance activities.

Hunting

> Q; do you feel glad about killing for a living?
> A; I'm a hunter-gatherer.
> Q; but your also, like, a hippy-environmentalist. How can you be

> both?
> A; I don't think it's possible not to be both unless your just ignorant about where food comes from.
>
> - Eating Alaska[39]

> *We are space-needing, wild-country, Pleistocene beings, trapped in overdense numbers in devastated, simplified ecosystems...the sanctity of nonhuman life was a normal part of small-scale societies for thousands of years [yet] the 'world religions' with their messianic, human-centered, and otherworldy emphasis, trampled those traditions [with which was lost a fundamental] sensitivity to human membership in natural communities and affirmation of and compliance with the biological framework of life. Greek ethics and biblical morality, organically alienist to begin with, cannot cope with our circumstances.*
>
> - The Others [40]

If food, and knowing where it comes from, is "the physiological link to the larger thermodynamics of the universe", rewilding must be a core component of our pathway towards food self-sufficiency.[41] To that end developing a hunting practice is fundamental.

We are who we are as humans because we learned to hunt and we must hunt to go feral. Hunting; the scouting, the chase, the stalk, the catch, and the dismembering, is a far more robust rewilding activity than fishing or fur-trapping, and certainly more robust than growing.[42] I hunt not just to learn subsistence, self-sufficiency, and to obtain ultra-nutritious healthy wild food, but also for all of its holistic teachings and realignments with wildness.

The eminent human ecologist Paul Shepard often made note that a hunting practice is critical to our connectivity, our knowing, and our deepest insight. At base, hunting, processing, and consuming animals represents a foundational element of a non-domesticated and ecologically centered humanity:

> *Continuity between animals' lives and our own reinforces a profound and enduring metonymy, a lifelong shield against alienation...A rich literal knowledge of animal life is fundamental... generating a respect for the natural community as a higher language, as clues towards wisdom in the immense panoply of nonhuman life.*[43]

Shepard maintained that the true depth of this relationship is obtained through wild food foraging, particularly hunting, and that to truly know ourselves as animals at all we must not only hunt non-human animals but also dismember and consume them because the "butchering of large prey [leads] to autopsy, comparisons, and reconstructed lives."[44]

For any omnivorous species, hunting is not simply killing and human predators behave quite differently than do other animals. Almost all recorded real-time observations of hunter-gatherers has displayed elements of holistic relatedness and reverence in the perspective of the hunters. "Perhaps the real evolutionary outcome of humans taking up hunting is not a violent brutal killer instinct but rather the ability to empathize with other beings, an attempt to put oneself in the animal's place and see the world from its perspective", suggests anthropologist Rane Willerslev.[45]

It can be expected that some readers new to rewilding and primitivism and of progressive or urban backgrounds will cringe at this topic.[46] When I first decided to transition from militant vegan to primitive hunter I romanticized the process. I made a vow to myself to only hunt with a longbow and idealized the mythical kill where the animal just offered itself to me. But a hunter quickly realizes the uncontrollable dynamic ways of the wild world and this becomes an important lesson in separating ones perception of what is 'ideal', a generally domesticated mind set, from the fact that wildness tends to always play out in wild, uncontrollable ways.[47]

The ideological need for a controlled scenario, which is virtually incompatible with life in wildness, has been suggested as one possible psychological impetus towards animal domestication and ritual animal sacrifice in the indigenous cultures that practiced these things. Here an attempt is made to do away with wildness and replace it with domestication and control because "the actual conditions of hunting make it difficult and often impossible to live the ideal."[48] In opposition to this, to become a successful feral hunter, one must effectively embrace the uncertainty and learn to live within a wild dynamic flow. This serves to further bring out the animality and adaptability within us, as we increasingly learn the arts of mimicry and travel into deeper primality.

If you choose to hunt, how you choose to hunt matters. Baiting wild animals and then dispatching them with a firearm represent the most domesticated, control driven method and persistence hunting the most feral. It took me 3 years to take my first deer with a handmade longbow. The lessons about wildness, myself, my reality, and my humanity were plentiful and I was proud of my accomplishment.

The following year, after being unsuccessful during archery season, I found myself missing the previous year's supply of wild food, hide, and other materials. And after spending a month with bow in hand wandering the land in search of game, I didn't want to stop. So I took a hand-me-down rifle from a relative and decided to continue the hunt during firearm season. There was so much to experience and learn and I realized it was important to stop being idealistic about my weapon choice. However, at the same time I vowed to continue bow hunting and continue learning to make primitive bows. Since then, every year I spend time shooting and walking with a bow but also always prepare to hunt with a firearm later if necessary. This has been highly beneficial because of the food and materials and extended experiences rifle hunting has provided me. Nonetheless, I fully understand the true consequences of firearm dependency – that the paranoid mentality of the gun rights crowd is ultimately a symptom of domesticated dependency and alienation from wild, truly self-reliant, ways of being.

The gun can only take one in a specific direction and only so far. When entirely dependent upon it, the gun is a massive obstruction to going feral and is thus a detriment to defeating civilization in the long term. The story of The Arrow People makes this clear:

Projectile-point technology was particularly well suited for human survival in the tightly closed forests of the Amazon...: blowguns for taking vertical aim at canopy birds and monkeys, arrows for shooting sideways through the trees at ambulatory, four-legged targets. And two-legged ones as well. Arrows may have been no match for repeating rifles in the village clearings and along the beaches where the rubber bosses' armies struck. But the gunmen who pursued fleeing Indians into the forest soon found themselves enveloped in a terrifying world of moving shadows where they did not belong, picked off silently, one at a time, by an enemy they could not see and could not hear. Small wonder it's been the impulse of whites on every frontier to level the forest.[49]

Obtaining and maintaining the skill set to build and effectively use primitive weaponry, with materials sourced primarily from local ecologies is a critical component for enduring wild subsistence, self-defense, and thus resistance. Therefore, I suggest a pathway which utilizes both modern and primitive weaponry, for the time being at least, but with the intent to immerse oneself fully in the primitive to the furthest extent possible while not letting oneself slide into complete firearm dependence, a mode of apathetic convenience, as this is domestication, not rewilding.

Returning to camp with the last load after a successful hunt with friends. Our band will be eating well this winter and we will defend this habitat, these mountains, this forest, and this river into eternity. Photo by Thinhorn.

Much more can be discussed on the topic of hunting, whether or not to pursue it, omnivory vs. veganism etc. For readers who grasp the argument for a hunting praxis and any who have an interest in getting started, I hope this brief discussion will serve as an impetus. Much information can be found within the countless anthropological research reports on the topic as well as in related writings. There is a lot to learn here. Even then, nothing else can replace what you will holistically gain as you stand up and walk into the forest in pursuit of wild animals for food.

Advanced Land Travel: Distances with Weight

Long ago, when a band of nomadic hunter-gatherers successfully took down a large animal the group would often move to a feasible campsite in close vicinity to the kill and stay there for a time. For a good portion of the world's remaining hunter-gatherers this is no longer the case as most have been settled into villages and property ownership and fences curtail the ability for both humans and wild ungulates to move. In North America at least, most indigenous people who continue to practice a partial hunting and gathering lifeway travel the lands and waters with fossil energy fueled machines. In the sub-arctic and arctic of Canada and Alaska, when motorized transport became available, the transition away from foot travel and dog team and canoe transport began, and younger generations were raised without the experiences of using non-mechanized means of transportation. This shaped their modern worldviews regarding the means and methods by which hunting, fishing, and gathering are accomplished. As a result, entire cultures have lost any reference point to a past where human powered travel on the land and water was primary and these cultures now depend almost entirely on fossil energy to travel, hunt, fish, and gather. The same can be said for virtually all Euroamerican hunters. This story represents another element of our domestication. For those of us in opposition to civilization's destructive tendencies and who are hunting to maintain our indigenous traditions or to begin a new lifeway centered on wildness, acceptance of this reality and doing something about it is critical. In the long-run uncivilized life cannot occur as long as people remain tied to oil. Ultimately, to defeat the programmers and domesticators, we must develop the capability to operate without the products which they profit from and that they enslave us with.

Chances are that if you are successful in hunting large game today you will be faced with the choice of either utilizing an ATV or snowmachine or instead to haul heavy loads of meat, bone, and a hide across trail-less terrain for long distances on foot. Choosing the later path is one of the most physically difficult tasks a person can experience, totally outside most civilized people's physical and mental boxes, but is also extremely rewarding and strength and spirit building for the rewilder, and also entirely in alignment with our land-based hunter-gatherer legacy.

Across the 3rd world today many people have maintained the ability to carry large loads on foot for long distances. It is always impressive to see an elder woman carrying 100 lbs. of wood on her back, buckets of water on a wooden pole balanced over her shoulder, or balancing a basket of fruit on her head while carrying a child on a dusty road. Who in Western culture can accomplish such things at 70 or 80 years of age? The Ona's ability to carry heavy loads of guanaco meat long distances across harsh terrain was noted by E. Lukas Bridges and he reported witnessing an Ona travel across "a mile of wet clay and stony moor with a load weighing well over three hundred pounds."⁵⁰ For training, Ona *klokten* were sent off alone or in pairs on expeditions into the forest to find and carry back meat killed by the older hunters. They were assigned loads to carry that would be equal to their own body weight and instructed on a specific route to follow on the return which was purposely made the most difficult and arduous route possible, they were "ordered to make long detours over certain hills or around lakes, both on outward or return trips."⁵¹

Carrying meat and hides is one example of the psychical ability and state of mind necessary for land-based rewilding activities. In general, activities such as hauling wood for shelters and fire etc., and simply backpacking with large, heavy loads are great trainings for our minds and bodies and also useful in breaking some aspects of our domestication. Rewilders should not balk at such tasks but fully embrace them, and thus our domesticated enemies shall find themselves at a great disadvantage against us when in the future their access to machines becomes increasingly limited.

Hard Work

> *The overpasses and exit ramps were monsters, concrete brachiosaurs, their backs lifting trucks and cars, the people in cars were veering together...My nose drowned in fumes. A man held a scrawled cardboard sign; WILL WORK FOR FOOD. Exactly what [our father] had taught us to do.* **You kids want to gut that caribou and hang it under the cache and then we'll go after cranberries?"**
> - Seth Kantner, relaying his observations from his first ever trip to a city, during his twenties, after being raised as a hunter-gatherer in remote bush Alaska.⁵²

> *Whenever the work of a beaver was encountered along the river the people were supposed to pick up some of the wood chips and put them in their pockets so that they would absorb the spirituality of the beaver, a hard worker. This is because there is no way around hard work on the land and to survive you must have the spirit of the beaver.* - Ahtna Athabascan elder speaking to the author on the topic of traditional work.

In *Feral Foundations* I declared that hard physical work is required if we wish to unhinge our domestication, that we must be fully committed to hard work if we are serious about rewilding.

Based on data from anthropological studies, primitivists have often cited a relative lack of work associated with foraging lifeways, when compared to agricultural adaptations.[53] While important for contextualizing differences between work requirements for established hunter-gatherers and the work loads of agriculturalists, as well as noting how all this compares to work requirements and overall quality of work in techno-industrial lifeways, the anthropological findings on these issues are partially irrelevant to our discussion here, being that we as rewilding practitioners in the 21st century are starting from almost scratch.

We don't have 500 generations of ancestral foundations and pedagogy at the material and landscape level from which to build upon. We were not born into stable land-based lifeways and raised to exist, survive, and thrive within such social and ecological contexts. We are tasked with establishing a cultural foundation from-the-ground-up, usually in places with very different spatial, temporal, and ecological contexts than available to past non-domesticated peoples. We are attempting to occupy much more heavily impacted and limiting landscapes. All of this means that we will be working harder. For those of who have now spent considerable amounts of time experimenting in the field, this is an unavoidable reality. Our challenges are immense, the mental and physical tasks ahead are sheer and there is no easy lackadaisical way out.

There exists a suite of physical, psychological, social, and technical constraints to this endeavor, each of which fall into the category I refer to as 'hard work', it is an entire package of willful sacrifice and determination which requires a massive leap away from our current state of domestication. Moreover, we must keep in mind that our ability to be lethargic today stems almost entirely from externalizing the work required for our survival to the poorest manually laboring classes, both in the 'developed' and 'undeveloped' worlds, and principally, externalizing it to the some 30 metaphoric slaves we each own due to our ability to plug into fossil energy.

In civilization, whether one works hard physically in a field or factory, or 'works hard' for 8-12 hours sitting in a chair staring at a screen all day, work within a state of domestication (aka 'employment') is generally spiritually degrading and ultimately debilitating for our minds and bodies. In this context, no sane person would desire to 'work'. In contrast, autonomously driven hard work in the context of wildness and primitive skills activities provides monumental benefits to our mental and physical health and our overall quality of life. Here, the amount a person works is not as important as the overall quality of life associated with obtaining a material existence from the outdoors in a natural human environment, in deep moment-by-moment immersion in wildness, under the guise of one's own autonomy, and in cooperation with other humans within a face-to-face community.

I speak from experience as a person who has made considerable efforts over the last decade to obtain a large portion of my food needs and other basic needs from wildness. In this pursuit I have worked immensely hard at times and suffered accordingly. Many times I have just wanted to give up, or have taken shortcuts to lesson my labor requirements and paid the consequences accordingly - with failure.

Spending up to 18 hours straight on the hunt, traveling the land, butchering game, carrying loads with very little time for rest or to eat is always far more physically and spiritually rewarding than civilized modes of work for me. As tough as dedicated rewilding work can be, in the face of the alternative; life inside of civilized 'work' environments, the physical and spiritual squalor of the office and trying to keep life together inside of a complex mass society, I do not see rewilding work as drudgery. The more I become accustomed to hard work in wildness and primitive skills oriented work the more I find it agreeable in comparison with 'work' as the majority of those in civilization experience it. I feel intuitively healthy and human, my body and mind send deep messages that I am following the correct path. What is also absolutely critical is the health and healing within me which the autonomy of primitive work allows. You are on nobody's schedule but that of your own adaptive flexibility. In flow with the dynamics of the wild world. It is wholeheartedly connective. It is authentically living within the present and being present.

It is important to note that much of my most difficult work experiences in rewilding have been because I have taken on ponderous tasks alone. Work required by single individuals, or just 2-3 people, is obviously much more demanding than work accomplished by communities. A more leisurely pace and overall enjoyment of work applies especially to established land-based communities with a long history in having the skills and organizational capacities required for survival in a specific ecology. Accordingly, even when we do establish our own 21st century rewilding community groups, while not alone any longer, we will still be working harder.

While having face-to-face community will certainly assist a needed change in our perceptions of 'work', from one of drudgery to one of presence, intimacy, physical health, and mental satisfaction, we are generally not beginning this with adequate skill bases, tools, and intact communities living within intact wild ecologies, and we need to be dedicated to the often uncomfortable hard work required to make this happen. And, if the anthropological findings on the workloads of hunter-gatherers are to provide an indicator, the physical reality of non-domesticated life will remain even after we have established our communal and subsistence foundations.[54]

In 1968, based on the information available from ethnographic observations and measurements, and a suite of comments in reports by explorers and missionaries, the most prominent hunter-gatherer scholars of the era emerged from the *Man the Hunter* conference with a general consensus that a hunter-gatherer lifeway seemed to require relatively little amounts of work.[55] This revelation was followed in 1972 by Marshall Sahlins' publishing of *Stone Age Economics* which documented the limited hours of work required for survival by some foraging peoples.[56] Sahlins' effort was vital, making a statement to the world regarding the great socio-evolutionary success of hunter-gatherer adaptations, an analysis which remains extremely valid today. Yet, Sahlin's conclusions on low work effort have since been disputed by other anthropologists who pointed out that some of the complexities of the matter were overlooked in Sahlins' analysis, which was based on too brief of a timeframe of observation, did not account for seasonal variability, and relied only on a small number of samples. When other factors were considered, such as food processing and tool/shelter maintenance, analysts ended up concluding that, on average, hunter-gatherers work around 5-7 hours per day rather than the 2-4 hours of work per day suggested earlier.[57] From this a new consensus arose positing that the low work thesis does not apply to all hunter-gatherer populations globally, and generally only applies to specific temporal, seasonal, and/or ecological contexts, and that where it does apply, there are undoubtedly periods of heavy work (normally followed by periods of heavy rest).[58] While these updated analyses have made it clear that a foraging lifeway is not and never has been simply one of leisure, an overall consensus remains that foraging lifeways generally require considerably less effort and drudgery than do domesticated lifeways.

Even for those hunter-gatherers reported to have only worked 3 hours per day, there is no doubt that, compared to most of us, they were on an entirely different plane in terms of knowledge, skills, physical and mental endurance, and overall resilience. No matter how much time was spent working on average we cannot avoid the fact that wild hunting and gathering activities "require considerable strength and stamina, visual acuity, and other aspects of good health."[59] There is no doubt that all non-domesticated people throughout history faced high levels of pressure at times and they were well adapted to enduring through these situations. We need to begin making ourselves prepared for these conditions as well.

Diverse environmental and personal circumstances will create diverse outcomes in the physical efforts required. It is logical that there will be differences across many different ecosystems, seasons, and specific activities. And the level of time and work required is greatly enhanced when people commit to all this while also continuing to require an income from which to purchase other necessities of survival that cannot currently be obtained in wild communities.

No matter which way we look at it, to undo domestication, great fortitude is required. However we choose to go about it, we should expect that we will routinely face circumstances that require physically and temporally demanding workloads. Let's stop romanticizing lethargy. We cannot dumpster our way out of domestication. Although I fully support and practice occasional raids on Taker caches, it is key not to develop a mode of total dependency on such tactics. We need to learn for ourselves how to take care of one and other, from the-wild-ground-up, and this requires firm commitment to physical work.

Weather and Climate

The same Ahtna man cited above told me that, for survival training in a harsh and cold northern environment, "elders used to tell kids to run outside in the snow without moccasins and build a fire, so that they would learn a lesson about their relationship with the snow and cold weather." E. Lukas Bridges reported on the immense resilience of the Ona in the cold waters and snows of Tierra Del Fuego. With moccasins made from the leg skins of guanaco "an Ona might walk for hours through icy water, often above the knees." Even though the wet fur on the outside of their robes and moccasins would freeze stiff at night, wrapped only in these, an Ona "would pass a comfortable night, despite the fact that the temperature might be many degrees below freezing point, with his bare legs exposed from ankle to knee to the stars."[60] Non-domesticated humans who lived in the coldest reaches of our planet managed these types of scenarios for thousands of years before there was such thing as a cigarette lighter.

I have practiced staying out without a sleeping bag in sub-zero temps in the dead of winter in Interior Alaska. In order to successfully do this I have needed to spend anywhere from 3-5 hours gathering the necessary materials for adequate shelter and suitable amounts of firewood. These have been the most difficult experiences of my life, a true in-the-face realization of how fragile our lives are, but also thoroughly rewarding for the realization of what we are actually capable of if we begin to attempt shedding our domestication. Other primitivist friends have gone well beyond my experiences, attempting to spend entire winters in the boreal forest camped out in the snow and cold. These are the types of people I look towards for inspiration, community building, and reliability; for rewilding and resistance.

Because of the vast amounts of wild land available and the relatively in-tact resource base, a good number of rewilders have chosen cold and wet northern environments for making their feral stands. Others theorize that we might be better off in more temperate environments or in tropical ones. If the deep cold of the north and the winters of the mid-ranges present great challenges, so do the tropics. Over the last several years I have spent considerable time exploring the prospects of primal living in tropical climates. While getting rid of the great weight of burden that is the constant worrying about body heat and stockpiling calories for the winter, the tropics present their own great challenges for the domesticated; dangerous insects which bite, sting, and carry deadly diseases. In the north I am comfortable drinking wild unfiltered water from almost any stream. In the south this all changes and obtaining safe drinking water requires a different approach and skillset. There really is no way out of our domestication except to accept and persevere through the risks, discomforts, and uncertainties of wildness, no matter what the weather, climate, and particular ecology.

Take into deep consideration the climatic conditions in your area. Study the old, non-domesticated methods used to adapt to these conditions and attempt to practice them. If the particular climatic conditions and related challenges of a specific bioregion seem to be more appealing to you, seek out land projects and rewilding-minded communities in those areas and relocate yourself there for a time to see how it works for you. Just remember, no matter what, a specific weather and climate adaptation will be required and it usually won't be easy getting comfortable right away.

Additionally begin a practice of paying careful attention to the daily weather in your area, the clouds, the sun, the moon, and the wind. As indigenous people did for thousands and thousands of years, attempt to read the signs and receive messages from these wild elements. From here a capability to predict future weather conditions, by the hour or the day, can become possible.[61]

Community and Sharing Balanced with a Need to Break Free of Debilitating Group Inertia

> *Indeed, what is most characteristic of hunting societies everywhere is the emphasis not on accumulation but on its obverse: the sharing of the kill, to varying degrees, amongst all those associated with the hunter.* - Tim Ingold[62]

Thus far I have attempted to make clear that through all this we should prioritize rewilding within the context of a community and not simply as solo artists, for without intact and functioning face-to-face community we can never successfully defeat civilization. Primitive living is a communal activity and thus rewilding and resistance needs to always incorporate a focus on social relationships.

I long for community. I long not only for relationships with ecology, but with humans. Still, in my quest for wildness I have often become more isolated as relationships with humans, particularly the domesticated type, seem to always be getting in the way of my rewilding pathway, because most just do not understand, don't want to see it, think it is too 'extreme', and cannot get themselves to even cross the mental threshold towards breaking free of their domesticated enslavement. Because of this I have often chosen to forgo social deference in exchange for strengthening my relationship with wildness. Sometimes we have to do this, but also with every accomplishment, every step forward into a feral future we should be doing our best to share it all with those around us, no matter their reticence, and whether these rewards are material, spiritual or both.

There is much we can accomplish alone and I maintain that having no communal options and being a lone rewilder should not limit one from making the greatest efforts possible. Nonetheless, a lone traveler in an unknown place was probably more often than not an anomaly for primitive peoples, so the lone feral voyager is breaking new ground. Even in cases where a very prepared and educated person did travel alone, it was very well possible that they could get into trouble and potentially meet their end. These are risks that some of us should be open to taking, but in terms of resistance our energy might be much better spent on efforts to create intentional feral communities than simply taking off as a lone traveler *into the wild.*

As the introductory story to *Feral Foundations* relayed, after accomplishing the learning of important skills on my own I was only able to find purpose and move further forward by sharing what I foraged and making an effort to build community. One purpose in the Ona's training of the *klokten* was also the teaching that a hunter should always share his catch so that "a man should not be greedy, because it would make him corpulent and lazy and he would cease to be a successful hunter" and that "a man should give meat generously to old people, even if they were not his relations. It might then be that, when he himself was old and could not hunt, some young man would bring meat to him."[63] This is just a single citation of many which attest that hunter-gatherers maintained gift economies, and not only this, but also that the practices of sharing went far beyond economics. Sharing practices solidified the entire social system and made a wild and free life of dynamic flow on the land possible and also kept hierarchy from rising, with all of its calamities. Key to this was an avoidance of commodifying foraging yields:

> *A return gift made too soon would seem like a trade, not like a gift made from the heart, and thus would not strengthen the social bond, which was its purpose. This concept was so strong that the Ju/wasi never traded with one and other...trading was too likely to stir up bad feelings...the Ju/wasi avoided the practice.* [64]

None of this means complete sacrifice of the individual and his/her autonomy to an idealistic and inert communal superstructure. The egalitarianism of hunter-gatherers meant that individuality was on an equal playing field with community, neither was privileged over the other, unless an individual was doing gross harm to others or to the whole.[65]

While attempting to organize our communities it will be easy for us to be idealistic about how things should go and thus fall into modes of debilitating, bureaucratic groupthink where the needs of some individuals are overlooked and neglected. And then, when a person takes a stand for themselves they end up being shunned, as evolved politically correct behavior keeps most of the group passive and silent. This is groupthink morphing into authority.

In order to avoid this unfortunately common situation, which ultimately translates to failure of our efforts here, individual autonomy needs to be consistently bolstered within our communities.

Hunter-gatherer mechanisms for coping with this include individuals going on vision quests or walkabouts under their own accord, temporary dispersal into smaller bands, upkeep of intra-band social networks where a person/persons could live with others for a while to cool off, and the division of labor and ritual dances along gender lines as mechanisms for healing tensions between men and women.[66]

All of this need to be taken into consideration in regards to community building for our feral future.

Mobility/Flexibility vs. Property

> *The entire cultural system of the Ju/wasi...was based upon the ability to relocate..."I live here. I'm staying on the spot come hell or high water. If you make that hard for me, I'll kill you" is a post-Neolithic concept. It is not a message from the Old Way.* - The Old Way [67]

A primary trait of all wild peoples in history has been flexible mobility. Hunter-gatherers base the location of their residences and their time of occupation on an ongoing pathway of social and ecological flow, in opposition to inertia.[68] As hunting, fishing, and foraging resources change, through ecological shifts, human use, or both, wild people shift location, allowing recovery of the older location. Sometimes, to avoid resource or social conflicts, members of a band will breakaway and go off alone or travel to the temporary location of another band and take up residency there with others for a time. A hunter-gatherer "can always move to join another band if he feels that his autonomy is unduly curtailed."[69] Life in wildness is a spatially, temporally, and climatically adaptive flow and is the evolutionarily proven optimal system for human populations, as it was the primary means by which we utilized landscapes for over 99% of our species history.

Through mobile lifeways in wildness, a deep ecological awareness and knowledge is constantly bolstered and maintained. In contrast, "village farmers" are only "linked to the outside world by middlemen" [domestic animals and plants] and thus while still "close to 'nature' they perceive their relationship to it in terms of growth and control."[70] This is antithetical to the far more robust and deep relationship nomadic hunter-gatherers have with the world. Wild and mobile lifeways result in a cultural psychology which views the world...

> *...less in terms of opposition than complementarity. But with sedentism the known world became smaller, bringing the outside closer. This presence of an absence of chaos became an obsession to be*

confronted by victory. There is evidence that duality and the problem of evil became more important in the cosmologies of agricultural and village life, as opposed to that of nomadic peoples.[71]

Not only is maintaining a capacity for mobility psychologically, socially, and ecologically optimal it also tends to impede the formation of hierarchy, wealth, and endemic violence. As anthropologists have verified, "a primary constraint on material-wealth accumulation and inequality in hunter-gatherer societies is the degree of residential mobility, which in turn is heavily influenced by spatiotemporal variability."[72]

Among hunter-gatherers degrees of mobility vary according to particular ecological niches, and more or less, so does the occurrence of inequality and conflict. In the north, people are forced by climate to work hard caching food for winter and then usually maintaining one residency during the coldest months.[73] Nonetheless, up until the occurrence of agriculture our human evolutionary legacy has always been one of movement, not of the *unkcemna*, which, a Lakota elder once explained to me, is not only a word for human excrement but also translates to a word used to describe a permanent settlement.

A truly sustainable human ecology dictates that ultimately there is no sedentary, village-based 'garden of Eden' (whether wild or cultivated). Throughout history total sedentism for wild peoples has only come by force or through self-domestication.[74] Hunter-gatherers would never "remain sedentary as a security-seeking strategy unless forced to do so."[75]

Regardless of our modern limitations, this ability to move and flow and to never be chained down to one location is core to rewilding and resistance against the sedentary totality and its psychology. Yet, in the developed places of the world which most of us inhabit today, the ability to move nomadically and survive is extremely limited both in terms of resources and legalities. Thus property ownership becomes a goal for many anti-civilization rewilders and permaculturalists. There are many reasons why this is a legitimate desire and need, but as property owners we should never forget that property is an extremely important element in the formation of control-oriented domesticated mindsets and thus the overall totality which we confront. We should be very careful about absorbing and internalizing the control and domination logic of the property owner. World history shows clearly what side of the Leviathan the privileged propertied class usually ends up being on and we should always first view them as enemies, no matter how 'communal' or 'green', until we can verify their actual orientations and intentions. Perhaps more important, on a personal level, we should also be quite careful about purchasing property for a land project and becoming so invested in that one place and project that we fall into a more or less sedentary survival inertia that we cannot bring ourselves out of. In the end, we cannot avoid the fact that property is in many ways a hindrance to an actualized feral anarchy. Nonetheless, rewilding oriented land projects should be supported, especially those which are attempting to operationalize a nodal concept which encourages flow between various properties and locales.[76] And don't overlook the fact that temporary squatting on wild lands is always a very feasible option, if you do it thoughtfully.[77]

No matter what our residential situation is, in the long run we should be continually building our capacity to move quickly across the land or water at a moment's notice. Mobile capacity is needed for our skill building, rewilding, and resistance praxis and it is also needed for our security culture. Rewilders should place focus on reviving and learning the ancient art of silent indigenous evasion. Hunter-gatherers are known to be experts at staying unseen and avoiding being tracked. The Ona were noted for:

...the care with which they would examine anything that looked like a footprint; by the caution with which they hugged the forest shades and avoided crossing open spaces, where long shadows cast by the low sun were seen from far away; by the anxiety with which they would notice a flock of birds rising in flight, or guanaco running as though startled, and speculate on the cause. Much time would be spent lying motionless on some height, intently scanning leagues of forest and blue distance, searching for the slight variation of tint that would betoken smoke rising from some encampment in the woods.[78]

Feral oriented security culture should take inspiration from such accounts and those who own property should have an escape plan blueprint in place, in case of unwanted guests, which will become increasingly likely during the course of this century as the domesticated masses go searching for a means to survive on the backs of others, just as they always have done.

I've tried to make clear that rewilders should never discount the importance of mobility. Tactics, logistics, and tools for land and water travel for the specifics of camps, whether extended-use, multi-use, or one-time-use, are all important considerations that readers should investigate and discuss further. If you're new to wilderness travel, at the very least grab some like-minded friends and some backpacks and take off for a multi-day camp-to-camp excursion in wildness for a few days or more. Mobility starts here, and I promise you won't be disappointed that you went on walkabout.

Rejection of Brain-Dead Bureaucratic Thinking, Symbolic Obsessions, and the Immiseration of Technological Dependency

> *Around our feet lay the beautiful land, enchanted in the twilight's weakening glow, cold, silent, unprepared. Suddenly the past was over. It would never come back to protect us. We'd been pretending as well as any actors. The chasm between legends around the fire and surround-sound TV, snowshoed dog trails and Yamaha V-Max snowmobiles was too overwhelming, and no hunting, no tears, no federal dollars could take us back across. I felt an avalanche of grief, and momentarily thought I'd lost...I pulled the rope starter, squeezed the throttle. My gas was gone. I couldn't make it home... Progress against progress. Whatever progress really was.* - Ordinary Wolves[79]

Rigid bureaucratic thinking and resulting attempts to administer and govern the organization and activities of our projects is quite often antithetical to wildness. Obsessions with numerical analysis, proper grammar, and politically correct language are generally non-liberating abstractions that take us continually to nowhere. The hyper symbolic elements of alienated civilized societies: uniform language, writing, code, time, and number have played key roles in hominid domestication. Calculations, lists, and codes related to trading requirements are some of the key initial symbolic elements which domesticated our minds. As our reliance on symbolic interpretations for essentially everything regarding our relationships with the world have become enhanced within technological civilization, we have experienced an immense "shift towards greater 'abstractedness', towards the decontextualisation of knowledge."[80]

This situation of being dominated almost entirely by domesticated modes of thought and modes of communication is one that a viable rewilding and resistance movement must strive towards doing away with. Yet the calls by progressive leftists and futurists to reform industrial economies to be more even-handedly distributive and 'green' and simultaneously maintain the all-engulfing order of symbolic and technological alienation of the current age are, in reality, civilization-reinforcing and self-domesticating.

Anthropologist Jack Goody once remarked that characteristics marking distinctions between 'savage' and domesticated thinking "can be related to changes in the mode of communication."[81] While Goody was speaking of the initial forms of human symbolic culture; writing, lists, numbers etc., the entire digital world is a massive further enhancement of the psychological and physical domestication initiated by symbolic culture.

Becoming robots who have nothing substantial to offer but computer skills, the futurists and digital technology fiends now look eerily similar to us as did the colonizing Spaniards to the indigenous inhabitants of the New World, "as demons, embodiments of depravity, [offering] nothing…no skills, no food…no knowledge of even the most fundamental elements of the natural world."[82] We need to face up to the fact that, in the end, total dependence on and constant use of the Internet is truly antithetical to resistance against civilization. It is generally quite pitiful to hear those who seem to care about the human trajectory attempt to cloak the current mass-alienation of our species within an unapologetic, do-no-wrong characterization of the digital matrix's 'great capacity' as a 'tool' to help us all 'communicate' 'network' and 'spread ideas.'

In the context of healing human relationships, community building, and land projects, some of the above can be alleviated through making efforts to pursue intimate face-to-face communication and cooperation rather than through digital alienation. Similarly, pursuit of economic individualism is representative of another factor in our psychological domestication as opposed to economic wildness via immediate return oriented procurement and consumption.[83]

Urban Pathways – Foothills

> *Every time I get a grip on what matters, then I'm all confused again. A white-person career, with insurance? And a pension? Something is missing in me – that feels like being born a wolf and choosing a dog's life.* - Ordinary Wolves[84]

For those of us stuck in the chaos and confusion of urban life (chained to employment which takes away the majority of our time for reflective healing, let alone going feral) maintaining our physical health and mental sanity is a day-to-day, moment-by-moment struggle. This is especially true in regards to the deep cognitive dissonance experienced by urbanites who become aware of the root causes of our world's troubles, namely civilization, itself a way of life dependent on cities, and then develop feelings of desperation that there is really no way out, that there is really nothing which can be done. In the face of this the answers are not apparent or easy and the options for any action are extremely limited and daunting. Yet, as removed from wildness as we are, some of us must embark on the struggle forward – to fight for our lives every moment of each day, for the possibility of a feral future.

It would be unfair and unbalanced to not attempt to address the concerns from those who care immensely for wildness and who connect with anarcho-primitivist thought, but who are trapped in urban environments. Some of us already have considerable access to relatively viable 21st century wildness. It's sometimes hard to believe that it still exists somewhere, that there are places where a person can live feasibly almost entirely on wild food and wander for weeks without ever crossing a road. In a few pockets around the world such places do exist and I acknowledge that I am writing from the context of some life experiences in such places. But what might be some pathways for those of marginalized urban environments who have no access to wild and free places?

There are many ways to practice rewilding in urban environments. One can find a way to practice all types of primal-oriented physical fitness and dietary rewilding steps inside of cities. When I have lived in cities I would spend as much time as possible in the *natural areas* close to home, parks and feral spaces. Wild plants exist in almost all domesticated places so I would study ethnobotany. Urban environments often have access to fishing opportunities and one can use this to learn the rod-and-reel method of catching fish, followed by cutting and drying them, and even tanning their skins. I have made shelters from downed wood in the groves of city parks. I perfected my fire drill skills here. I also spent a lot of time at the archery range in one of the other parks shooting a longbow. With a small hatchet and a sharp knife quick-bows can be made from saplings cut from disturbed areas. If one can obtain a stave, advanced bow making can be pursued in a backyard or home workshop. And this goes for many other primitive skills. Once you have the materials, you can easily work on projects from an urban base. You'll be slowly training yourself and others, especially children, for a life engaged in relationship with natural materials and both mental and physical acuity.

If you travel far enough towards the periphery of most urban environs you will encounter an edge where pockets of secondary, and

I have often encountered scenes like this on the outskirts of cities, where, believe it or not, it remains possible to spend one's evening sitting in the grass with a band of wild deer. Photo by 4LH

even primary, wildness exist. On days off from my urban job I would ride my bike out to the city's margin, to the abandoned fields and find sign of white tails and foxes and see eagles there. If I went further I could reach the foothills where there are elk, bear, moose, and lions, dozens of species of edible and medicinal wild plants, all mere remnants of what once was, but elements that brought me into deeper and more profound opportunity to learn what it means to be a human without civilization. I brought back what I was learning to my activist and punk friends in the city. I applied this new energy and awareness to various resistance schemes we were involved in and I like to think I inspired a lot of people before I left and took on a new life in a wilder place.

At the very least, even from the vantage of city life, a primitivist perspective on the world, based on minimalism, community self-reliance, deep ecological awareness, and physical fitness, will be very valuable and coherent for resistance and in coping with the changes we might be forced to make in the coming decades. So do whatever you can from wherever you reside and recruit as many friends as you can to join you.

Conclusion

This article cannot cover all of the many variables and factors involved with a feral path, nor can it cover the many hundreds of writings which could be references to back up its main points. The observations I've presented here are by no means a comprehensive list; they are suggestions for inspiration and for getting people thinking. I am certainly not the first person to recommend similar baselines and pathways for rewilding. Several essays and books have been written on similar topics, more can be written, and, from the perspective of what people learn from their own on-the-ground experimentations, more should be. We each have our own valuable perspectives and experiences to share. Yet none of these in themselves will ever provide the 'ideal' or perfect formula.

Above all, the purpose here, while being very real and unflinching about our challenges, is to inspire an actualized rewilding and anti-domestication praxis as core amongst the broader communities of conscious and passionate persons fighting against the dominant order and all of its destruction. A fundamental point is to drive in the reality that the Leviathan will continue to live as long as we keep feeding it, and it is our domestication and dependency that feeds it. I've attempted to suggest some purposeful psychological and physical approaches which we can use to move forward in stopping that. It is very important also to reiterate my message from *Feral Foundations* that all of this should be seen as multi-generational and that a core objective need be passing on all of these messages, teachings, and activities to children. This is where the ultimate hope rests.

If I were only to present some very distinct, basic principles and guidelines for approaching the organization and psychology of our resistance, I would urge that in any way possible rewilders, anarchists, and all resisters, at the very least, adopt the following features of hunter-gatherer societies which, through comprehensive analysis of the known record, anthropologists have determined have allowed hunter-gatherer groups to consistently defy the tendencies of civilization and capitalism[85]:

- Limited Production Effort
- Immediacy
- Autonomy
- Routine Sharing
- Lack of Interest in Material Accumulation

Living in whatever context we now find ourselves in (wild, urban, or rural) the five features listed above are absolutely some of the top things we should now be putting our intention towards. They are simple guidelines verified from the bulk of human existence on the planet living in a foraging mode of production, which if psychologically and culturally operationalized could help translate our entire world into a new paradigm.

No matter what, however, it's going to take serious work to undo domestication: a diligent, intensive, concerted effort from willing individuals of high personal integrity working as team players. In this regard, I cannot overemphasize that, as currently being projected within the anarchist milieu, inward looking idealisms such as egoism and nihilism have little role here.

All of the facets presented here, based not in philosophy but in physical action, are foundational for imparting in "people a respect for wildness, a sense of human limitations and of biological community, a world of mutual dependency."[86] And lastly, never overlook the fact that all of the above, - pursued with intensity - absolutely represent trainings, conditionings, and tools for the primal war battlefield, no doubt indispensable to the potency required for our defeat of civilization.

Endnotes

1 *The wind roars ferociously: feral foundations and the necessity of wild resistance*. Black and Green Review, Issue #3, Spring 2016. Hereafter referred to as *Feral Foundations*.
2 L. Van Der Post, *A far off place*. Harcourt Brace & Company, London, 1978. Pg. 302
3 P. Shepard, *The others: how animals made us human*. Island Press, Washington D.C., 1996. Pg. 221
4 M. Harris, *Cultural materialism: the struggle for a science of culture*. Altamira Press, Walnut Creek, 2001. Pg. 58
5 It is important to note that all of this is meant to be complimentary and foundational to resistance in the forms of various types of actions, including attacks against the infrastructure of civilization. But I shall refrain from discussing these aspects here. For various reasons, this article is not meant to be about those forms of resistance.
6 E.M. Thomas, *The old way: a story of the first people*. Picador, New York, 2006. Pg. 48
7 W. Davis, *The wayfinders: why ancient wisdom matters in the modern world*. House of Anansi Press, Toronto, 2009. Pg. 178-179
8 L. Luddite and M. Skunkly, *Fire and ice: disturbing the comfortable and comforting the disturbed while tracking our wildest dreams*. Apeshit Press. 2004. Pg. 85
9 For example see: C.S. Coon, *The hunting peoples*. Little Brown and Company, Boston, 1971, A. Massola, *The aborigines of south-eastern Australia: as they were*. Henemann, Melbourne, 1971, D. Everett, *Don't sleep there are snakes: life and language in the Amazonian jungle*. Pantagon, New York, 2008, J. Diamond, *The world until yesterday: what can we learn from traditional societies?* Viking, New York, 2012, and T. Ingold, *On the social relations of the hunter-gatherer band*. In R.B. Lee and R. Daly (eds), *The Cambridge encyclopedia of hunters and gatherers*. Cambridge University Press, Cambridge 2004, Pg. 54-71.
10 Everett, 2008, Pg. 90
11 Davis, 2009, Pg.174
12 Ingold, 2004, Pg. 65
13 Diamond, 2012
14 Everett, 2008, Pg. 90
15 Diamond, 2012, Pg. 208-209
16 Shepard, 1996, Pg. 37

17 For example see Harris, 2001and Davis, 2009.
18 E.L. Bridges, *Uttermost Part of the Earth: History of the Tierra Del Fuego Indians.* Overlook/Rookery, New York, 2007, Pg. 421. In a recent review of my previous article *The wind roars ferociously: feral foundations and the necessity of wild resistance.* Black and Green Review, Issue #3, Spring 2016 I was accused of brushing over the fact that the Ona were documented to be violent and patriarchal. The reviewer apparently failed to notice that I had never attempted to present the Ona as a 'noble savage' stereotype. My sole intention of referencing the Ona is to display first-hand documentation of the enduring resilience and wildness of the Ona people and also their thought-out and sophisticated minimalism. I have elected to continue using the Ona here as an excellent example of wild, resilient self-sufficiency. The Ona have long been considered a 'savage' and 'fierce' group of people and I do not romanticize them or any other hunter-gatherers I reference. A bit more information on Bridges and the Ona is in order here. Bridges was a sheep farmer born on the island of Tierra Del Fuego and raised by British parents in the 1800s and is thought to be the first European to make contact with the Ona. He proceeded to live and hunt with various bands of Ona for several decades. He and the Bridges family as a whole also attempted to missionize them. While quite sympathetic to the Ona, Bridges' account is partially rooted in his own colonial and agriculturalist bias. Nonetheless he seems to have recorded the Ona's characteristics quite objectively. Bridge's account displays the full-spectrum of the Ona's humanity, much that is beautiful and much that is sorrowful, including numerous incidences of murder and violence amongst different Ona bands. Incidences of brutalizing women were also documented. Yet overall, the record seems to be quite mixed on these matters, as there seems to be just as much, or more, documentation of Ona caring and loving for one and other at the small-band level. It has been noted that many of the observations of violence amongst the Ona stem from the context of colonialism and that violence increased greatly as a result of contact, particularly amongst distinct Ona bands competing for dwindling food resources and hunting territories. While Bridges was one of the few colonists who tried to protect them, the Ona were almost hunted to extinction by European and Mestizo miners and sheep farmers. In the 1970s the last Ona was reported to have died. Also see M. Gusinde, *Folk literature of the Selknam Indians,* University of California Los Angeles, 1975 and J.M. Cooper, *The Ona.* In J.H. Steward (ed.) *Handbook of South American Indians,* Smithsonian Institution, Washington D.C., 1946, Pg. 107-125.
19 Van Der Post, 1978
20 Bridges, 2007, Pg. 453
21 Ingold, 2004 . Also see A.Y. Artemova, *Monopolization of knowledge, social inequality and egalitarianism: an evolutionary perspective,* Hunter Gatherer Research 2.1, Liverpool University Press, 2016, Pg. 21 who ascertains that "truly egalitarian societies were the result of conscious and persistent efforts over many generations" as well as J. Lewis, *Where goods are free but knowledge costs: hunter-gatherer ritual economics in Western Central Africa.* Hunter Gatherer Research 1.1, Liverpool University Press, 2015, who explains that all BaYaka people are expected to contribute to the group's needs according to their ability but that those who cannot contribute at an equal level are still provided for.
22 See K. Tucker, *Hooked on a feeling: the loss of community and the rise of addiction.* Black and Green Review, Issue #3, Spring 2016.
23 T. Ingold, *The perception of the environment: essays in livelihood, dwelling, and skill.* Routledge, 2000, Pg. 25
24 R. Willerslev, *On the run in Siberia.* University of Minnesota Press, 2012, Pg. 117.
25 For example, see P. Agland, *Baka: People of the Forest.* Channel 4, 1987. https://www.youtube.com/watch?v=QhU_3Dz9Z9g
26 Bridges, 2007, Pg. 379
27 Davis 2009, Pg. 41. Hawaii and New Zealand were exceptions, not included in this map.
28 Davis 2009, Pg. 61
29 D.A. Kircheff and H. Lukas, *Being Maniq: practice and identity in the forests of southern*

Four Legged Human: Towards a Feral Future

Thailand. Hunter Gatherer Research 1.2, Liverpool University Press, 2015, Pg. 143
30 Shepard, 1996, Pg. 4
31 E.A. Smith et al., *Wealth Transmission and Inequality among Hunter-Gatherers.* Current Anthropology, Volume 51, Number 1, February 2010.
32 See Bridges, 2007, Thomas, 2006, and C. McDougall, *Born to Run: A Hidden Tribe, Superathletes, and the Greatest Race the World Has Never Seen.* Knopf, 2009.
33 Thomas, 2006, Pg. 94-95
34 McDougall, 2009. Another example is D. Lieberman, *The story of the human body: evolution, health, and disease.* Pantheon, 2013.
35 Thomas, 2006, Pg. 29
36 B. Bower, *Modern feet step back 1.5 million years.* Science News, February 26th, 2009.
37 Obviously, larger bodies of water and serious rivers will require watercraft and advanced skills not to be discussed here. Readers are encouraged to educate themselves about canoe and raft travel if so inclined.
38 Davis, 2009
39 E. Frankenstein, *Eating Alaska: a wry journey for the 'right thing' to eat.* Frankenstein Productions (film), 2010.
40 Shepard, 1996, Pg. 317
41 Shepard, 1996, Pg. 327
42 At risk of sidetracking the important discussion of hunting here, I should add that foraging is even keel with hunting in terms of its connective experience, but in different realms than is hunting. In foraging, the scale of relation and focus becomes, in a sense, more microscopic. For example, when laying on the ground picking berries from low shrubs, one becomes immersed in a meditative state within the fine details of the groundcover; the various species of plants, lichens, mosses, the dirt, the smells, flowers, insects, and of course the berries. Foraging humans are very animal-like in movement, thinking, and behavior. Alongside hunting, foraging is highly recommended as a continuous practice.
43 Shepard, 1996, Pg. 88-89
44 Shepard, 1996, Pg. 24
45 Willerslev, 2012, Pg. 110
46 There is also a contingent of so-called 'anti-civilization/primitivist vegans' who seem to be hell bent that the traits of civilization can be abolished via 'vegan permaculture' and/or that survival can be accomplished purely via fruit and vegetable foraging and who, in order to maintain their narrative, seem to be unabashedly willing to ignore the entire anthropological record post *Australopithecine*, the first known hominid, with an origination and extinction timeline of approximately 4 million-2million BP. This means ignoring the following 2 million years of omnivorous hominid history as well as the approximate 1.5 million years before that where hominids were very much omnivorous, not vegan. It also means ignoring the fact that there is no documentation whatsoever of any hominid species (including *Australopitheicus* who very likely at least consumed insects*)* which can be verified as maintaining a 'vegan' adaptation. Additionally it means ignoring the legitimacy of the very heavily documented extremely long-lasting and robust omnivory of all known self-sufficient indigenous peoples of the world, hunter-gatherer or otherwise, and thus blatantly attempts to delegitimize a core feature of ALL indigenous cultures worldwide, a feature which ALL non-civilized indigenous cultures consider central and sacrosanct. Yet we hear these otherworldly, ideological, dogmatic, so-called 'vegan primitivists' also make mention of 'indigenous rights' and call for a halting of civilization's destruction of indigenous cultures? One can only find all of this extremely humorous. As a person very experienced in living amongst indigenous cultures I can assure all factions that not only will the world's indigenous peoples laugh at such a prospect as 'vegan primitivism', they would find ANY proselytizing of veganism's 'virtue' a highly offensive attack on their cultures and view proselytizing 'vegan primitivists' not as allies but simply as another group of progressive, futurist, civilized invaders. As Paul Shepard made very clear in his work, the moralistic ide-

al that humans of any type have lived and can live without total participation in the actual life-and-death, predator-and-prey cycles of earth ecology (and yes, herbivores also prey on wild beings) is rooted entirely in alienated, post-domestic, civilized thought. It is high-time for vegan ideologues to get real about earth ecology and human ecology, especially the so-called 'anti-civilization/primitivist vegans'. Civilization is a (failing) effort to escape ecological reality and veganism is inherently progressive and futurist and is thus highly civilized in its psychology. *Australopitheicus* is not *Homo*. Evolution to homo begins with omnivory and then develops from there to full-scale pursuit and consumption of mammals; long, long before *sapiens* emergence. There is no escape from evolutionary-ecological reality, no escape from your omnivorous foundations.

47 An 'anti-civilization vegan' who authentically attempts to rewild outside of civilization may, in that experience, quickly come to realize that their veganism was also just that, an 'ideal' which does not hold when confronted with survival outside of support by the infrastructure of domestication. They too shall learn to separate what is 'ideal' from what is adaptable and what has endured, and they will have to choose either to sacrifice themselves to domestication's gods or to live, and thus to prey on something and consume it.

48 R. Willerslev et al., *Sacrifice as the ideal hunt: a cosmological explanation for the origin of reindeer domestication*. Journal of the Royal Anthropological Institute. 2014, Pg. 9.

49 S. Wallace, *The unconquered: in search of the Amazon's last uncontacted tribes*. Crown Publishers, 2011. Pg. 264.

50 The load was almost two guanacos including bones and skins. Bridges, 2007, Pg. 258

51 Bridges, 2007, Pg. 419

52 S. Kantner, *Ordinary wolves*. Milkweed Editions. Minneapolis, 2004. Pg. 175

53 To be clear, here I am referring to autonomous physical work by individuals and small-groups, not to work in the form of "employment" or "wage labor".

54 Anarchoprimitivists have been criticized in the past for brushing over the fine details of this in the anthropological record and I want to set the record straight that we are not brushing over it. Those of us who have spent considerable time in the field of land-based survival know from experience not to generalize on the complexity of this topic.

55 R.B. Lee and I. Devore (editors), *Man the hunter*. Aldine, Chicago, 1968, particularly M. Sahlins, *Notes on the original affluent society*, contained in this volume.

56 M. Sahlins, *Stone age economics*, Aldine, Chicago, 1972.

57 K. Hawkes and J. F. O'Connell, *Affluent hunters? some comments in light of the Alyawara case*. American Anthropologist 83, 1981, Pg. 622-626.

58 Various reanalysis of the 'primitive affluence' thesis can be reviewed in Coon 1971, Hawkes and O'Connell 1981, E. Cashdan, *Hunters and gatherers: economic behavior in bands*. In S. Plattner (editor), Economic Anthropology, 1989, Pg. 22-23, and B. Winterhalder, *Work, resources, and population in foraging societies*. Man, New Series, Volume 28, Issue 2, 1993, Pg. 321-340.

59 Smith et al., 2010, Pg. 21

60 Bridges, 2007, Pg. 369-370

61 An excellent reference from which to draw on for inspiration in this practice is A. Fienup-Riordan and A. Rearden, *Ellavut: our Yup'ik world and weather, continuity and change on the Bering Sea coast*. University of Washington Press, Seattle and London, 2012.

62 T. Ingold, *Hunters, pastoralists, and ranchers*. Cambridge University Press, Cambridge, New York, New Rochelle, Melbourne, Sydney, 1980, Pg. 144

63 Bridges, 2007, Pg. 422

64 Thomas, 2006, Pg. 223. Thomas notes that Bushmen did trade with settled Bantu people but generally always ended up with a bad taste in their mouths regarding the practice, due to the relationship being generally always one of their being taken advantage of by the Bantu.

65 For example, see Ingold, 2004.

66 See R. Katz, *Boiling energy: community healing among the Kalahari Kung*. Cambridge,

MA: Harvard University Press, 1982, C. Knight, *Blood relations: menstruation and the origins of culture*. New Haven and London: Yale University Press, 1991, M. Biesele, *Women like meat: the folklore and foraging ideology of the Kalahari Ju/'hoan*. Johannesburg and Indiana: Witwatersrand University, 1993, Thomas 2006, J. Lewis, *Ekila: blood, bodies, and egalitarian societies*, Journal of the Royal Anthropological Institute (N. S.) 14, Pg. 297-315, 2002, T. Skaanes, *Notes on Hadza cosmology: epeme, objects and rituals*, Hunter-Gatherer Research 1, Pg. 247-267, 2015, C. Power, *Reconstructing a source cosmology for African hunter-gatherers*, presented at the Conference on Hunting and Gathering Societies, Vienna, September 2015. And K. Tucker, *Hooked on a feeling: the loss of community and the rise of addiction*. Black and Green Review, Issue #3, Spring 2016.
67 Thomas, 2006, Pg. 162
68 For one of many examples, see Ingold, 2004.
69 Ingold, 2004 Pg. 66
70 Shepard, 1996, Pg. 295
71 Shepard, 1996, Pg. 64
72 Smith et al., 2010, Pg. 22
73 L. R. Binford, *Willow smoke and dogs' tails: hunter-gatherer settlement systems and archaeological site formation*, American Antiquity, Vol. 45, No. 1, 1980, Pg. 4-20.
74 For a discussion of the self-domestication process see *The wind roars ferociously: feral foundations and the necessity of wild resistance*. Black and Green Review, Issue #3, Spring 2016.
75 Binford, 1980, Pg. 19
76 See *Feralculture: discussing nodal land projects with Andrew Badenoch* and *Wild healing: talking about building wild communities with Sky* in Black and Green Review, Issue #1, Spring 2015. Also see https://feralculture.com/
77 I have stealthily tent squatted for months at a time on wild forested public lands. In one instance this was accomplished within 25 minutes walking distance of my place of employment at the time, where I was required to show up with a 'professional' looking business appearance. No one had a clue that I was simultaneously living a secretive double-life as a 'homeless' person camping and foraging in the forest. Highly recommended for spirit enhancement, skill building, and for avoiding rent payments!
78 Bridges, 2007, Pg. 390
79 Kantner, 2004, Pg. 273
80 J. Goody, *The domestication of the savage mind*. Cambridge University Press, London, 1977, Pg. 13.
81 Goody, Pg. 13
82 Davis, 2009, Pg. 38
83 See my article *The commodification of wildness and its consequences* in Black and Green Review, Issue #1, Spring 2015
84 Kantner, 2004, Pg. 286
85 For example, see Ingold, 2004 Pg. 63 and Winterhalder, 1993, Pg. 336. Ingold notes that the terms *immediacy, autonomy*, and *sharing* "appear together in the ethnography with such regularity and consistency as to suggest a distinctive form of sociality." Winterhalder notes that throughout their history hunter-gatherers seemed to not have developed material reifications and instead have maintained within their psychology an aptitude to consistently differentiate between "scarcity as a perception of inadequate provisions or as material fact."
86 Shepard, 1996, Pg. 223. Shepard asks if human observations/relationships with zoo animals provide any venue for this whatsoever and concludes that only in relationship with wild animals is this possible.

Modernity Takes Over
John Zerzan

What were modernity's origins and what has been its trajectory? In this very brief critical survey, let's start with the Renaissance. Ever since Jacob Burkhardt's *The Civilization of the Renaissance in Italy*, the word immediately brings other words to mind: "individual," "self," "personality," usually thought of as modern. Western individualism, and a new age of domination, begin with the Renaissance.

Oswald Spengler used the word "Faustian" to designate a further realm of control. "Renaissance, Rinascita, meant...the new Faustian world-feeling, the new personal experience of the Ego in the Infinite."[1] Of course, he refers here to the so-called Age of Discovery, when emerging European national states reached out to colonize far-flung continents.

"Humanism" is another term that points to the future, with its emphasis on individualism. An individualism that must be seen as corporate, firmly embedded in collective networks of power and wealth. And the "self-confident artistic utopianism of 15th-century Renaissance Florence"[2] existed in the context of a noisy, dirty, violent, typhus- and malaria-ridden city. Along with self-confidence there was much discontent–even despair. As Edgar Wind put it, "the most splendid release of artistic energies was attended by political disintegration."[3]

Merchant bankers dominated the urban politics of the Renaissance, often wielding near-absolute power. In Florence the Medicis amassed huge wealth and authority, but lacked legitimacy. To make interest-bearing loans (usury) was a mortal sin, Dante's favorite target. And Medici wealth was fairly recently obtained, usually by fraudulent and violent means. It fell to artists to create an artificial aura of legitimacy (e.g. Rubens' Medici cycle of paintings). Patronage of art and architecture succeeded at this task on a grand scale, also in the service of an especially corrupt and violent Papacy (e.g. Alexander VI, Pius II).

The glories of Renaissance culture also papered over a surge of anti-semitism in Florence that "would not be matched in Italy until the rise of fascism."[4] High culture was also deaf to the fact that European expansionism involved consigning entire peoples to non-human status. These atrocities were accompanied by what Alexander Lee termed "the most deadening artistic silence of all time."[5] In fact, mastery of color, perspective, and the like often served the opposite of what we might think of as Renaissance values.

Spengler rightly concluded that "the Renaissance never touched the people."[6] Case in point: the several years' rule over Florence by Dominican friar Girolama Savonarola in the waning years of the 15th century. Simplicity and repentance were the watchwords of his near-revolution. Thousands of youth ran through the streets smashing anything that appeared to be arrogant wealth. It was a virtual theocracy, ISIS-like to some degree, but plebian in character.[7] Savonarola's social and cultural bonfire did not endure; in 1498 he was hanged, then burned to ashes on the spot.

Half a century later, according to J.B. Singh-Uberoi, "the modern chapter of man and nature as well as of natural science [owed] as much (or more) to the Reformation as it did to the Renaissance."[8] Protests against abusive practices of the Catholic Church by Luther, Calvin, Zwingli, and others became a revolt against Papal authority. Protestant denominations were the result: a full break with Catholicism. And the anti-authoritarian spirit of the Reformation was not limited to doctrinal matters. In Germany, home of the Reformation, anger at Church landlords ran high; appeals to the people by Luther and other reformers brought more radical results than these preachers intended.[9] The radical Reformation was exemplified by Thomas Müntzer, who broke with Luther early on, announcing an imminent apocalypse wherein freedom and equality would reign. Müntzer preached dispossession of the nobility, echoing the Taborite millenarians and social revolutionaries of 15th century Bohemia. The great peasant revolt in southern and central Germany (1525-1526) was the most important event of the Reformation period and one of the biggest mass movements in German history.[10]

But sadly, the Peasants' War is not what was arguably modern about this era. The seeds of modernity are found instead in writings of people like Ulrich Zwingli. He preached the necessity of regular, industrious habits, and warned of "the danger of relaxing the incentive to work."[11] The origin of this modern, now-internalized ethos is the main subject of Max Weber's classic, *The Protestant Ethic and the Spirit of Capitalism*.

The rise of Protestantism relied upon the print culture introduced by Johannes Gutenberg's invention: a printing press using moveable type. Printed books were available in the early 1500s, accompanied by a striking increase in literacy. For Marshall McLuhan, print was a founding aspect of modernity: "With Gutenberg Europe enters the technological phase of progress, when change itself becomes the archetypal norm of social life."[12]

Typography made possible the first assembly line, the first mass production. Not only did authorial ownership commence, but, according to Roberto Dainotto, "By embedding language in the manufacturing process of mass-produced books, the printing press transformed words and ideas into commodities."[13] Walter Ong observed another key outcome: "Before writing was deeply interiorized by print, people did not feel themselves situated every moment of their lives in abstract, computed time of any sort."[14] A changed sense of time seems related to a growing "passion for exact measurement"[15] in the late Renaissance. The emphasis on precision shows that the domestication process is speeding up and tightening its grip.

The privatization of this medium through silent reading, an enormous change in itself, also altered the balance among our senses. Touch and hearing became much less important. In antiquity and in the Middle Ages, reading was social–reading aloud. Some saw typography as a powerful, alien force. Rabelais and Cervantes declared it "Gargantuan, Fantastic, Suprahuman."[16] Print and literacy led to a marked increase in the social division of labor. Illiterates became subordinates, subject to the greater effective power of specialists, and witness to a steady dissolution of community.[17] Community became less important than one's place in the division of labor hierarchy.

A cognate of *public* is *publish*. We come now to a foundation of mass society: mass media as a means of social control. Print greased the wheels for national uniformity and state centrism; yet at the same time it facilitated individual expression and opposition to the dominant order.

Humanism is the watchword of Renaissance thinking. *Huma-*

nitas is its Latin reference, opposed to *immanis*, or savage. Humanism's proponents stressed individualism, but that covered a multitude of sins. An individualist spirit of inquiry and adventure helped fuel overseas invasions and territorial expansion. Humanists were often silent about the deeds of colonialist explorers, but occasionally there was a direct connection. Amerigo Vespucci, for instance, was an explorer and a humanist writer. He had also worked for the Medici bank in Florence.

Many humanists sanctioned the subjugation of women. Renaissance power was inherently masculine. During the Renaissance period, women lost status compared to their medieval sisters. although women of the middle and poorer classes retained more self-determination than those of higher rank.[18] Between 1480 and 1700 (the heyday of humanism), large numbers of women were condemned and executed as witches.

Renaissance humanists were filled with zeal to rekindle the Crusades and wipe out Muslims. The early and much-cited humanist Petrarch was especially venomous against Islamic infidels.[19]

As always, intellectuals were called upon to legitimate the dominant order, and humanists performed this service. Michel de Montaigne, a 16th century magistrate and essayist, is principally noted for his project to question everything--a very modern idea. He is seen as the first fully humanist writer, the first to express a coherent version of the doctrine. He denied that commoners and women could engage in the search for self-knowledge.[20]

The earthy François Rabelais, Montaigne's contemporary, was the rare antinomian figure of the period. His utopian Abbey of Thélème was a place of pleasure and freedom, not of sanctioned individualism.

As 1600 approached, humanism's legitimacy was challenged. "Late humanism was beset with a crisis of confidence," in Katherine Eggert's words.[21] Something seemed to be missing. Something human was being lost. But what would take its place?

In 1582 time was brought up to date with the introduction of the Gregorian calendar, which reigned over a time of "a general malaise"[22] and active disaffection in Europe. The late 16th century was marked by serious peasant revolts. France and the Netherlands experienced urban disorder, not forgetting the great 1585 rising in Naples. In 1600 Giordano Bruno was burned at the stake in Rome's Campo Fiori for defending Copernicus and espousing dangerous ideas of atomic theory and an infinite universe.

17th century thinkers dethroned scholastic Arisototelianism and indeed, theology itself. Not only Church orthodoxy, but animism and magic that had survived into the Renaissance were rejected. The mental universe was still animate rather than mechanical, though, despite the concept of conquest of nature whose roots lay in the Renaissance.

The scientific revolution of the 1600s was a decisive break with the past, a thorough re-evaluation of what had come before. Francis Bacon (1561-1626) has come to represent the shift. Inaugurating methods of induction and experimentation, his project was to restore the dominion over creation that had been lost with the expulsion of Adam and Eve from the Garden of Eden. Bacon saluted America's first colonizers, their work in a "Newfound Land of inventions and sciences unknown."[23]

But Bacon did not achieve a full break with Church scholasticism (of Thomas Aquinas and others). That task fell to René Descartes, and Michel Serres' words are worth noting: "Mastery and possession: these are the master words launched by Descartes at the dawn of the scientific and technological age, when our Western reason went off to conquer the universe. We dominate and appropriate it: such is the shared philosophy underlying industrial enterprise as well as so-called disinterested science, which are indistinguishable in this respect."[24]

A self-proclaimed original, Descartes was an arch-rationalist who refused to trust his own senses. His dis-embodied approach sought to derive sensory information from mathematics instead of the other way around, and virtually equated math and natural science. Having created analytic geometry, he wanted to mathematize thought. Descartes' famous formulation of mind-body dualism is consonant with his view of reality as immutable and inflexible mechanical order. It should come as no surprise that he saw humans, among other living beings, as fundamentally machines.

The Cartesian project did much to initiate modern thought and at base, still obtains. Now we witness the Artificial Intelligence technicians striving for Artificial Consciousness, pursuing a machine model. And contemporary philosophy seems to take seriously hyper-estranged Alain Badiou's mathematics-equals-ontology concept. Descartes subverted humanism, and gravely worsened the un-health of the West.

Among Descartes' contemporaries was Gottfried Leibniz, whose new system of "pre-established harmony" offered a mechanistic explanation of Creation–a further move in the onslaught on scholasticism. John Locke, founder of the modern liberal, individualist tradition, rejected Descartes' dualism as too God-oriented. Locke attacked political absolutism for the non-productivity of the land-owning aristocracy. He argued for a more modern form of exploitation, the enclosure of communal land into privately owned property. The 17th century backdrop to these published ideas was burgeoning occupation and enslavement on other continents by European profiteers. Thomas Hobbes was party to this through his involvement with the Virginia Company. He condemned life in the state of nature as "nasty, brutish, and short," and termed indigenous people "savages," providing ideological justification for conquest and slavery.

Price hikes and tax increases provoked resistance, such as the 1630 rising in Dijon and revolts in Aix-en-Provence between 1631 and 1638. Silk workers in Amiens attacked their masters' establishments in 1637. Bayeux tanners rose up briefly in 1639, and sailors' wives went on the offensive in Montpelier in 1645, to cite a few insurrectionary incidents in 17th century France.[25] During this period the Thirty Years' War (1618-1648), Europe's last mainly religious war, ravaged a third of the continent, with millions of casualties.

1648 was a year of revolts, particularly in the context of the English Civil War. Levellers, Ranters, Diggers, and others espoused radical, anti-authority, anti-enclosures orientations. But Oliver Cromwell's Protectorate prevailed over the resistance, establishing mercantile capitalism as the core of the economy.

By this time, and commencing in earnest around 1600, division of labor was transforming the ground of social existence.[26] New production techniques ushered in proto-industrialization, especially in rural areas.[27] "Proto-industries arose in almost every part of Europe in the two or three centuries before industrialization."[28]

The ideas of Bacon, Descartes, Leibniz, and other mathematical and scientific thinkers interwove with and supported technological innovation during the 17th century. As Margaret Jacob notes, "The road from the Scientific Revolution to the Industrial Revolution...is more straightforward than we may have imagined."[29]

What we call the Enlightenment of the 1700s owed much to the canon of 17th century empirical philosophy and natural science. Denis Diderot's iconic *Encyclopédie* was based on his "tree of knowledge," derived from Bacon's 17th century ideas.[30] Although initially an English phenomenon, Enlightenment is best known for its flowering in Paris, between the death of Louis XIV in 1715 and the onset of the French Revolution in 1789. Its most important figures were Voltaire, Montesquieu, and Rousseau.

During this period, protests and riots continued to flare (e.g. Geneva experienced risings in 1717, 1738, 1768, and 1782). Newspapers and commercialized leisure became part of everyday life. In the 1750s and 1760s the modern chronological timeline was first introduced,[31] and modern education forms (such as measurable results via written examinations) became common.

Enlightenment voices decried superstition and tyranny. Christianity came under fire, most forcefully by the programmatic disbelief of Diderot and David Hume, among others. The Church retreated, dissolving the militant Jesuit order (it would not be re-established until 1814). The new outlook overturned the Renaissance belief that what came first was best, replacing it with faith in progress and the future. A favorite target of Enlightenment's materialist orientation was animism; the once-prevailing conception of a living spirit in nature was denounced as superstition.

The supposed anti-tyranny credo bears a closer examination. Voltaire and other leading Enlightenment lights were friendly with Frederick the Great, despite his despotism and support of feudalism.[32] Frederick's proclamation of the Enlightenment as Prussia's official ideology[33] seems like a strange fit.

Enlightenment reason certainly did some demythologizing, but it also installed new myths along with its claims and promises. One such myth held that history, in Couze Venn's words, as "the universal and rational project of the becoming of humanity as a whole"[34]--a myth with grave implications and consequences for indigenous people. There is an evident connection between imperialist expansion as a system of power, and the diffusion of Enlightenment thought as a global pattern of culture.

A forbear of dissent from the vision of universalizing Progress was Rabelais. He declared his "enduring affinity with the alien spirits, of whom there are always some in every society, who at any sacrifice resist, or rather, quietly elude, all pressure towards conformity, towards standardization and mechanization of thought."[35] In his utopian Abbey of Thélème, there are no clocks; a swimming pool and other non-monastic features are inspired by the abbey's all-encompassing watchword, Do What Thou Wilt. 18th century philosopher and novelist Jean-Jacques Rousseau took a dim view of civilization and proclaimed the natural goodness of humankind. He refused abstract geometry and its method, preferring the promenade as a way of visiting "idle and lazy" nature, as Michel Serres put it.[36]

Central to Enlightenment thought and probably the most important modern philosopher, Immanuel Kant did much to shape how people understand reality even today. He also revealed something of the less than liberatory side of Enlightenment. Silke-Maria Weineck placed his thinking "on the side of certifiable calculations, of the exchange of goods, of sound economics."[37] Similarly, Heinrich Heine referred to Kant's "petty-bourgeois values."[38] Theodor Adorno took this further, observing that "All the concepts...[Kant's] Critique of Practical Reason proposes, in honor of freedom–...law, constraint, respect, duty–all of these are repressive."[39] He found that "Kant's moral philosophy...will not let him visualize the concept of freedom otherwise than repression." And "reason itself is to Kant nothing but the lawmaking power.... He glories in an unmitigated urge to punish."[40] Montesquieu is closely aligned with Kant in this: "Law, generally speaking, is human reason."[41]

The empire of Reason also liquidates difference, in the direction of the "total, perfect political unification of human species," in Jacques Derrida's words[42]–a cold, universalizing agenda. The German poet Novalis found a conformist spirit of disenchantment in the "harsh, chilly light of the Enlightenment."[43]

Its supposed higher form of rationality provided cover for Europe's "civilizing mission" and for Western hegemony. Without the new imperialism, as Paulos Gregorios saw it, the Enlightenment "could hardly have taken place."[44] Ideas and actions deeply influence each other.

In France the Enlightenment emerged after the reign of Louis XIV, when it "began to set the tone in polite society."[45] Enlightenment *philosophes* felt confidence, at least in part, because of their close relationships with bourgeois notables. Not only Frederick the Great, but other ministers and sovereigns looked to them for guidance and legitimation. The patronage of absolutist princes created influential positions for them; as J.B. Bury reminds us, "They never challenged the principle of a despotic government, they only contended that the despotism be enlightened."[46] Before the Revolution that began in 1789, Enlightenment standard-bearers were "part of the new ruling elite."[47]

It is also true that the modern understanding of citizenship is a creation of the Enlightenment. But as Voltaire said, "Better not teach peasants how to read; someone had to plow the fields."[48] Yet Voltaire also passionately denounced slavery, as did Condorcet and Raynal. There were also protests against the oppression of colonial peoples, though not against the practice of colonization itself.

Summing up their mid-20th century critique of the Enlightment, Max Horkheimer and Theodor Adorno declared that the "fully enlightened earth radiates disaster triumphant."[49] Modern exploitation of nature and modern, atomized mass society commence with this epoch.

Enlightenment thought was an ideological bridge between a pre-industrial, aristocratic culture and an industrialized, consumerist society. Some large-scale production facilities existed in mid-18th century Europe: examples include van Robais' textile factory at Abbeville, the Lombe brothers' silk mill at Derby, and the iron industry initiated by Peter the Great in the Ural Mountains.[50] Some Enlightenment proponents were directly involved in these enterprises. Diderot studied the mechanical order of production; Vaucanson designed efficient silk mills. Early manufacturers breathed the air of the dominant liberal, humanistic creed of the Enlightenment. Its spirit of classification and analysis was a practical aid to industry. Enlightenment materialism fostered "mastery by technological and commercial means over the material world."[51]

The principle of individual autonomy, even with the necessary qualifiers, gained acceptance during the Renaissance and the Protestant Reformation. But as Bruno Latour argues, "modern" only applies to societies in which artisanal, personal kinds of making are superseded by broad-scale, impersonal modes.[52] Modernity is an Enlightenment word, and Latour's watershed distinction can be found in that era. The Enlightenment was the first take-off point of the non-conscious praxis of amoral technicism.

Major claims and promises were made. There would be an end to religious intolerance, and a Brave New World ushered in by science and technology. Given the evident failure of these promises, it is little wonder that there is now "a global backlash...against the Enlightenment itself," as John McCumber has put it.[53] I concur with Onora O'Neill's assessment: "A world of isolated and alienated individuals who find to their horror that nihilism, terror, domination, and the destruction of the natural world are the true offspring of the Enlightenment."[54]

We are still in the Enlightenment era, and its "light" is spreading everywhere. The fully enlightened world, the fully civilized world, is indeed disaster. The prospect of modernity without end faces each and all of us.

Endnotes

1 Oswald Spengler, *Decline of the West*, Vol. II (New York: Alfred A. Knopf, 1926), p. 191.
2 Alexander Lee, *The Ugly Renaissance: Sex, Greed, Violence and Depravity in an Age of Beauty* (New York: Doubleday, 2013), p. 42.
3 Edgar Wind, *Art and Anarchy* (New York: Knopf, 1964), p. 6.
4 Lee, *op.cit.*, p. 308.
5 *Ibid.*, p. 350.
6 Spengler, *op.cit.*, Volume I, p. 233.
7 Thomas Cahill, *Heretics and Heroes* (New York: Doubleday, 2013), p. 79.
8 J.P. Singh-Uberoi, *The European Modernity* (New York: Oxford University Press, 2002), p. 26.
9 Peter Burke, *Popular Culture in Early Modern Europe* (New York: New York University Press, 1978), pp. 260-261.
10 Michael Hughes, *Early Modern Germany, 1477-1806* (Philadelphia: University of Pennsylvania Press, 1992), p. 45.
11 R.H. Tawney, *Religion and the Rise of Capitalism* (New York: Harcourt Brace and Company, 1926), p. 115.
12 Marshall McLuhan, *The Gutenberg Galaxy: The Making of Typographic Man* (Toronto: University of Toronto Press, 1962), p. 155.
13 Roberto M. Dainotto, *Europe (in theory)* (Durham, NC: Duke University Press, 2007), p. 35.
14 Walter J. Ong, *Orality and Literacy* (London: Methuen, 1982), p. 96.
15 McLuhan, *op.cit.*, p. 166.
16 *Ibid.*, p. 194
17 See Agnes Heller, *Renaissance Man* (Boston: Routledge & Kegan Paul, 1978), e.g. pp. 206, 291.
18 William Caferro, *Contesting the Renaissance* (Malden, MA: Wiley-Blackwell, 2011), pp. 15, 68, 76, 86.
19 Lee, *op.cit.*, pp. 318-319.
20 Caferro, *op.cit.*, p. 33.
21 Katherine Eggert, *Disknowledge* (Philadelphia: University of Pennsylvania Press, 2015), p. 8.
22 Alexander Cowan, *Urban Europe 1500-1700* (New York: Oxford University Press, 1998), p. 189.
23 Loren Eiseley, *Francis Bacon and the Modern Dilemma* (Lincoln, NE: The University of Nebraska Press, 1962), p. 59.
24 Michel Serres, *The Natural Contract* (Ann Arbor, MI: University of Michigan Press, 1995), p. 32.
25 Cowan, *op.cit.*, pp. 44, 176-179.

26 John Zerzan, *Future Primitive* (Brooklyn, NY: Autonomedia, 1994), p. 147.
27 Peter Kriedte, Hans Medick, Jurgen Schlumbohm, eds., *Industrialization Before Industrialization* (New York: Cambridge University Press, 1981).
28 Sheilagh C. Ogilvie and Markus Cerman, "Proto-industrialization, economic development and social change in early modern Europe," in Ogilvie and Cerman, eds., *European proto-industrialization* (Cambridge: Cambridge University Press, 1996), p. 227.
29 Margaret C. Jacob, *The Cultural Meaning of the Scientific Revolution* (New York: McGraw-Hill, 1993), p. 7.
30 Jeffrey S. Ravel and Linda Zionkowski, *Studies in Enlightenment Culture*, vol. 36 (Baltimore: The Johns Hopkins University Press, 2007), p. 55.
31 Robert Darnton, *The Great Cat Massacre and Other Episodes in French Cultural History* (New York: Basic Books, 1984), p. 194.
32 Alexander Rüstow, *Freedom and Domination: A Historical Critique of Civilization* (Princeton, NJ: Princeton University Press, 1980), p. 330.
33 T.C.W. Blanning, *The Culture of Power and the Power of Culture* (New York: Oxford University Press, 2002), p. 201.
34 Couze Venn, "Altered States: Post-Enlightenment Cosmopolitanism and Transmodern Socialities," in *Theory, Culture & Society* 19:1 (2002), p. 65.
35 Albert Jan Nock and C.R. Wilson, *Francis Rabelais* (New York: Harper & Brothers Publishers, 1929), p. 358.
36 Pierre Saint-Armand, *The Pursuit of Idleness: An Idle Interpretation of the Enlightenment* (Princeton, NJ: Princeton University Press, 2011), p. 14. Similar cases Chardin's distraction, Rameau's vagrancy, Joubert's laziness, p. 16.
37 Silke-Maria Weineck, *The Abyss Above* (Albany, NY: State University of New York Press, 2002), p. 10.
38 Anthony Pagden, *The Enlightenment: Why It Still Matters* (New York: Random House, 2013), p. 387.
39 Theodor Adorno, *Negative Dialectics* (New York: Continuum, 2007), pp. 230, 232.
40 *Ibid.*, pp. 255, 256, 260.
41 In John W. Yolton, et al, eds., *The Blackwell Companion to the Enlightenment* (Cambridge, MA: Blackwell, 1991), p. 258.
42 Quoted in Venn, *op.cit.*, p. 74.
43 Ulrich Imhof, *The Enlightenment* (Cambridge, MA: Blackwell, 1994), p. 270.
44 Paulos Mer Gregorios, *A Light Too Bright: the Enlightenment Today* (Albany, NY: State University of New York Press, 1992), p. 63.
45 Darnton, *op.cit.*, p. 208.
46 J.B. Bury, *The Idea of Progress* (New York: Dover Publications, 1955), p. 176.
47 Robert Darnton: *The Case for Enlightenment: George Washington's False Teeth* (New York: W.W. Norton, 2003), p. 5.
48 R.G. Saisselin, "Philosophes," in Yolton et al., *op.cit.*, p. 397.
49 Theodor Adorno and Max Horkheimer, *Dialectic of Enlightenment* (New York: Verso, 1997), p. 3.
50 Norman Hampson, *A Cultural History of the Enlightenment* (New York: Pantheon Books, 1968), p. 46.
51 Aram Vartanian, "Diderot and the Philosophes," in Yoltan et al., *op.cit.*, p. 316.
52 Julian Yates, *Error, Misuse, Failure* (Minneapolis: University of Minnesota Press, 2003), p. 5.
53 John McCumber, *On Philosophy: Notes from a Crisis* (Stanford, CA: Stanford University Press, 2012), p. 10.
54 Onora O'Neill, "Enlightenment as Autonomy: Kant's Vindication of Reason," in Peter Hulme and L.G. Jordanova, *The Enlightenment and its Shadows* (New York: Routledge, 1990), p. 189.

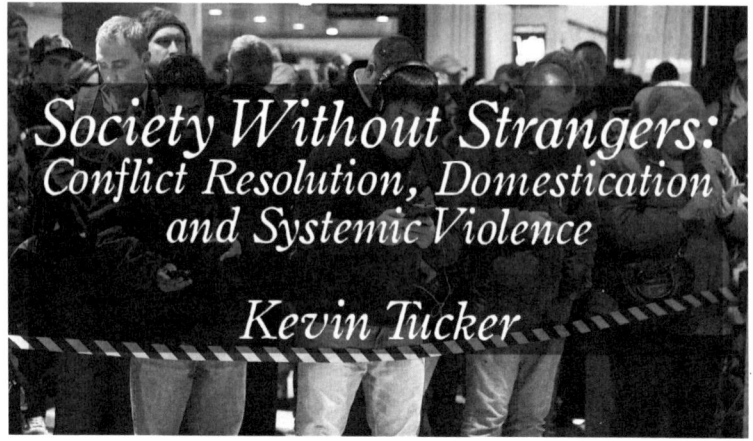

Society Without Strangers:
Conflict Resolution, Domestication and Systemic Violence

Kevin Tucker

> Sahlins has called the state a society especially constituted to maintain law and order. The vast administrative hierarchies of the state are, of course, absent in band and tribal societies. An alternative but complementary view is to regard the process of social evolution leading to the state as one of externalizing violence rather than controlling or eliminating it. Such a view enables us to see the evolution of social control in a different light.
> -Richard Lee, *The !Kung San*[1]

/Twi was a dangerous man.

Living amongst the /Du/da clan of the nomadic foraging !Kung San of Namibia of 1940s, /Twi stood out. Violence amongst the indisputably egalitarian !Kung has been both well-documented and largely over-stated. But /Twi was particularly violent. By his own family's telling, he was possibly psychotic.

Amongst his contemporary !Kung this was well known.

Fed up, /Xashe, another !Kung man at /Du/da, one day ambushed /Twi, shooting him in the hip with a poisoned arrow, their preferred hunting weapon. They grappled and /Xashe's mother-in-law held /Twi and told /Xashe to run. Other residents at the camp gathered around /Twi as he pulled the arrow from his hip. Some tried helping him by cutting the wound and attempt extracting the poison out.

/Twi took advantage of the situation. He snapped. He flung a spear which ripped the cheek of a woman named //Kushe. //Kushe's husband, N!eishi, came to her aid and /Twi shot him in the back with a poisoned arrow.

At this point, everyone took cover, shooting arrows back at /Twi.

None sought to give aid to /Twi. They had decided, collectively, that he had to die.

/Twi walked out to the center of the camp and sat, calling out, "are you still afraid of me? Well I am finished, I have no more breath. Come here and kill me... Do you fear my weapons? Here I am putting them out of reach. I won't touch them. Come kill me."

As /Twi's younger brother, ≠Toma, recalled:

Then they all fired on him with poisoned arrows till he looked like a porcupine. Then he lay flat. All approached him, men and women, and stabbed his body with spears even after he was dead.

/Twi was buried and the camp split up.

All going their separate ways.[2]

Within civilization, we have a very strange relationship with violence.

For anthropologists Nancy Scheper-Hughes and Philippe Bourgois violence "defies easy categorization. It can be everything and nothing; legitimate or illegitimate; visible or invisible; necessary or useless; senseless and gratuitous or utterly rational and strategic." It is a small term for a range of actions and provocations.

In their summation, "violence is in the eye of the beholder."[3] You know it when you see or experience it.

Violence is an outburst. It is a response to emotions, to anger, and to fear.

As animals, violence has a place.

As animals, violence also has its thresholds.

When we remove the distance between our lives and our actions: violence is just one part of our experience of the world. It is a trait, an ability, but hardly one that defines our existence. In the civilized perceptions of the world, *nature* is a passive place.[4] For the escapist backpacker or the spiritual zealot, wilderness is a place of peaceful reflection. We carry these voyeuristic perceptions of the world, of the ecology of life, because they are comforting. On a surface level they stand in stark contrast to the systemic, organized violence and anxiety of civilized life.

As technology intrudes, this contrast only becomes louder.

Our perception of wildness echoes our understanding of what it means to be an animal, of what it means to be human. Embracing that wildness is neither a simple nor an easy process, but it gives us the ability to know who we are, what we need, and what stands between us.

Wildness is a state where passivity is not an option. To borrow a phrase from Tamarack Song, wildness is a state of *dynamic tension*.[5] In this all beings are aware, ready, and reliant on the songs of birds, the movement of leaves, the sounds of the environment. Here we inhabit a state that is neither entirely peaceful nor warring, but of *being*.

This is a place where humans are neither angels nor demons.

This is a place where power, be it social, political, or economic, does not exist. And this is the place where our nomadic hunter-gatherer bodies and minds evolved.

This is also the place where the /Du/da camp of the !Kung collectively decided that /Twi must die.

He had become a liability.

And so they killed him. Immediately and without remorse or anger. It needed to be done so that life could continue on, as it had and as it would, without unnecessary violence.

Within civilization, our relationship with violence is schizophrenic.

Those of us unfortunate enough to have been born within this era of hyper-technological, modernized civilization live in the most violent society that has ever existed. And we have the fortune of almost never being confronted directly by any of it. We are so accustomed to not seeing the violence inherent in our daily lives that we can convince ourselves that it isn't there. We convince ourselves that we are better off: as individuals, as a society.

These are the lies that are sold to us by programmers, the architects of Modernity, like Steven Pinker. In his widely upheld 2011 book, *The Better Angels of our Nature*, he makes the claim that our past, human history, is "a shockingly violent one." He states that it "is easy to forget how dangerous life used to be, how deeply brutality was once woven into the fabric of daily existence."[6]

And yet we kill.

We subjugate and suffocate the earth, our home. We colonize the periphery, we tear down forests, we scrape the life off the bottom of the oceans while we pour toxins into the air and dilute chemicals into the soil. We wipe out entire species methodically. This happens every time we turn on the light switch. Every time we get into our cars, turn on our phones, buy food at the grocery store; as I write these words on a computer and as you read them in a book: the earth and all its inhabitants feel the consequences.

And so do we.

We've just been trained to not see them.

We use technology to distance ourselves from those impacted.

We use the technology and politicking that Pinker upholds to feel as though we've braved the worst of our own humanity, our primal animality, to become civilized.

In the eyes of the State, violence is a violation of our supposed codes of conduct: a transgression from law and order. It happens when individuals act without involving the government-sanctioned mediators.

In the hands of the individual, violence is an unjust, uncivilized response to conflict.

All institutions, all vestiges of political power, require a monopoly on control. They require a monopoly on the justness or unjustness of violence. They must control it. They determine how an act of overt force fits with prescribed rules of conduct for any given society. And in doing so, they create *systemic violence*: the violence considered just and necessary to maintain a civilization.

What is happening in this process is the reification of violence. We turn it into an external entity, a *thing*. Violence becomes the property of the state; mitigated by its military and police. We remove violence from human emotion because, as Pinker's forbearers have told us, our innately nasty and brutish humanity demands taming. Without control, our wild selves would uncaringly seek to lash out and destroy anything that stands in our way.

In their defense, you get what you wish for.

In any society where power exists, social or political in nature, it is wielded over others. Power is always defined by who holds it as much as it is by who does not; be they individuals, ecosystems, other animals, or any other created groups. Power is the necessary precursor for politicians. And for those with power, the system serves well. Everyone else is left with varying degrees of disempowerment, without a voice or redress.

The demands of the state weigh heavily. Stagnancy fosters unrest. Robbed of the means to mitigate conflict, the disempowered lash out, violating the presumed sanctity of the law. The state calls it violence and uses the digressions as evidence for its own necessity. Criminals are to be punished.

Throughout all of this, violence, like the law, remains a thing: separated from flesh and soul. Violence becomes something we can object to, quarantine, divert, control or reject. It is removed from any and all context. Radicals uphold it. Pacifists reject it. The State arbitrates it.

Violence becomes the *subject*.

In the process, we completely miss the point. The discussions remain in the hands of the domesticators, the programmers: what level of violence is just? What level is unjust? We accept the premise of civility: this is how things are, this is how things must be.

Violence is a reaction to circumstances.

And our circumstances are the problem. Those circumstances are civilization: the domestication of our world and our beings. The pacification of our animality and the passiveness we put upon the world around us. We become spectators instead of agents within our own lives.

Nomadic foragers, the immediate return hunter-gatherers that all of our ancestors were, understood the importance of this. The complexity of being an animal, with a full range of emotions and needs, remained central to their relationship with the world and each other. That dynamic tension didn't cause their lives to be overrun with fear of violence and a need for retaliation, but they accepted the possibility and probability of violence in many forms.

These societies, these egalitarian communities living in primal anarchy, work because they were built upon fluidity, with accepting the complications of our emotional states and giving the space to address and confront them. I didn't open with the story about /Twi's execution to rationalize it away nor to say that this story is exemplary of nomadic forager societies.

The case of /Twi was the exception, not the norm. And it is by understanding how egalitarian societies respond to such exceptional situations that we can shed light on our own circumstances: what does it look like to live without the State? As our society continues to spiral through an epidemic of mass killings, to constantly expanding its killing technology, and to embrace the fractured mentality of eternal war, typified by militarized police systemically targeting non-white communities and individuals, it is not enough to call the organization of violence implicit in the State into question.

We need to understand what life lived on our own terms, on the band level, looks like.

We need to understand what it means to be free.

And that means we need to grapple, with openness and honesty, with how we deal with each other without the State and its infrastructure.

But it also means questioning the perceptions we have of violence.

It means confronting our circumstances. /Twi's violence didn't shake the core of /Kung communities. He attacked them, but they were not terrorized by it to a place where they could no longer return. /Kung society, like all nomadic forager societies, understood violence not to embrace it, but to learn to cope with it: to diffuse it.

Written into books, isolated from time and place, we can extract and imply our fears. That is because our understanding of violence only knows retaliation and punishment. The /Kung, like all other wild beings, know reconciliation and dissolution.

For us, tensions constantly mount. Our violence is born of a brooding hatred.

And it swells.

Short of external force and mediation, our societies know only of peace as toleration. Circumstances aren't changed: policy is mitigated. The fluidity of egalitarian societies is stilled in sedentary lives and the need for stagnancy that fields and storehouses demand.

Our lives, carried out before an audience of strangers, each of us boiling over in our own minds, is steeped in violence that we likely will never see nor experience. And our ability to take part in or resolve our tensions is robbed from us by a system that requires obedience.

It is us who have to confront violence, to understand its circumstances, so that we can learn to live without fear of it. Just like our nomadic forager ancestors and cousins.

For the nomadic forager, violence exists, but it is not a defining trait of society. It is one type of conflict resolution and most often it is the last resort. When it arises, it often passes without escalation. And society moves on.

Like all wild things, the community must move on.

Reconciliation and the Society without Strangers

> *Our bodies and minds are made for social life, and we become hopelessly depressed in its absence. This is why next to death, solitary confinement is our worst punishment.*
> -Frans de Waal, *The Age of Empathy*[7]

It can be disheartening to read biologists' accounts of the importance of community, within human societies or any other. As social beings, we have an innate need and deep fulfillment that comes from simply belonging to something larger than ourselves.

That doesn't typically translate well for scientists. It's simply not logical enough.

And so you have biological and anthropological accounts of why we are social animals that must contest with the overt brutishness granted by Richard Dawkins assertion that "we are born selfish." That we should "understand what our own selfish genes are up to, because we may at least have the chance to upset their designs."[8]

The presumption that biologists, whose field cut its teeth during periods of colonization and war, are working with is exemplified by Dawkins who extrapolated from Charles Darwin: we exist to do what is best for ourselves. We reflect the survivalistic individualism of life within civilization upon the world.

And so biologists feasted upon work like that of Jane Goodall discussing the brutal warfare of chimpanzees.[9] They disregarded the fact that Goodall's encampment at Gombe created unprecedented hierarchy among wild chimps, much like early colonizers amongst uncontacted indigenous societies.[10] This is what the biologists were looking for: evidence that human nature was the "nasty, brutish and short" existence ascribed by Hobbes.

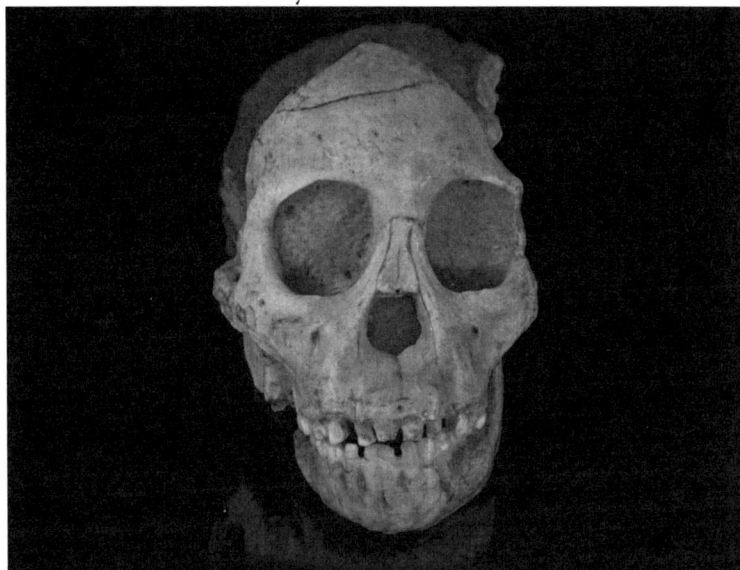

The Taung Child skull.

Despite the fact that humans share equal genetic ancestry between violence-prone chimpanzees and the pacifistic bonobos, a new wave of biologists bolstered the notion of innate human warring, partly, as primatologist Frans de Waal observes, "based on a single puncture wound in the fossilized skull of an ancestral infant, known as the Taung Child."[11] That puncture wound, it turns out, was caused by an eagle.[12]

This reinforced a one-sided view of animality: as beings evolving with a machine-like drive towards self-preservation and self-interest. A distraction that kept biologists from seeing an important part of violent outbreaks within animal populations: reconciliation.

For de Waal, that distraction was lost while observing chimpanzees at the Anaheim Zoo. A high-ranking male lashed out and fiercely attacked a female. The chimpanzees reacted loudly to this, other apes coming to the female's defense:

Suddenly the entire colony burst out hooting, and one male produced rhythmic noise on metal drums stacked up in the corner of the hall. In the midst of this pandemonium, two chimpanzees kissed and embraced.[13]

This was more than an act of empathy; it was a sign of momentum. A violent outbreak had occurred, a chimpanzee was injured, but along with coming to her aid, there were acts of reconciliation. The violence hadn't innately changed the group, it had broken out within it, and then it was over.

This incident happened in captivity, but the observations were then found in the wild. Ethologist Peter Verbeek observed that in both "the wild and in captivity chimpanzees regularly make peace after fights within the community or group" and "console victims of aggression."[14]

Acts of reconciliation were seen not only amongst monkeys and apes, but in wolves, dolphins, hyenas, and elephants.[15]

35 years after de Waal's observation, ethologists had case studies of post-conflict resolution in "close to 40 nonhuman primate species." And then the door was open to observe reconciliation in humans. Ethologists found that "across cultures young children tend to make peace following peer aggression and conflict." These acts of reconciliation decreased only when adults intervened in the situations.[16]

The crude biologist's basis for not being able to see reconciliation following acts of violence is a reiteration of how violence is perceived within civilized societies. It is here that violence, or even the threat of violence, are grounds for mediation or decisive judiciary or military action. There is no de-escalation without force or arbitration.

Within civilization, there is neither incentive nor grounding for de-escalation. There is only punishment.

The problem with civilization is the problem of mass society. There are a lot of people, far more than the band-networks of nomadic foragers. When violence breaks out, it is largely faceless and nameless. With so many people so tightly wound that their unraveling might be imminent, it is not surprising when strangers unleash on each other, but shocking when it doesn't happen.

Anonymity doesn't exist within band societies.

If you do something, you are unquestionably responsible for your actions. There is no technology to buffer accountability or causation. There is no sea of people to fade into, nor is there the ability to flee without leaving a trace.

For the most part, this simply comes down to scale. The average hunter-gatherer band consists of roughly 25 people.[17] That band will consist of men, women and children affiliated with a group of other hunter-gatherers who share languages, customs, and proximity. The average size for that larger group leans around 500 people though that can vary.

Anthropologist John Bodley puts 500 as the number of people an individual can typically sustain relationships with.[18] The number game gets a bit tricky as the "scale differences are so vast that they cannot be comprehended or visualized within our ordinary perception." But to continue putting numbers out for the sake of comparison, 500 is the average number of people within band or tribal level societies, 50,000 for chiefdoms, 50,000,000 for agrarian empires, and 500,000,000 for colonial empires.[19]

Lofty though these numbers may be, they are evidence of the fact that population, as Thomas Malthus famously observed, grows exponentially when left unchecked.[20] But that number, 500, is barely a drop in the bucket of the global society that technology has created where we are quickly approaching a population of 7.5 billion people.

Naturally speaking, numbers are tricky and reductionist. The typical nomadic forager band could look vastly different for ecological or social reasons. Average band size amongst the Penan of Borneo ranged from 32 to 50 and 25 to 40.[21] In 1968, the Hadza living east of Lake Eyasi in Tanzania an average "camp contains about eighteen adults," sometimes that meant a camp of an individual, other times a camp of a hundred.[22]

This variation is far from inconsequential, but we will return to that point. What matters here is that when any camp generally consists of a range of 18-40 people, nothing goes unnoticed. No *one* is going to go unnoticed. There is no need for secrecy here, because for all intents and purposes, there is none. As individuals from that camp intersperse and travel amongst their affiliation of roughly 500 people, the ability to simply fade into the background disappears.

Strangers, as we have come to know most of the people we personally interact with, simply don't exist here.

They simply *can't*.

Affiliations, relationships, friendships, feuds, shared food, communal rituals; all of these things create bonds. It doesn't mean that they always end well, but it means that you know who your neighbors are, often being intimately aware of or exposed to them. That plays a huge role in understanding and interacting with your world. One that we have easily ignored as people living in places like New York City with its population of nearly 24 million people or Tokyo nearing 38 million or Jakarta just over 30 million could potentially cross paths with thousands or hundreds of thousands of *strangers* every day.[23]

My point in juxtaposing these numbers, arbitrary though averages may be, isn't to approximate a sustainable number of people on earth, but to reflect on the kind of scale that we, as humans, as social animals, are psychologically capable of co-existing with. It's a sense of our reach, as individuals, to impact others, typically without negatively harming them.

That is a balance that is impossible within mass society. Be it agrarian kingdoms or hyper-technological, post-industrial consumerist ones, the complexity of social relationships becomes intertwined with the machinery of a society based on extraction and production.

Even as technology infuses the mirage of narcissism as self-worth, we fade into the fabric of the quilt of Ego. Each of us is unique, all of us are special; all of us oblivious to our impacts upon the world.

And all of us unknown to the other Selves we are thrust upon.

When we push beyond that 500 person threshold, when we are born into a world with 5 billion others and see the world hit 7.5 billion people, we have no sense of place or community other than the notion of what we are sold.

Yet civilization ensures that all of our lives are enmeshed.

500 people says nothing about the carrying capacity or thresholds for humanity. It just says: this is an approximation of the number of people I can interact and empathize with. Nomadic forager communities are built on that axiom and they can deal with each of those 500 people, their moods, their attitudes, their joys, and their grief.

None are lost here.

And none of those people live in a way that blindly impacts everyone outside of that sphere. Within the society without strangers, you are responsible for you own actions, for mending ties or seeking resolution, just as you are expected to be able to provide for yourself and the band. There is no place to hide and no reason to cover up your actions.

This is why band societies value methods of conflict resolution that don't include violence, but also anticipates that violence can and will happen. That's a complicated web for our minds to wrap around: nomadic foragers are peaceful in the sense that warfare does not exist, they seek to avoid escalations of hostilities, but they are also able to move past violent incidents when they inevitably do occur.

To the more liberal of sensibilities, this response to violence or even homicide should be a direct challenge to the notion of nomadic forager societies as the most egalitarian societies to have ever existed. The existence of violence is a trait of social animals: it doesn't make us fascist. Fights can be broken up or avoided entirely, but that isn't always the case.

Egalitarianism is about equality of access to subsistence, the freedom to exist on your own terms. It is the absence of systemic suppression that grants certain segments or individuals within society access to a subsistence base, food, ritual knowledge, shelter, or anything else. Nomadic foragers are notably capable of self-subsistence and they are raised from an early age knowing and accepting this. Band life exists because self-reliance doesn't fulfill our emotional needs as individuals: we are social beings; we want and need community.

And we don't always get along.

Arguments happen, fights may break out, but being fully capable and able to move on, to settle, diffuse, or reconcile disputes on your own terms is a hallmark of egalitarianism, contradictory though it may seem.

It is the absence of overarching political and socio-economic conditions that force people to stay within one society or circumstance. It is the absence of the ability of others to determine what you must do or not do that epitomizes the loss of freedom inherent in non-egalitarian societies.

Outbursts of violence are not a threat to egalitarianism; they are a latent understanding and acceptance of our animality. One that is understood so that it can be curtailed rather than simply controlled as an emotion.

Violence is something that may happen, but for nomadic foragers, it is not a defining trait of society.

Violence within the Society of Strangers

> Thus the point to make about the Ju/wasi and their murder rate is not that they didn't have one, not that they were peaceful by nature, and not that our species isn't violent or hasn't always been violent since we parted from our sometimes violent relatives, the chimpanzees. The point is that the Ju/wasi knew only too well what the human animal is capable of doing. The point is that they knew how to suppress anger and aggressive impulses, and placed a very high priority on doing so.
> - Elizabeth Marshall Thomas, *The Old Way*[24]

Much has been said of the homicide rate of the !Kung.

In nearly every discussion about the role of immediate-return hunter-gatherers, it is not uncommon for the !Kung to take the exemplary center stage. And as a case point in egalitarian societies, rightfully so. Yet their homicide rate, famously comparable to 1970s Detroit, was touted as evidence of a seeming oversight in violence within the "state of nature." Elizabeth Marshall Thomas came under scrutiny from anthropologists for having titled her ethnography on the !Kung of Nyae Nyae as the "Harmless People." A claim she has supported as a translation of how the !Kung of Nyae Nyae saw themselves and also, generally true, as a statement of fact. In her mother, Lorna Marshall's words, "The !Kung are strongly set against violence, and accord it no honor."[25]

Nonetheless, socio-biologists and other engineers of civilization grabbed on to the statistics. Pinker makes it instrumental in his laughable argument for the notion that civilization has resulted in a net decrease in violence. He also touts the Master's Narrative by flattening the violence among the !Kung by listing fights with intruding Bantu neighbors or European colonialists as evidence of their "pre-historic" violence.[26]

This cannot be overlooked.

As much as discussion of the !Kung and other nomadic foragers has been accused of "romanticism," it is absolutely apparent that the opposite is far more widely and insidiously spread: the notion that violence is interchangeable with warfare and that eras of colonization are a reflection of a society's pre-contact behavior.

The 22 cases of homicide that Richard Lee found amongst the

!Kung occurred during a period of intensive contact and colonization by Europeans and their neighbors, including the Bantu. This is an important point that we will return to. But before White people actually came into the Kalahari in the 1930s, their path was exacerbated through the previously contacted and embattled Tswana and Herero pastoralists and Bayei and Mbukushu agriculturalists.[27]

To add to the context and give a glimpse of the reality behind intrusions upon the !Kung at this time, the Herero and Nama (Khoisan pastoralists, ethnically and linguistically tied to the !Kung) were subject to militaristic extermination at the hands of German colonizers. Between 1904-1907 alone, the Germans reported killing "more than forty-five per cent, 7,682 of approximately 17,000 Herero and Nama."[28]

Victims of the Namibia genocide.

It is befitting for us, as the descendants of such genocidalists, to later draw an increase in violence as a justification for berating human nature, just as it had been used to justify the extermination to begin with. I would hope that no one would fault the !Kung for fighting back against intrusion. Brutal oppression came at the hands of Whites and the Bantu then, just as it continues to today. The !Kung were "taken as slaves, hunted down like animals, and, wherever possible, forced from their land."[29]

The violence of colonization increases pressure on even the most intact of communities. And the increased contact with neighboring pastoral and agricultural societies can also influence social behavior. Of the 22 cases of homicide documented by Lee, 15 occurred as parts of feuds, a form of retaliation typically occurring in delayed return societies.[30] That most certainly includes the Bantu.

Not surprisingly, the !Kung had stories of pre-contact times when blood feuds did not exist. As a result of fights, parties would "hang up their quivers", *//gau!kurusi*, so they could "announce symbolically that the fighting was over for good." The elders would split the group to keep tensions and further violence from mounting.[31]

Again, my point is to contextualize the period of violence in which the famously echoed rate of homicide amongst the egalitarian !Kung occurred. Colonization didn't create violence among the !Kung, but it unquestionably amplified it. Regardless of not placing social value on violence, "the Ju/wasi had violence in them," as Thomas points out.

"We all do."[32]

And so we have stories like the one we opened with: the murders committed by /Twi and his ultimate execution. There are certainly others. Even without colonial pressure, it is likely that they would have existed. With or without a state, with or without external pressure, a society without strangers is forced to confront its own when they become dangerous.

In looking back over the stretch of time Marshall and her family had spent amongst the Ju/Wasi, she was made aware of five homicides, two of which she considered "safety measures." One case was similar to the one already told of /Twi's execution after causing three of the five homicides.

The other was of a man who began hiding in an aardvark burrow, jumping out and startling those that passed by. Clearly, to the group, he had lost his sanity. In their assessment, it became unquestionable that he was too dangerous. A few men went out into the veld and killed him with poisoned arrows.[33]

It can be difficult, coming from our own disconnected society, to see such a response to what is clearly mental illness. In the society without strangers, however, there are no mysteries. These aren't faceless people.

Nor are the potential victims.

Within this society of 550 people, here is an accounting of 5 murders, 3 of which were committed by one person who was subsequently killed as a "safety measure." In our own assessments, executing someone for jumping out of burrows seems overwhelmingly excessive. In light of the situation as the Ju/Wasi saw it, as those who would have ultimately had to lose and bury their own family members and loved ones, as those who could not bring sense back to the man in the burrow, there was no question and no vengeance in their decision making process: they were faced with the likelihood of worse outcomes and chose, collectively, to mitigate the risk.[34]

Life beyond the state requires action. There is no infrastructure to fall back upon. No prison to lock up the excessively violent.

Everyone knows this, just as they know each other.

And for the most part, homicide is the exception, not the rule.

Fighting amongst hunters is largely discouraged and avoided when possible. A hunter is exceptionally skillful at killing. For the !Kung, the use of poison tipped arrows for hunting ensures that the weapons capable of taking lives are widely available within camps. Like all weapons, they can be used indiscriminately.

The use of such weaponry is the most extreme form of violence, the fallback when emotions spiral beyond all social mechanisms, beyond the reproach of others in the encampment to intervene. The !Kung have three levels of fighting; *talk*, *fight*, and *deadly fight*.

A talk *is an argument that may involve threats and verbal abuse, but no blows. A* fight *is a dispute that includes an exchange of blows but without the use of weapons. A* deadly fight *is one in which the deadly weapons-poisoned arrows, spears, and clubs-are used whether or not someone is killed.*[35]

Of the arguments observed by Lee, less than half involved the use of weapons. It is most likely that many other arguments or talks would have occurred without being reported, as the use of weapons is likely to cause physical harm that is hard to overlook. Verbal arguments, as we shall see, are a more aggressive form of joking that is typical throughout non-state societies, be they immediate-return hunter-gatherers or semi-nomadic horticulturalists. In the case of the !Kung, it "is often punctuated by a joke that breaks the tension and leaves the participants rolling on the ground helpless with laughter."[36]

If the joking only escalates the tension and others haven't been able to step in and break it up, physical fights are likely to break out. Fights without weapons aren't unlike the kind of flaring that de Waal mentions amongst chimpanzees and as anyone who has fought with friends or siblings when joking went too far can attest. Lee explains:

Fights are of short duration, usually two to five minutes long, and involve wrestling and hitting at close quarters rather than fisticuffs. Fighters are quickly separated and forcibly held apart; this is followed by an eruption of excited talking and sometimes more blows. Serious as they appear at the time, anger quickly turns to laughter in Ju/'hoan fights. We have seen partisans joking with each other when only a few minutes before they were grappling. The joking bursts the bubble of tension and allows tempers to cool off and the healing process to begin.[37]

We see again this emotional flare leading to an outbreak of violence and then acts of reconciliation. This is an escalation of arguments more than a precursor to the potentially lethal fighting with weapons.

It is worth pointing out that these fights typically involve men, but can involve or be strictly between women as well. The kind of violence inflicted is not the kind of battery typical of one damaged person trying to physically dominate and suppress another; these fights aren't particularly effective in that regard. Even though men are more likely to fight with women than vice versa, there is no presumption that women are innately victims of male violence. Women are much more likely to start fights with men than other women. Since women don't use weapons they are rarely used in fights where women are involved.

Patriarchy has as much to do with the pacification of women as it does the oppression of women as a whole. Even in the far more hierarchical societies of Australia's hunter-gatherers, women are equal in terms of fighting and the expectations of violence as men.[38]

In the case of deadly fights, those involved in the argument are likely to reach immediately for weapons instead of grappling.

In that moment, whether built up or spontaneous, the individuals have crossed that line and are willing to risk, often before the entirety of the band, the probability of lethal violence. The presence of poisoned arrows makes the lethality of !Kung fights far greater. Though the poison used is relatively slow, often taking six hours to kill someone, the person struck with the arrow typically will receive help from the rest of the band. Knowing the likelihood of death as a result of being hit with an arrow, it is rare that the fight goes any further.

Others will cut the wound and try to extract the poison from it. They will talk and begin the *kia* healing trance ritual,[39] attempting to aid the victim and to soothe social tension arising from a fight. Regardless of whether the victim lives or dies, the immediate task is to try to heal all bonds. The attacker will leave the camp.[40]

As a community, whatever the outcome of a fight may be, the immediate goal is reconciliation.

There are no secrets here.

There are no random murders or unknown suspects. Fights

typically occur in camps before the rest of the band. They will take part in the arguments, interjecting jokes, trying to break up physical confrontations, or yelling about the "yikkity-yack" of arguments. The goal, for everyone, is resolution, ideally without violence.

But there is always the expectation that violence may arise.

There is the expectation that it may have to be dealt with.

It is because of the seemingly exceptional homicide rate of the !Kung, the self-described *harmless* people, that I chose to open with them. In particular, I chose to focus on some of the more exceptionally violent incidents that we know of. Egalitarianism is, I believe, in our nature. It is written into the primal anarchy of the nomadic foraging lifeway that we have evolved to. It is a part of the social lives that we live as wild animals.

One that is particularly unfit for captivity.

These incidents give a glimpse of what can happen in a society without strangers, a society without a state, when the fail-safes don't work. More often than not, they do. But egalitarianism doesn't mean that everything works in angelic form or fluidity. Everyone within a nomadic forager society has the skills, ability and access to choose to remove themselves from tense circumstances.

They also have the choice to stay.

But what is most important, is that they accept, without delusion and without lament, the nature of being a social animal: that arguments may occur and that, as a community, they will have to be able to deal with unpleasant and even potentially lethal situations.

In the !Kung case, the oft-cited example for egalitarian societies also tends to have the record of being the more violent. As such, what we've just looked at, warts and all, is more the exception than the rule.

Among the Hadza of Tanzania, between 1967 and 1997 there were 2 homicides by Hadza against other Hadza.[41] Among the South Indian foragers and the Batek, no homicides were recorded within these societies. For the Batek, the *talks* of the !Kung involve the whole of the group "in a direct discussion between the person involved or in the form of loud complaints made to anyone who was willing to listen, sometimes done during the evening hours in cross-camp arguments, discussions, or simultaneous monologues."

And if resolution cannot be reached, then movement is the response.[42]

The Orang Asli of Peninsular Malaysia are openly hostile towards violence, a stance that has bolstered their refusal to succumb to attempted conversions to Islam and to domesticate animals. As one individual states,

> *I don't know how it feels to hit someone or be hit by someone. ... I never felt angry or knew how to get angry enough to want to fight with others. When I was angry before, I always felt, it's all right if that person wants it his way, I will let it go.*[43]

The Hill Pandaram of Southern India espouse a particularly non-competitive nature which instills a virtue of avoiding violence through movement.[44] The Rautes of Nepal see individual disputes as a threat to the entirety of band integrity and seek to resolve tensions through camp-wide nightly discussions.[45]

Within the Mbuti, the arguments taking place within camp are considered *noise* by the band elders who step in and "demand silence, on the grounds that the noise is offending the forest." It is then the elders who mediate the arguments and determine a resolution, typically, again, consisting of movement either of the band or of individuals.[46]

What becomes obvious from running down this list is one thing: violence is one form of conflict resolution, but hardly the only one.

In being aware of and sometimes accepting the probability of violence, it becomes equally essential to hunter-gatherer communities to learn how *not* to resort to violence. Granted, as we've seen, that doesn't always work, but that's because we've gotten all too used to seeing and accepting homicide statistics.

The problem is that this goes beyond numbers.

As Frank Marlowe observes about the Hadza statistics; "The murder rate among the Hadza is roughly the same as that in the United States. The U.S. murder rate in 1997 was 5.5 for every 100,000 people."[47] To famously meet the *per capita* murder rate of Detroit in the 1970s, it took 30 years of monitoring !Kung society to make the statistics work. And that while active colonization was happening.

It is unquestionably and undeniably true that homicide can and does happen in nomadic forager societies. Clearly far more in some than others, though the reality of forced settlements have taken their toll. As Thomas noted:

> *Although the Ju/wasi dealt with anger and violence very successfully as long as they lived in the Old Way, their mechanisms for doing this broke down after the 1970s, when change came and Western civilization overtook Nyae Nyae. Then, when there really were police and government officials, when the Ju/wa population become concentrated at a government post where they lost their ancient*

Hadza healing dance. Photo by Sofia Yu.

lifestyle, when hunger, alcohol, drugs, disease, and poverty overtook them, they began killing one another like madmen.[48]

There are cases like the Orang Asli settlement Air Bah, where the non-violent virtue has given rise to active resistance to alcohol consumption as it breeds violence.[49] This is also seen amongst the Paliyan of Southern India.[50]

But as Douglas Fry points out, "as alcohol becomes available to nomadic forager societies violence goes up. Often the traditional mechanisms of social control and conflict management are not effective in dealing with drunken aggression."[51] The reality of this is just another part of the colonization process: a finalization of the ethnocide that results from attacking indigenous communities spiritually, physically and ecologically.

The infusion of intoxicants only feeds the perpetuated mythos of the violent savage in need of civilization. This morbid view of humanity, and the animality it arises from, spews from the mouth of the domesticator's pulpit. From Hobbes to Pinker, the intent is clear: violence is violence, and it is the duty of the state to protect you from it.

And yet here we have hundreds of thousands, if not millions, of years of evidence to the contrary. The nomadic forager lifeway is peaceful in the sense that there is no war. But it is peaceful in its acceptance of violence and refusal to allow hierarchical institutions to arise to mitigate it.

Instead, they default on the egalitarian version: amongst free people, disputes will arise. It is a testament to the enduring strength of their society that they neither hide from it nor let the potential of violence dictate their existence.

This is our open and willing acceptance of the human condition.

And it is our ability to cope with the presence of violence through understanding that there are other forms of conflict resolution without the state.

How to Cope with Violence: Conflict Resolution and Dissolution

> *Conflict is an inevitable feature of social life, but clearly* physical aggression is not the only option for dealing with conflict.
> - Douglas Fry, *The Human Potential for Peace*[52]

Of the various forms of conflict resolution amongst nomadic foragers, none is more pervasive than mobility.

On the ecological level, movement keeps bands from over-harvesting areas; it can follow the movement of hunted animals, it can follow the shifting seasonality of foraged foods, it can lead to streams seasonally overrun with fish. It lets the ecosystem recover while the refuse composts. It ensures that the people living within a living landscape are aware of the population flux of flora and fauna within the region.

On the biological level, the movement of camps, like the movements latent within foraging, it pushes back the onset of menses in young women and helps reinforce birth spacing for children: both of which greatly check the band population.

On the social level, mobility is the epitome of freedom.

The movement from camp to camp, the fluidity of moving between groups, the chance to bring the camps together for periods; all of these things reinforce not only the ties between individuals, they ensure that people who don't get along with each other have their options open.[53] As arguments arise, the offending individuals will split apart. If fights or homicides occur, the perpetrators will split off. If whole camps are feeling ecological pressure from outsiders, they will even "typically move apart or settle in unpopulated areas, even if these are less desirable, or avoid or reduce conflict."[54]

To a certain degree, sometimes ecology becomes an excuse for mobility.

There are two types of Mbuti groups; the net-hunters and archers. Net hunting is a communal activity based around driving game towards a net where hunters then take them. Archers, by comparison, are more solitary when on the hunt. By virtue of methodology, net hunting bands have more people, which carries more potential for possible conflicts. Their typical group size and potential for conflicts play into how each group views honey season: the ecology of honey plays into their justification for banding together or splitting up. The net hunters claim it "is a time of such plenty that the game can easily be caught by hand, and so there is no need for the large cooperative net-hunt." Conversely, the archers *only* hunt in larger bands during the honey season, which they claim is "a time of poor hunting, and thus, maximum cooperation is demanded."[55]

Logically, both can't be true, but it's an ecological justification for social actions. The want is to break up how bands and camps exist most of the year, get a bit of variation. It is to have a reason to come together if it's not what they typically do or to split up for a bit for those with higher population densities.

They get the chance to dissolve tension through flux.

As James Woodburn observes, it is always possible that
members of a camp all move, they may go together to a new site; they may split up and form camps at two or more new sites; they may go as a body to join some existing camp, or they may divide, some joining an existing camp at a particular site, the composition of the camp changes: some people move in and some move out.[56]

This is the ingenuity of nomadic forager, immediate-return hunter-gatherer, communities. This is what strangers can simply ignore: we can't and won't always get along *and* we all get along better when we can move and cycle through areas, camps, and gatherings.

Proximity is not an argument for mutual aid. That is an innate problem that sedentary societies are forced to deal with and none have nor will be able to cope with appropriately. It is a part of the domestication process stripping down our innate needs as social beings and redirecting that into a notion that any people are good to be around.

That is, so long as you have the right attitude about it. Can't we all get along, right?

The answer is no. We can't.

But the beauty of the primal anarchy of nomadic forager life, the way of existence that literally wrote into us how we see, feel and interact with the world and all its inhabitants, is that we don't have to. Ecologically, biologically, socially, and spiritually, we're better off being nomadic.

We're better off when we embrace our fluidity.

This is a lesson so vital to nomadic forager life that it is consistently the most profoundly iterated virtues taught to children.

This is a point I want to focus on: for us to be able to isolate violence requires that we ignore the causation. Violence, as we have abstracted it, within domesticated societies is always to be avoided, unless it is coming from the hands of the state or hidden through the day-to-day violence inherent in civilized living. It is always *uncivilized*.

Hunter-gatherers, trained and equipped to kill by livelihood, know that violence is something they'll have to deal with, to respond to, and that it likely can become lethal. This is a practical concern. This is a practical reason to instill and uphold other forms of conflict resolution that bring the society closer together rather than to draw it apart. Violence, in this context, is not something abstract: it is the result of other forms of conflict resolution failing to mitigate an individual dispute. In so far as there can be a "goal" asserted onto their approach to avoiding violence, it would be that the intent is to resolve conflict rather than to penalize its outbursts.

Even in incidents where a homicide does occur, the killer is either chastised or resolves to relocate to another camp until the tensions soothe over and the healing has occurred. Other members of the group may choose to shun them. Life is flowing, fluid. A society that choses stagnancy, as we all know, is stuck in an endless cycle of self-perpetuated escalations on one hand and punishment on the other.

If we're being honest about it, I think that's something we all can recognize as horribly unhealthy.

But let's get back to the children.

Anthropologist Tim Ingold observed that "hunter-gatherers act as self-conscious agents endowed with subjective intentionality."[57] From a civilized perspective, that sounds counter-intuitive as a foundation for functioning and egalitarian communities. We simply take everything to its furthest extent: buying into the narcissistic cult of the individual or a religiously dogmatic refusal of any personhood.

It should be a given that both aspects are pushed into overdrive as technology becomes smaller and more pervasive in our own lives.

For stateless indigenous societies, this kind of identity crisis is dealt with between childhood and adolescence. You learn who you are in the world with other children, mimicking parents, slowly taking over your own subsistence, playing and exploring the wild, as a group, as individuals.

It is telling that coming from a society such as ours, where survival is such a flaunted virtue, that we make much of the skills that hunter-gatherers learn instead of understanding the context in which they learn them. Seeing children hunt or catch shell fish, to start a fire and cook them, is certainly impressive, but only noticeable if you lacked that context in your own upbringing, as I'm sure is the case for many of us.

The skillset of nomadic foragers or any self-sufficient person or group, is absolutely fascinating, but within their own context they can easily be taken for granted. There is no specialization here, there is no industry: this is about exploration, child's play. It is about replicating relationships with each other and with the larger community of wildness that surrounds them, the materials are just tools.

Within this context, they are a given.

Self-sufficiency, learning the ins and outs of these lifeways is a comfortable expectation. You should be able to provide for yourself. There are no lifeguards on duty. None are necessary, children learn by watching their parents, getting guidance where needed and then interpreted through play with other children in a mixed age group.

So what lessons do the parents spend time upholding? Passing on the importance of mobility and conflict resolution. Namely, mobility *as* conflict resolution.

"Teaching," amongst the nomadic forager Nayaka of Malaysia, "is done in a very subtle way." As anthropologist Nurit Bird-David writes, "Knowledge is inseparable from social life."

I believe knowledge in this context has to do with learning how to behave within relations, in order to keep these relations going, rather than with knowing things for their own sake, as a known detached from the knower. Young people learn their skills from direct experience, in the company of other children or other adults, in the course of everyday life.[58]

Infants within nomadic forager societies are cared for greatly by parents and surrounding groups. Affection is openly displayed; fathers and mothers take to tending children instinctually and without hesitation.[59] As an infant becomes a toddler and young child, that affection remains as they increasingly turn towards their peers in their social life.

Amongst the Nayaka, "a person becomes a child when he or she starts socially engaging with others, independently, responsively, and responsibly."[60] To a certain degree, the case has been made by Paul Shepard that domestication stunts this process of becoming independent, leaving most of civilized individuals stuck within a childhood level of development and awareness.[61]

Within the Nayaka, the role of the parent "connotes an emotional sort of caring." This is the same kind of relationship that their society expresses between themselves and the forest. When they refer to themselves as *children of the forest*, it is a statement of "an emotional attachment, a shared living, a shared sense of identity and mutual responsibility."[62]

Amongst the !Kung, toddlers typically start integrating into play groups of mixed ages and sexes by the second half of their second year.[63] For the Agta of the Philippines, communal coddling and care begins at birth. Parents lead by example, allowing the children their own group:

When a child learns to walk he turns more and more toward the companionship of peers, who are not only playmates, but also teachers. They teach games of skill and dexterity which prepare a child for his adult economic roles. They instruct each other in how to swim, fish, and gather vegetables and shellfish and generously share their treasures, food, secrets, and knowledge.[64]

It is reiterated again and again through the accounts of children's play groups that the interventions of adults typically revolve around one central aspect: fostering cooperation and resolution. Within the Hill Pandaram, "Children are treated as autonomous individuals, and are not taught, or expected to obey their elders."[65] The play group of the Mbuti children have their own camp, the *bopi*, where "they are learning the fun and beauty of working and playing *with* not *against* other, they are in a positive way learning by prescription rather than proscription." The "children will find that mobility is one of their prime techniques for avoiding or for resolving a dispute, for once they move elsewhere their spheres move with them and the dispute is discarded."[66]

The games played within the *bopi* are meant to manifest situations of conflict so that they can learn to resolve them. And if resolution fails, they simply walk away.[67] But the bonding that occurs strengthens their resolve. Those limits of resolution, tested within the safety of the *bopi* and instilled into their interactions with the world at large, brings the circumstances which foster violence directly into the light. They learn to identify and respond before they boil over.

Violence isn't something external or looming within context, it is

simply an emotional reaction.
And, more to the point, one that can be avoided.

This circumstance, this primal approach to parenting, reaffirms the lived primal anarchy of nomadic forager bands. It breeds egalitarian societies based upon mutual aid and respect. By embracing the facets of life that cause tension, it frees the individuals from becoming paralyzed by them.

So while the homicide rate of the !Kung was famously and unjustly being compared to that of 1970s Detroit, it's easy to see why the comparisons fail: violence, within egalitarian societies, is largely mitigated through resolution, but its existence is not forgotten. Outside of external pressures, random and horrific acts of faceless violence do not occur, so there is no need to live in fear of them. When violence does occur, there are ways of healing and reconciling it.

For the most part, the means of mitigation work. But what is most important is that in the confrontation with these unpleasant aspects of social existence, they give those within a given band and society a lot of room to freely be themselves, to uphold laughter and joy as a given in life. These are societies that dance and sing to bring themselves together. They aren't locking themselves away at night.

It comes back to childhood. It comes back to being affectionately and lovingly held by the camp as infants. Kin or not, there is acknowledgement, care and interaction. There is comfort and acceptance.

And these are the circumstances we have evolved into, as *Homo sapiens*. This is what is written into us: a world where we are given the space to exist and therefore actively create our own lives, with others.

This is freedom.

This is what egalitarianism comes down to: we come together not because we need to, but because we want to. As stated about childhood among the Batek of Malaysia:

> *Despite occasional parental worries, as long as children remained within earshot they were allowed to do almost anything they pleased. They chopped down trees. They built fires and cooked food. They pretended to smoke porcupines out of holes. They carried sticks on their shoulders like bundles of rattan or firewood. Many children enjoyed pretending they were moving camp.*[68]

And just in case anyone wants to stand in the way of that, they also learn to laugh.

The Anarchist's Laughter: Sharing Jokes and Meat

It is difficult to be dangerous or violent if you are laughing so hard you cannot stand.
   -Colin Turnbull, *The Human Cycle*[69]

For the Inuit, anger is something that was expected with children, but unacceptable for adults. Hugh Brody found the question, *"Ningngarpit?"*, or "Are you angry?" to lie somewhere between "a tease and reproach."

Anger, simply put, was for children.

There are many aspects of life, be it that of an immediate-return hunter-gatherer or a hyper-technological, post-industrial consumer, that are difficult. There are aspects of being alive that can bring euphoria and aspects that can result in endemic depression if they aren't resolved. Social life, for all its joys and comforts, also creates tension and can allow an individual to bring out all of their unresolved conflicts into this situation.

As we have seen, that can be lethal.

The question *Ningngarpit?* is a gut check. This simple question, half jest and half ridicule, is a reminder: the purpose of community is to help resolve those tensions, not to amplify them. As Brody puts it:

> *To laugh, to be happy, to feel welcome or welcoming, to experience shyness, to be nervous about dangers in the world or society, and to feel ilira, the mix of apprehension and fear that causes a suppression of opinion and voice: all these states of mind are spoken of and exhibited with real freedom. They have helped to shape the stereotype of the Inuit as a people with unfailing goodwill, good humor, and generosity. Yet the intensity of feeling that can exist within this restraint and dignified self-control, breaking through at times of extreme difficulty, is also remarkable.*[70]

Laughter and humility are virtues taught through childhood. Nearly every violent situation that has been mentioned among nomadic foragers already is precipitated by attempts of either the individuals involved in fights or those around them to try and keep the "yikkity yak," as the !Kung call it, on the lighter side. That the ridicule leads to more laughter and less anger.

This doesn't always work, but more often than not, it does.

Returning to the *bopi* of the Mbuti children, arguments quickly "revert to ridicule which they play out until they are all rolling on the ground in near-hysteria." Which echoes into their adult life as a primary form of resolution. "Chortles quickly become laughter, and this laughter becomes the Mbuti's prime weapon against conflict, aggression, and violence."[71]

Hadza hunter returning with his share of a kill.

Band life, in nearly all non-state societies, consists as much of joking around as it does singing and dancing. Communities elicit joy and comfort; otherwise they wouldn't exist at all. This is an aspect that is easy to miss when revolutionary perspectives become so dogmatic about what the ideal society might be and how it might deal with unpleasant circumstances that it strips the life from situations which may potentially arise. The tension of the struggle often overshadows the coercive aspects demanded of many intentional communities: again, based in the liberal notions that we can all get along and the agrarian squalor of sedentary life.

Removed from those constraints, it's easy to see more about the organic nature of life without the state, freed from the tension and presence of its infrastructures. As anarchist and anthropologist Pierre Clastres observed amongst the Yanomami, they enjoyed a good dick-joke or waking the lulled sleepers with a sneaky fart in the face.[72]

Having spent over two decades attending anarchist conferences and gatherings, it's obvious that people living in anarchy, less preoccupied than anarchists, seem like a lot more fun to be around.

Jokes aside, ridicule is often seen as a means of social leveling.

To an extent it's true, certainly as societies become more stratified, but there have been arguments made that the presence of such mechanisms is an indication of the fragility of egalitarianism.[73] However, the idea of keeping individuals from getting a big head about what they've done is a far cry from a big head resulting in non-egalitarian situations and the presence of social power. Without property, being capable of packing up and leaving while being fully self-sufficient, it's hard to imagine the ability to create a structure for power being that simple.

In other words, "social leveling" in this case is really just about checking, habitually and hilariously, any time someone thinks their contributions to the group are greater than any others. It is a testament to the degree to which egalitarian societies value the contributions of everyone. Early ethnographers sought out the "big hunter" as they presumed, with patriarchal zeal, that in a hunter-gatherer society, the hunter rules the roost. Among complex hunter-gatherers, those who were sedentary or had domesticated animals to store or carry a surplus (respectively), they were able to find a semblance of that.

Among nomadic, immediate-return hunter-gatherers, however, not so much.

To the extent that ridicule is used to check the potential narcissist, it quite often seems to go to young men as they become successful at hunting larger game. For the Orang Asli, "it appears that 'leveling mechanisms' designed to challenge self-aggrandizers, such as joking, shunning, meddling, demanding, and mocking, only apply when the perceived 'self-aggrandizer' is a younger man."[74] Outside of this, heckling is just a way of airing out irritations as jokes instead of attacks.

And it becomes habitual.

A famous case for habitual heckling as a means of reducing potential areas of tension or, simply, socially irritating people has been made by Richard Lee, who learned about it first hand amongst the Ju/Hoansi. At the end of a lengthy stay among them, Lee wanted to share his gratitude from their generosity and hospitality, choosing Christmas as a time to celebrate them: to give back to the community that had hosted and tolerated his presence.

He ended up purchasing a large cattle from a neighboring Herero pastoralist. An "ox of astonishing size and mass," for a feast at the /ai/ai camp for roughly 150 !Kung. He had hoped telling his hosts about his purchase and plans would be graciously received.

It didn't play out as he had anticipated it. The following conversation occurs right after he confirms his plans and which ox he had chosen:

"I have purchased Yebave's black ox, and I am going to slaughter and cook it."

"That's what we were told at the well but refused to believe it until

we heard it from yourself."
"Well, it's the black one." *I replied expansively, although wondering what she was driving at.*
"Oh, no!" *Ben!a groaned, turning to her group.* "They were right." *Turning back to me she asked,* "Do you expect us to eat that bag of bones?"
"Bag of bones! It's the biggest ox at /ailai."
"Big, yes, but old. And thin. Everybody knows there's no meat on that old ox. What did you expect us to eat off it, the horns?"[75]

Having spent years studying the social life of the !Kung, Lee still missed an essential feature: the degree to which egalitarianism was innate within their society. He hadn't been prepared for it even though he was effectively seeing it in action daily.

Unprepared for this kind of response, he was devastated. Coming from the apex of civilized society within America, the structure of power along with the tyranny of the gift is so ingrained that it can be an unshakeable core of how someone relates with the world. Like the problem of thinking we can always get along, the nomadic foragers, those living in a state of primal anarchy, thought of that too.

Upon discovering the core of meat insults from those at /ai/ai, Lee asked one of its residents, Tomazo, to clarify its universality:

"We refuse one who boasts, for someday his pride will make him kill somebody. So we always speak of his meat as worthless. This way we cool his heart and make him gentle."
"But why didn't you tell me this before?" *I asked Tomazo with some heat.*
"Because you never asked me," *said Tomazo, echoing the refrain that has come to haunt every field ethnographer.*[76]

For nomadic foragers, heckling, like joking, is as latent as it is lacking in our society where hierarchy is constantly reinforced.

Along with heckling the hunter are intentional complexities around meat "ownership," built to obscure the relationship between the hunted animal and the hunter who fired the arrow which itself may "belong" to someone else.

As the Inuit saying goes, "Gifts make slaves like whips make dogs."[77] Gifts are refused because sharing is expected. "Ownership" is, by and large, a façade. Paired with the lack of stored or storable meats, it's equally impractical. Children's demands for meat are respected which feeds the ongoing and self-perpetuating role of sharing: the essence of the communality within communities.[78]

This is the aspect of the society without strangers that Tim Ingold reiterates is the "central attribute" of "face-to-face relationships":

> Far from being an index of the submission of the particular man or woman to the authority of the social collectivity, sharing underwrites the autonomy of the person, who thus remains wholly accountable for his or her actions. In short it is not in spite of their mutual involvement, but because of it, that people in hunting and gathering societies enjoy a fundamental autonomy of intention and action.[79]

Just as egalitarianism centers on equal access to a subsistence base and society, egalitarian societies are "underwritten by a principle of collective access": "The band is conceived as one big household, whose members enjoy unrestricted use of the resources of its country and who labor in common to draw a subsistence from them."[80]

It is property that complicates this ecology of social relationships, not the tendencies of self-aggrandizing young men.

Without property, they have nothing to harvest but an ego.

As Tomazo reminds us, the fostering of egos is exactly the kind of circumstance that can lead to the violence that nomadic foragers uphold avoiding.

Society Against the State and Mitigating Tensions

> Faithless, lawless, and kingless: these terms used by the sixteenth-century West to describe the Indians can easily be extended to cover all primitive societies. They can serve as the distinguishing criteria: a society is primitive if it is without a king, as the legitimate source of the law, that is, the State machine.
> - Pierre Clastres, *Society Against the State*[81]

Property, namely in the form of stored foods or domesticated plants and animals, among non-state societies does in fact create tension. But this isn't an on/off switch. The changes, in many ways, are subtle.

Sedentary life further creates a more malicious form of property: territory.

It is the very functionality of conflict resolution: the ability to move, to laugh, to splinter after a fight and cool down, that keeps nomadic forager life fluid and flowing. Horticultural societies, that is, typically speaking, gardener-hunters rather than small-scale farmers, don't completely break with these methods, but they are forced to adopt them to new circumstances. As they lose the ecological benefits of nomadic life, they start to feel the pressure of an increasing population.

As anthropologist Marvin Harris noted:

Were it not for the severe costs involved in controlling reproduction, our species might have remained forever organized into small, relatively peaceful, egalitarian bands of hunter-collectors. But the lack of effective and benign methods of population control rendered this mode of life unstable.[82]

The problem is that the ecological balance of the nomadic forager band is no coincidence. This is the lifeway that has been written into us going back, potentially, millions of years. This primal anarchy is etched into our mind, body and spirit.

It is no surprise that this is the society where we thrive the best and are defined by egalitarianism.

That primal anarchy isn't easily shaken. The domestication process, the ongoing attempt to subjugate our innate egalitarian, nomadic spirit, is a constant reiteration of a totality. It is a retelling of the world as it is through the mouths of specialists and segmented into the mirrored world of production and division of labor.

But none of this comes quickly or universally.

Martin Fried identifies four levels of what becomes "political society." The primary level is the "simple egalitarian society" of nomadic foragers. Then there are "rank societies" noted by limited "positions of prestige without affecting the access of its entire membership to the basic resources upon which life depends." Notably these are largely slash-and-burn horticultural societies.

Maori Pa, or fort.

There are "stratified societies" where members of the same sex and equivalent age status do not have equal access to the basic resources that sustain life. By and large, this type of society is harder to pin down, though it seemingly exists in the build up among sedentary hunter-collector, mounted hunter-gatherer, or early agrarian societies.

They become hard to pin down because these are societies in flux, typically towards the next type of society, "the state". In Fried's words: "Once stratification exists, the cause of stateship is implicit and the actual formation of the state is begun, its formal appearance occurring within a relatively brief time." Rarely in human history is the notion of "Progress" or "social evolution" a given nor does it follow the prescribed paths offered by early historians and social thinkers, but in terms of John Bodley's politics of scale, the state is itself a response to Harris's dilemma of population expansion and its required intensification. The state is "better viewed as the complex of institutions by means of which the power of the society is organized on a basis superior to kinship."[83]

The path from egalitarian nomadic foragers to hyper-modernized consumers is hardly a straight one, but there are clear distinctions in the rise and nature of political society here. Simple egalitarian societies deal with conflict on the band-level because it's realistically the only "level" of society that exists. Rank societies, and some stratified ones, typically have both property and territory. These are tribal societies and chiefdoms that we're speaking of.

Through the production of surplus, either in the form of stored grains and proteins or in the form of domesticated plants and animals, the flux of group identity and residence is largely losing out to affiliation based on kinship, place, and locality.

Or, as Harris puts it, "Permanent houses, food-processing equipment, and crops growing in the field sharpened the sense of territorial identity."[84]

This leads to increasing social and ecological pressure on the group and the primary means of conflict resolution succumb to the need for reliability upon static groups. If fights break out, splitting up the camp or group is increasingly less of an option. It becomes the role of individuals to mitigate conflict and to offset its rise.

In practice, this looks like the rise of Big Men or Headmen, individuals who wield influence, but lack the leverage of the state. In Marshall Sahlin's assessment, "A big-man is one who can create and use social relations which give him leverage on other's production and the ability to siphon off an excess product."[85]

Unlike chiefs or kings, the Big Man is a position of respect, not power. They are a leader without authority and without permanence.

As Fried states: "In rank society leaders can lead, but followers may not follow. Commands are given, but sometimes they may not be obeyed."[86]

This is where egalitarianism is hard to shake loose.

The Big Man, and to some degrees, a Chief, are still rooted in a society where the essential power of the state: the ability to organize and coerce individuals to work or to war does not exist. These roles of leadership exist because the position offers a talker, someone who is willing to insert themselves into disputes and areas of contention because the society, as a whole, needs to find resolution to tense situations otherwise it would dissolve into roaming bands again.

It is in that laughter, the heckling implicit in egalitarian societies, once used against self-aggrandizing young hunters that could be used to put a leader back in their place. In Pierre Clastres' words, this is the essence of the "society against the state", one that refuses an economy, refuses political power and the power of coercion:

This mode of constituting the political sphere can be understood, therefore, as a veritable defense mechanism for Indian societies. The culture asserts the predominance of what it is based on – exchange – precisely by treating power as the negation of that foundation.[87]

While the social mechanisms of egalitarianism may remain intact to some degree, the ecological consequences of settled life remain. The Big Man and Chief may not be able to coerce individuals to work, but in their influence, through their giving back to society and mitigation of disputes, they become the instigators of war.

Like all sedentary and domesticated societies that follow, the inability to mitigate tension through movement, laughter, dancing, and even outbursts of internal violence, means that the source of tension must be externalized.

Removed from the ecological contraceptives and diverse food stores that come with nomadic life, societies grow and intensify. It becomes inevitable that other societies, whether they are nomadic foragers, slash-and-burn horticulturalists, totemic kingdoms of hunter-collectors, or the technologically infused drive of twenty-first century corporate-colonizers, the *others* become an intrusion.

It is arguable that the tribal identity is only created as "a consequence of external force," perceived or real.[88] In a stateless rank society, warfare becomes the way to bring the group back together: there is no greater unifier than a common enemy. In Harris's words, "Having external enemies creates a sense of group identity and enhances espirt de corps. The group that fights together stays together."[89]

And as we are emerged into an era of rampant nationalism and xenophobia in response to economic and political turmoil, this is a concept that we ought to be familiar with.

It is the nature of domesticated societies to externalize, to *otherize*, the sources of our tension.

This process might only be seen in minutiae within slash-and-burn horticultural societies, but the innate loss of the means of primal conflict resolution is central to the function of all societies. Relatively egalitarian though many of these societies may be, their palatability is another issue.

I don't say any of this to judge the supposed morality or lack thereof in stateless societies, but my own preference to avoid war comes from living in a society where constant war is a prerequisite. The scale is greatly different, but in all regards, warfare is a long shot from the way disputes are handled and resolved within nomadic forager societies.

The insurmountable feeling of tension felt within the society of strangers is a historical creation.

It is one that we have been born into, but it has a beginning and it will have an end.

The society without strangers is not a sudden or immediate loss, but, as we are sadly all too aware, situations arose that allowed it to continue growing. Through the organization of violence, the externalization of aggressions, empires can become created and boundaries pushed. Left unchecked, we enter a social and ecological downfall into the political economy: the State.

We lose sight of each other and, in turn, lose sight of who we are. Of where we belong.

We lose each other at the moment that we desperately need each other the most. Entering into untold new places and roles that we were never adapted for. We cling to created identities. We create *Others*.

And we lose sight of our own causation. We no longer assume the responsibilities of our own actions. Community succumbs to tribe. Tribe falls to country.

We kill, but we no longer are held to our own actions.

All of this is most prevalent in the organization of violence through the origins of war.

The Organization of Violence and the Origins of War

> *War does not go forever backwards in time. It had a beginning. We are not hard-wired for war. We learn it.*
> -R. Brian Ferguson, 'Pinker's List'[90]

Arguments among nomadic foragers, with or without violent outcomes, center on individuals, not groups.

These are personal grievances, "not fighting over land, for political power, or material wealth, and they are not raiding to abduct women from other groups or attempting to kill cultural outsiders should opportune situations for killing present themselves."[91] Furthermore,

> *The targets of homicide attempts are rarely randomly chosen members of other groups. They are offenders who have committed specific misdeeds or acts of abuse.*[92]

Lacking property and territory, group identity is a complicated notion. "Due to the cultural flexibility and contextual identity," Orang Asli foragers do "not perceive any more commonality with Orang Asli than within members of majority groups."[93] When societies settle down, this changes drastically. Among the sedentary hunter-collector Tlingit, there "was no such thing as a crime against the individual, only against his clan."[94]

It becomes the job of the Big Man and the Chief to foster that sense of group identity.

As populations grow, as gardens expand and shift, as fish and mammals become scarcer, a new ecological reality creates the need for a new social order. And so we get tribes. We get a firmer sense of group identity.

And in response to these mounting pressures, we get warfare.

War, as stated by anthropologist R Brian Ferguson, "by any definition, is a *social* activity, carried out by groups of people."

Beyond combat, war is about group mobilization. It is "organized, purposeful group action, directed against another group that may or may not be organized for similar action, involving the actual or potential application of lethal force."[95] As societies intensify socially and economically, "the deflection of aggressive behavior onto neighboring bands or villages would certainly be preferable to letting it fester within the community."[96]

In social and ecological terms, warfare serves as a means to spread out human populations, through deaths, slavery, or forced relocation which can ease pressure on the land. It leads to the redistribution of territories. It can be "preventative" to punish transgressions from the moral code of a tribe. And it can be cathartic in the sense of giving the release of anxiety, tension, and hostility that arise from sedentary life so that "domestic frustrations and other in-group tensions can be kept within tolerable limits."[97]

War requires a cohesive tribal entity and circumstances that permit the "internalization of a group identity." It requires planning, division of labor, and the sustained collective will to attack.[98] This is a far cry from the potentially, though not typically, fatal arguments that can break out amongst nomadic foragers.

Anthropologist Andrew Vayda has pointed out that it's best to understand warfare as a process: there are stages, phases, and varying levels of intensity.[99] Without the coercive power of the State and using the volunteer army of kin, warfare amongst horticulturalists can easily disintegrate if social and ecological tensions fade. Among the Yanomami, members of raiding groups have been known to simply drop off the raiding party complaining of sore feet or stomachaches. Easy enough to do when there is no system for reprimand.

As Douglas Fry put it: "Command structure and authority are very weakly developed within tribal society."[100]

Conversely, they don't exist among egalitarian bands of nomadic foragers.

To get a closer look at what warfare looks like among horticulturalists, let's look at the Maring of eastern New Guinea. Upon contact in the 1960s and 70s, there were roughly 7,000 Maring spread over roughly 190 square miles. The Maring had gardens and, most notably, they had pigs.

And they had lots of them.

The pigs and gardens go hand-in-hand. Aside from being a source of food, the pigs left in fallow gardens would dig out the scraps their human counterparts missed or didn't find worth it to dig up, their rooting kept the ground soft for replanting, eliminated weeds and seedlings, but the pigs also ate the human refuse that piles up from sedentary life.[101]

Self-contained though this may seem, the population of both the people and, even more so, the pigs created a perpetual socio-ecological conflict: they would run out of room and the efforts to maintain the hogs became too much work. The result: a perpetual cycle of warfare that centered on the ritual slaughtering and feasting of pigs. In Marvin Harris's words:

> *Every part of this cycle is integrated within a complex, self-regulating ecosystem, that effectively adjusts the size and distribution of the Tsembaga's human and animal population to conform to available resources and production opportunities.*[102]

The Maring follow a very common form of horticultural warfare: there is a period of truce and as escalations arise internally, they expand externally, resulting in less intensive battlefield warfare with low mortality rates and intensive battlefield warfare with high mortality rates. The underlying cause of warfare is population pressure, but it is the social consequences of that population pressure that lead to warfare.

Materialist and ecological analysis tells us a lot about why we do the things that we do, across all cultures. But rarely, if ever, do we speak in these crude terms. As social animals, we create a mythos to justify what it is we do and what we don't do. Just as the Mbuti archers and net hunters have varying ideas about the ecological bounty of hunting during honey season based on their camp compositions, the circumstances for war amongst horticulturalists are typically the same, but the social justification may vary.

For the Maring, the initiation of war can be set off by any of the following; taking women, rape, shooting pigs that have invaded gardens, stealing crops, poaching game or stealing wild resources, and sorcery accusations.[103]

Dani men of Papua New Guinea. Photo by Survival International.

The last cause is an essential one in non-state sedentary societies, chiefly states and kingdoms: witchcraft and sorcery. Effectively speaking, the witch or the sorcerer is the ultimate means of externalizing internal drama and tragedy. It's a harsh form of internal conflict resolution. And while those of us in the First World might shrug at these notions as antiquated and primeval, it's just because we've substituted witches and sorcerers with terrorists, immigrants and rogue states as Others.

"Witchcraft," writes Peter Wilson, "especially welds these elusive and diffuse effects people have on one another with the dramatic and tangible effects the natural world has on them in the form of illness, death, and misfortune."[104] The witch and sorcerer are the ultimate scapegoat; they are also the most typical cause of war and raiding cycles.

Not surprisingly, there is an intimate link between disease and warfare. Anthropologist Alexander Alland notes, "Disease may be linked to transgression of the moral code, to social enmity, or to super-natural power, with consequent treatment of these "causes" rather than of the disease-producing organism." This is something that is verifiable throughout our entire recorded history.[105]

Most of Maring life is lived during periods of prolonged truces.

The follow up to the battle cycle is a truce ritual, carried out by each tribe amongst itself, where *rumbim*, a small tree, is ritualistically planted at the borders of the territory. Part of the ritual is that all adult men of the group grasp the *rumbim* as it is planted, "symbolizing both his connection to the land and his membership in the group that claims the land."[106] This is the material representation of the tie that binds the sedentary together. It's how focus is kept on externalizing internal disputes and tensions.

It is the externalization of conflict resolution through killing as a group.

Maring warfare takes two forms: *nothing fights* and *true fights*.

Nothing fights have gotten a larger reputation. Fatalities do happen, but they are rare. Men from two groups will get within range of each other, bringing a bow-and-arrow and large wooden shield. Close enough that they can hear each other voices, but far enough that the arrows are largely ineffective.

More than launching arrows, they are throwing insults. The opponents are not complete strangers, but they are also not kin. They are neighbors with just enough distance to be Others, but also the kind of neighbors capable of maintaining decade long truces.

At this stage of battle, which can last days or months, it is possible to deescalate the disputes: to talk them out, to use mediators to settle arguments, or that a fatality might lead to an end of hostilities without revenge killings. The men go home at nights and come back in the morning until the fight ends or it grows into a *true fight*.

The true fight is close combat. The bows-and-arrows return alongside spears and axes. When the nothing fight escalates, the men retreat from the battlefield for days to prepare for the axe fight. The *rumbim*, planted to signal a truce and now grown, is symbolically uprooted. Pigs are slaughtered and roasted, the salted bellies consumed prior to going out to war. When fatalities occur the individual is mourned and more pigs are slaughtered for a funeral feast.

This too can last for weeks or months: a warrior is killed and pigs are slaughtered. Until the population of people and pigs have waned to sustainable levels. It lasts until the *rumbim* is once again planted.[107]

Brute though warfare may be, this is what non-state societies engage in to keep their numbers low enough to support otherwise relatively egalitarian situations. This isn't the primal anarchy lived by nomadic foragers, but it's also not the ordered hierarchy of the state: a place where this level of warfare can easily become an everyday reality rather than a ritualistic necessity.

Regardless, this kind of warfare is a cultural establishment. It changes the relationships within the bands and their relationship to the world at large. The dynamic tension of the wild and of life becomes something to fear and to fight.

And this is reflected in their social relationships.

Power Goes to the Head(Man)

> *Violence can never be understood solely in terms of its physicality – force, assault, or the infliction of pain – alone. Violence also includes assaults on the personhood, dignity, sense of worth or value of the victim. The social and cultural dimensions of violence are what gives violence its power and meaning.*
> - Nancy Scheper-Hughes and Philippe Bourgois[108]

The Jívaro are horticulturalists that live in the Amazonian basin of Ecuador. At roughly 100,000 people, they're solidly fitting in the chiefdom category that Bodley offers.

And the Jívaro are also notably violent.

Their reputation as headhunters put them on the global stage early in the colonization of South America for all the wrong reasons. In some regards, their warring nature nearly worked for them. By 1589, the Jívaro had been nearly wiped out by the smallpox and measles that the Spanish colonizers had brought with them. But ten years later, in

1599, the remaining Jívaro banded together and successfully threw the Spanish out.[109]

Unfortunately, they would come back, but this is a rare moment of decisive victory in a history of colonization far more deadly than the warfare the Jívaro practiced.

The Jívaro are a warrior culture of raiding parties. Being sedentary horticulturalists with such a high population leaves far less room for times of peace when compared with the Maring. And like the Maring, the social and ecological build up for warfare is never the stated reason for war. It is again the fear of malicious spirits and the want for social and political power that drives the men to war.

And they are out for trophies: the nefarious shrunken heads.

In this society, the chiefs and the shamans are intrinsically tied. Most men vie for both positions and they are allotted to the most outstanding killers.[110] And outstanding killers they are. Warfare is so pervasive and effective at curbing population here that the Jívaro practice polygyny, where men have multiple wives. Because so many men die in raids, the adult population is 2:1, female to male.[111]

That number is high, but not necessarily beyond characteristic of horticultural warfare:

29 percent of Dani men die as a result of injuries sustained during raids and ambushes. Among the Yanomamo village horticulturalists along the Brazil-Venezuela border, raids and ambushes account for 33 percent of adult male deaths from all causes.[112]

So who is the target of Jívaro warfare? They are after *arutam* souls.

Men are not born with them, but they possess them by killing other *arutam* men, who gain them both through hallucinogenic vision quests and killing. There are only so many *arutam* in existence, but "The Jívaro believe that the possessor of a single *arutam* soul cannot be killed by any form of physical violence, poison, or by sorcery." Perhaps a nod back to the unfortunate reality of 1589 however, "he is not immune to death from contagious diseases such as measles and small pox."[113]

An individual can possess no more than two *arutam* souls at one time, but they have a work around on this. The spirits will cycle out, the newest taking over for the older ones. But the warriors are capable of continually compounding the accumulated *power* from their bounty.[114]

Effectively speaking, in a society this large and entrenched in the warrior ethos, there is no need or reason to cap the amount of murder. This is the sheer externalization of the need for the kind of conflict resolution that nomadic societies are capable of.

When an *arutam* man is killed, the *muisak*, or "avenging soul" is unleashed. The *muisak* is thwarted only by the process of properly creating *tsantsa* by removing the head and hair from the skull, shrinking them through boiling, sealing the eyes and mouth to create a shrunken head trophy. This is all done within the *tsantsa* ritual ceremony. And if not done timely, the *muisak* will come for the head taker.[115]

Brute though it may be, the trophy carries its own powers. It is "believed to make it possible for them to work harder and to be more successful in crop production and in the raising of domesticated animals, both of which are primarily the responsibilities of women in Jívaro society."[116]

In contrast to the crude materialist or ecological reasons for why a sedentary chiefdom might seek outside assistance for "successful crop production" and the "raising of domesticated animals," we have a mythical one. As social animals, we prefer the better story. The *tsantsa* heads aren't unlike the flags of nations: a physical source of symbolic pride for their cultural values.

It becomes easy to judge this, as early colonizers surely had, as a form of savagery, a primeval act. We say that to feel better about our own forms of decimation. But as Modernity continues to turn the world into a singular, global culture it is important to remember that the beheadings of ISIS, made for social media, represent the same technological imperatives of the military drones.

We can excuse ourselves from the ecological consequences of lives lived out of the balance achieved by our nomadic forager cousins, ancestors and relatives because we can distance ourselves from the violence and tension our society is capable of externalizing. We ignore the causation of mounting tension and then watch the aftermath on TV or online in disgust.

I don't uphold the warring life of the Jívaro as an ideal, but I don't doubt for a single second that the Jívaro warrior and his victim, even though they may likely be strangers, both know exactly what they are responsible for at the moment when they meet in battle.

The same most definitely can't be said for us.

One problem that we run into when trying to understand, from a social and ecological perspective, about why societies do what they do, is that none of these societies exist within a vacuum.

I don't point out the warfare of horticulturalists to judge them, but to emphasize that these are the stakes that come with yearning for a non-state society, but denying the primal anarchy implicit in nomadic forager lifeways. As we have seen, they have violence and they have created and fostered means of conflict resolution to generally avoid it.

We see amongst warring horticulturalists, or among settled hunter-collector societies and agrarian kingdoms, an attempt to slow the scaling of society through curbing growth. While violence was once the result of options breaking down, we see the situation shift to where violence, namely homicide, becomes necessary for the future of society.

It is this situation that becomes the hallmark of domestication.

It has been argued that the basis for arising patriarchy is the social power granted to *man the hunter*. But this is a complete fabrication, one granted by a patriarchal society that sought to find a glimpse of itself in less complex societies.

That basis is found in *man the warrior*. The scale may vary greatly, but we know this is a historically created and self-reinforcing feedback loop that arises with sedentism and surplus. In some regards, these responses may work. Compared with the hyper-technological, fossil fuel dependent civilization we are a part of, these even appear relatively sustainable. We'll have to leave aside for now whether or not individuals would find them desirable.

The question of their sustainability faces an external threat. And in this regard warring societies have not fared well: if the infrastructure for externalizing the cause of social tensions is in place, what happens when new intruders come?

In this case, those intruders are a whole other level of strangers: militarized colonizers and their technology. As I have argued is the case amongst the Ju/'Hoansi, their uncharacteristically high levels of homicide coincide with the intrusion of colonizers, both directly and indirectly. Alcohol, steel tools and guns create the perfect trifecta of toxic social substances.

History is a living example of this.

In the case of the Ju/'Hoansi, their influx caused the override of potential conflict resolution through traditional means. But without a social infrastructure in place for warfare, they still largely did not escalate beyond personal grievances. Just as they always had.

In the case of the Jívaro, that warring and warrior culture did exist. And just as it always had, the influx of civilized tools and vices led to catastrophic escalation of what was meant to be a curbing mechanism and safety valve for social tension and ecological balances.

The ability to accumulate power from *arutam* while not retaining the spirits likely goes back to the demand upon intrigued Westerners for the *tsantsa* heads. Going back to 1870, the heads became a source of currency with Ecuadorians. The trade began of giving heads for steel tools, but by the early 1900s, they were trading heads for guns.[117]

Similar patterns of outside trade escalating hostilities resulted in genocidal loss among the Yanomami[118] and the complete annihilation of societies, as it had when the Haudenosaunee expanded their territory and networks for the European fur trade.[119]

For the Jívaro, chiefs and shamans became trade partners. Feeding into the role of the chief as one of social stature created a "trend to the desire of individuals to acquire 'white men's valuables,' especially machetes and firearms, and to distribute these goods in order to win friendship."[120] The role of the shaman was available for purchase; their services could be compensated for in trade goods.[121]

The outlawing of the head trade was paired with missionary intervention to pacify the Jívaro.

True to form, the old trade heads can still be found for sale on the internet.[122]

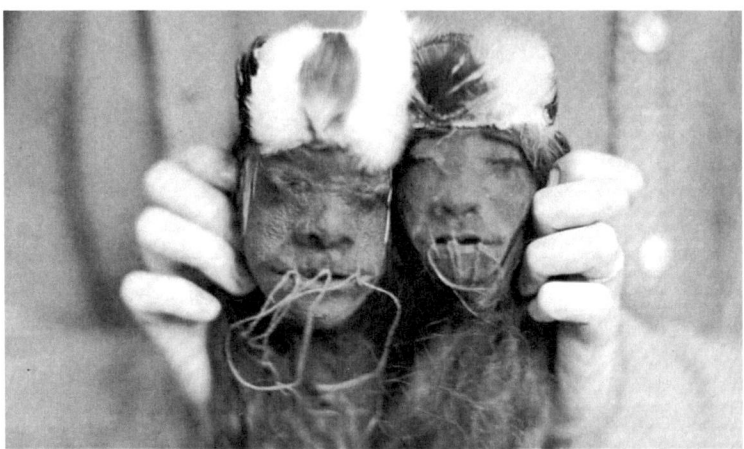

Jivaro shrunken heads.

This is tragic and toxic history, but it is important to point out that warfare as a mechanism scales with freakish ease. Once the social and cultural norms are established, they don't typically scale down.

The spread of these cultures looks like a distorted reflection of the way children are raised in nomadic forager societies. Jívaro childhood is almost the exact opposite of the *bopi* that the Mbuti child inhabits. Children are discouraged from play as "such behavior leads to a disinclination to work." Embracing the fears implicit in sedentary life, children do not interact with the children of other households. Which adds "to the child's sense of insecurity vis-à-vis the rest of the population" as "the frequent attribution of illness within the household to the bewitching activities of hostile shamans."[123]

Both mothers and fathers regularly strike children. Wrestling among boys is encouraged and approved of. Young boys may even begin to follow their fathers on raids as early as the age of six, but typically no later than when the sons are nine. And if the boys disrespect the authority of their fathers, they will make them drink the "the juice of the *maikua*," otherwise known as the powerful hallucinogen *Datura*.

If a child is being particularly bad, the parents may indulge a particularly harsh form of punishment: "This consists of dropping a large quantity of hot peppers into a small fire and forcing the child to remain over the fire under a large cloth until he becomes unconscious."[124]

There is no question that this is the domestication process.

Children are broken much like domesticated pack animals, but they are inversely instilled with the identity of the group and drawn into the allure of social power that is created. From a distance, it may be hard to see the correlation, but this is how we are raised in domesticated societies: refused the rite to self-subsistence, we are fed subservience and find our merit in the ideology of the tribe or the nation as our case may be.

The purpose of this upbringing is to uphold social power. It allows us to remain disconnected from ecology, even if we are reluctantly shaped by it. The will to power is the will to control the sustained stagnancy of sedentary life. And it is an uphill battle.

Warfare confirms this.

Fearing Others is the ultimate introduction to the world of strangers. It is the necessary step to assure that responsibility for your actions can be shouldered by the culturally constructed sense of justice and necessity.

Like the Jívaro, the Mundurucú are headhunting horticulturalists living in Brazil. Despite their equally perpetual state of war, it has been observed that:

> *The seemingly tranquil life of the Mundurucú is fraught with fears of the unseen and unknown. There is little violence, or even ag-*

gressiveness, among them, but violence and aggression are indeed present in repressed and residual form.[125]

This insulating relationship with the world and the ability to push all internal conflict onto others made it possible for the Mundurucú to consider all other tribes as enemies while being seemingly peaceful with each other. That externalized sense of us-versus-them just kept pushing them farther and more mercilessly out into the forest:

After perhaps months of travel through the forests, they would surround an enemy village by night and launch an attack at dawn. Burning arrows were shot into thatched roofs, driving the bewildered occupants outside—to the lances and arrows of the Mundurucú warriors. Enemy men and women alike were slaughtered and decapitated, and the trophy heads thrown into carrying baskets.[126]

Once the cultural infrastructure is there, these societies scale in one direction: growth, expansion; conquest. That is until they can no longer sustain themselves and they fragment. Or they collapse.

The same happens among sedentary hunter-collector societies, where "we see, as a pattern, an increase in the severity of fighting." Along the Pacific Northwest of North America, the Haida were considered the "Vikings of the coast," warring relentlessly with all neighboring tribes. To the south of them, the Klamath "warred for revenge, booty, and slaves."[127]

It is the nature of settled societies that their surplus makes them as likely to war with neighbors as they are to become targets themselves: "When food is stockpiled, it inevitably becomes a key military objective of raiding parties."[128]

It is the direct immersion in these acts that keep the communities intact. We are social animals. We are drawn towards each other. As we have all seen, we're willing to endure pretty horrible things to stay closer to other people, even if our relationships are just a fragment of what it is we are looking for.

We yearn for the fluid sense of belonging that comes with nomadic forager life. And we will grasp onto anything that bares it semblance.

So perhaps the question left to ask is: why?

The Society of Strangers: the Trauma of Isolation

The play goes on, more or less imperfectly. The person, so deprived, bears the consequences as unregenerate elements of immaturity, glossed by repression and compensation, distorted by unconscious yearnings for overdue fulfillment and resentments against the nurturers.

- Paul Shepard, *Nature and Madness*[129]

So why are we drawn to community? What pulls us closer to each other? There are many possible answers to these kinds of questions. We tend to focus on biological ones: stripping away the emotion and wants of our social animality. There are truths to the biological explanations, but those approaches don't really get at the heart of the matter.

I believe we enjoy the solace that we offer each other. We find joy in the company, care and companionship that we have to offer each other. In healthy communities, we can air our frustrations, we can sing and dance them away: we can ritualize the conflicts that arise from the reality of life and death.

We can rely on each other to help cope with the difficulties that can come with living.

And there are many things about living that can be complicated. There are many reasons why we might end up snapping, much like the aardvark burrow dwelling !Kung man. Or like the 18.2% of Americans who suffer from mental disorders.[130]

One of those reasons is a high rate of infant mortality among nomadic forager societies.

Stillbirths, miscarriages, and other sources of infant loss are suffered silently within Modernized societies. In terms of industrialized, First World nations, the United States is actually fairly high with an average of 6.1 infant deaths per 1,000. No doubt, the advancements of technology in terms of prolonging life play a huge role in this, but, like all things civilized, the U.S. stands out in terms of a massive gap in access to that kind of technological health care. Children of poor families are nearly five times more likely to lose a child within the first year compared to wealthy families.[131]

This is stark in contrast to the Batek where about 25% of infants died within their first two years. It is worth noting that during that same period, malaria was the prime killer and one that arose from contact with civilization.[132]

This kind of number is one that is hard to hear.

That is due, in large part, to the fact that within civilized societies, we don't speak about things like infant mortality. Statistically it is far less significant than in nomadic forager societies under active colonization, but 6.1 deaths per 1,000 births are not none. We carry these losses personally and, as a culture, refuse to acknowledge them.

In refusing to acknowledge tragedy, we create trauma.

It becomes easy to look at the society without strangers through the same kind of potential for punishment that we have been instilled with. Living without strangers shouldn't be seen that way. Losing anonymity means that mourning and loss become communally understood, felt and accepted. We care for each other, empathize with each other, and help deal with bad things that can happen.

We help with the bad things that do happen.

And within nomadic forager societies, infant mortality is one of those things.

As mentioned earlier, toddlers become children when they begin to have signs of autonomy: when they begin to interact with others within the community on their own. This is a coping mechanism. Once a nomadic forager child passes the test of the first couple years, their chances of living to old age increase greatly. "Young babies are," within nomadic forager societies, "an extension of the mothers' self, until they start to communicate and interact with others, independently."

There are cultural acknowledgements and beliefs to contextualize the potential for loss. The "Aka believe that dead young babies come back again reborn as other babies." Seen as an extension of the mother, the loss of infants "registers with the community as a failed birth, rather than as the death of a person."[133]

This recognition and acknowledgement of a potentially demolishing experience of losing a child doesn't take away how infants and toddlers are treated. As stated earlier, they are loved, coddled, held close, and engaged with passionately by the community at large.

The interests of the child to be are always upheld. It is part of the ecological awareness that comes with mobility that nomadic foragers will make decisions based on ensuring that children within the group are loved and never neglected. Infanticide, when it does occur amongst the !Kung, occurs "with the stated goal of enhancing the quality of care and survival of existing children and to avoid caring for seriously defective children, almost certain to fail."[134] Among the Batek, infanticide only occurred in cases of babies born with severe physical deformities.[135]

It is equally unfair to talk about the rates of infant mortality within nomadic forager societies, which seemingly are far greater than those within countries like the United States, without acknowledging some caveats: of the recorded instances of pregnancy in the US in 2012, 15% ended in abortions.[136] A fate that is arguably far less sufferable than being born unwanted by uncaring parents who feel the moral and social obligation to maintain the pregnancy.

If you include those statistics and consider the rate of unwanted children within civilized societies, it's hard to believe that we really have it better off.

From the perspective of the nomadic forager, there is an acceptance that not all children who are born will live and they have adapted for it. It may be impossible to say how much the realities of contact and colonization have increased rates of infant mortality, but considering scum like Pinker have included the killing of children among foragers by colonizing agents such as loggers and miners, it's impossible to think that both the direct killing and stress it carries haven't increased that number.

But the point remains, it is the understanding of what can happen and the readiness of the community to help heal, foster and move on, ushered with a cultural acceptance that the spirit of the child will likely return, that it wasn't ready, all turn a potentially traumatizing situation, one that I think every living being wishes to avoid, into something that isn't emotionally endemic.

The processes of mourning and healing are made public.

These losses, unthinkable as they may be, are not settled in isolation.

The care of children is tantamount to the survival of the group.

Alongside adultery, the primary cause of arguments among the Agta is "careless or irresponsible use of a bush knife or bow and arrow within a campsite where onlookers, particularly children might be injured."[137] Mothers have been known to even go to blows with other women for verbally reprimanding their children.[138]

Everything is out in the open. There are no personal problems that escape the empathy of the group. The community exists to nurture each other.

In our own society, we bury that pain, that conflict. We ironically live in fear of what may happen to us as a result of external forces while we blind ourselves to the things that are likely to happen.

Within the United States, the top ten leading causes of death have almost no reflection in the fear mongering politics of control. Almost all of those causes of death are preventable illness (cardiovascular, certain cancers, and diet related). "Accidents" are the fourth leading cause of death, which includes drug overdose, medical mistakes, and automotive collisions. But while suicide is barely trailing influenza and pneumonia, homicide (including terrorism) doesn't make the list.[139]

We return to the Others.

We focus on the common enemy so we can foster an artificial sense of group identity as we stumble through the motions of a social animal living in a sore replacement for community.

We suffer, alone. Together.

This is the society of strangers. Individuals, wound up, lost, and hurting, who are willing to externalize their own inner turmoil. A place where once healthy individuals seeking comfort through fluid movement and affiliation are left without recourse for a shattered process of personal growth and cognitive development.

This is the scourge of domestication.

Neoteny, as Paul Shepard explains, is the process of stunting our development into fully aware and active beings. That is into individuals capable of maintaining communities. This process of severing the competency of a capable adult is no accident; this is a need for agrarian societies:

> *Politically, agriculture required a society composed of members with the acumen of children. Empirically, it set about amputating and replacing certain signals and experiences central to early epigenesis. Agriculture not only infantilized animals by domestication, but exploited the infantile human traits of the normal individual neoteny.*[140]

Post Traumatic Stress Disorder, PTSD, is said to impact 7.8% of adults in the United States. It is two times more prevalent among women than men.[141] Because of technology, we can suffer historically unique forms of brutality. As we suffer alone, without a cultural preemption or recognition of that probability, it is not surprising that one of the wealthiest nations has such a high rate of PTSD. Considering our refusal to acknowledge the possibility of infant mortality and the silencing of women's voices through patriarchy, the disparity between men and women having PTSD should also not be surprising.

Surely as nomadic foragers our brains are built to withstand stressful situations.

Life in the wild may not be "nasty, brutish, and short," but that doesn't make it stress-free either. Infant mortality is a looming tragedy, but it's not alone. There are a lot of harsh ways to die living in the wild outside of homicide; falling from trees while collecting honey, being bitten by snakes, being attacked by predators, facing periods of hunger, and weather extremes. Most of the situations are not necessarily lethal, but, by and large, nomadic foragers aren't suffering from PTSD even though they may likely have dealt with a number of those situations.

I believe the difference comes down to the acceptance and acknowledgement of things that can happen. If the community is aware and capable of mitigating those tensions and possible sources of stress, then they need not become traumatic. No one suffers alone.

But the civilized do.

We become lost in our trials and tribulations, left to reiterate them or to refuse to cope with them in a dance of neoteny. We become strangers, mere neighbors: a concept that, prior to domestication "had no significance, no social meaning."[142]

And this permits us to both perpetuate and permit systemic violence. This allows us to remove our sense of responsibility from the world and each other. It keeps us from giving children the space to explore boundaries and find themselves among friends.

It keeps us from seeing and believing the violence of the state.

With 7.5 billion people, we have created 7.5 billion variations of how the domestication process has fucked with our minds. We all create our uniqueness through how we have endured as individuals. Dependent upon the law to control and mitigate our unresolved conflicts, we give away our ability to become self-sufficient, both physically and cognitively.

As Stanley Diamond stated, "schizophrenia is the process through which the inadequacy of the culture is concretized in the consciousness of individuals."[143] We become fractured. Our punishment becomes self-propagating. Diamond continues, the "development of the early civilizations as instruments of oppression was the result, not of some environmental or technical imperative, but of the new possibilities of power which men in certain positions found it necessary to cultivate and legitimate."[144]

Domestication is about dependency. And that is what we are: dependents of the custodial State.

Each of us is born to be a *child of the forest* and becomes a *child of the machine* through indoctrination. Our own pain becomes a justification for pushing further and further into the depths of the mechanisms of the State.

And as the power to respond and resolve is taken from our hands, it is given directly to the State.

The unresolved, unreconciled tension of existence tightens the shackles.

The Violence of the State

> *The hallmarks of civilization may be as much the conquering warrior, the armed guard, the city wall, the whipping post, the prison, and the gallows as they are the high arts, religious monuments, and writing.*
> - Timothy Earle, *How Chiefs Come to Power*[145]
>
> *I can't breathe. I can't breathe. I can't breathe. I can't breathe. I can't breathe. I can't breathe. I can't breathe. I can't breathe. I can't breathe. I can't breathe.*
> - Eric Garner, as he was suffocated by a NYPD cop on July 17, 2014[146]

Till this point, my focus has been on non-state societies. I've made it my goal to focus on violence, particularly violence within a society, because neither egalitarian nomadic foragers nor warring horticulturalists see violence as an ideal way to deal with kin, with family, with anyone where a personal relationship exists.

Nomadic foragers are not shaken by acts of violence, but they have instilled numerous coping mechanisms to try to stem off tension before it is overflowing.

Horticulturalists, by and large, uphold violence as an institution. Their means of internal conflict resolution are to ritualistically and habitually externalize the sources of social and ecological pressures.

And they do this so that they don't turn on each other because they need to all get along; to tend gardens, to keep their domesticated animals, and to fill raiding parties.

Though these societies may be polar opposites in many ways, they are tied by a refusal of *social power*. The members of these societies are willing participants in their cultures. They celebrate them without the cognitive dissonance afforded to state-dwelling nationalists who may never see the inside of a mine or have to stand armed on a battlefield.

As populations grow unchecked, as societies grow in number, as territory must continue to expand: the effective function of mobility or influential, yet powerless, leaders crumble. As the scale expands, "the number of decisions required by any node increases until it exceeds an individual's personal capacity to make decisions and requires an expansion in the hierarchy of decision makers."[147]

As horticultural societies grow, they take on the infrastructure of sedentary hunter-collectors and the technology of agrarian society. The role of the Chief becomes a specialization. And as the position grows into an occupation with subordinates, the growth "creates certain dynamics of competition, management, and control that underlie the eventual evolution of the state."[148]

War in societies without a state is waged for revenge, defense, land, plunder, and/or prestige. Within states, war is waged for political control, economic gain, social status, and defense.[149] War becomes an essential part of the ideology of the state: a self-justifying conquest of the world. "The form of political organization which we call the state," explains Marvin Harris, "came into existence precisely because it was able to carry out wars of territorial conquest and economic plunder."[150]

It is worth noting that there is nothing inevitable about this entire situation.

Our lineage is evidence of this. The hundreds of thousands, if not millions, of years of our combined ancestry is virtually all the lived primal anarchy of nomadic foragers. The problem is that when societies do settle, when they do domesticate plants and animals, they *must* grow. The speed and path may vary, but the results, left to their own devices, in time may all look the same.

And when the state does arise; it doesn't exist quietly.

The state arises when the coevolution of war and society merge. The segmentation of the world into an ordered hierarchy is the necessary precondition for the cornerstone of states: the law.[151]

The law stands in defiance of the conflict resolution implicit in nomadic forager life. Not content to merely externalize tension into warfare, as stateless horticulturalists do, the state absorbs the function of the war machine while it refuses the legitimacy of internal group tension. The group is given an outlet for aggression to build identity, but it is a lesson in subservience: a lesson in absolute domestication.

"The latent purpose of the law," as seen by Stanley Diamond, "was punishment in the service and profit of the state, not prevention or the protection of persons, not the healing of the breach."[152] The ambiguous influence of Headmen and Chiefs is now increasingly ineffective: power becomes absolute.

Hierarchy is cemented into the foundation of bureaucracy and production. The religious sanctions granted by shamans and priests lay the groundwork for the legal sanctions of kings. Within the stratification of the state are the roles and duties of its officiators. To take matters into your own hands is now a crime and a punishable one. The goal of the law is to punish and to make an example of the perpetrators.

The judge replaces the mediator.[153]

The law is the social construct of the society without strangers. It exists solely in the place where all other forms of conflict resolution fall into the pit of anonymity. True to the schizophrenic nature of civilized life as it seeks to dissociate circumstance and action, action and consequence. We continue to externalize our aggressions, but we are forced to fear our internal tensions. The law is order. And a violation of the law is personal failure.

And we are accountable only to the law.

This is where the true terror of the state becomes apparent: in the absolute refusal to grant us our own means of resolving and reconciling tensions, we become statistics. We become a broken record of violations of the stagnant and impersonal nature of legislated morality. Our subservience upon the state grants it the ability to exist by bending the moral code as it declares the justice of its own necessary evils.

Witihin this realm, homicide becomes the crème-de-la-crème of crime. To kill another person, to violate the sanctity of "thou shall not kill." We take this for granted, but it's because we deny all the circumstances where killing another person *just may be* the most peaceful form of conflict resolution.

Rare though those cases may be, they do exist.

The !Kung, for example, have no need for moral or legal codes because they have no distance between action and consequence. They mostly avoid violence, but if they were to impose anything resembling legal or religious sanctions against murder, then what would they have done with /Twi after he violated it? The society without strangers doesn't need law because if the law is to be enforced, the people who kept /Twi from killing more would be seen the same as /Twi: murderers.

The law is black and white to all who can't afford to bend it: the very people who governments pretend to protect and serve.

The state is the gold-bearer of double standards. Above all else, "the state and government are organizations for war." As anthropologist and anarchist Harold Barclay puts it, "No more efficient organization for war has been developed."[154] That double standard works because of our dissociation: first in production, then in warfare.

"War," writes Paul Shepard, "is the state's expression of social pathology."[155]

We simply follow orders. We don't connect the dots.

Resolved to refuse the rite of resolution, absolved from the flux of circumstances; we become the consumers of nationalized ideologies spread from pulpits and talking heads. We become the audience for programmers like Steven Pinker applauding our civility and restraint against our "savage" impulses.

And so we end up in a nation where the president evokes the notion of "a just war" while he receives a Nobel Peace Prize, simultaneously carrying out indiscriminate drone strikes and military operations globally.[156] We are absolved of our responsibility, our consequence.

This is how we become monsters, when we are so removed from the reality of our world that we can look at it with indifference. It is when we become the efficient cogs of the globalized machine that we can compare homicide rates, without circumstance or attentiveness, to feel good about our own notions of social progress.

As Stanley Diamond points out, it is here that we become the threat:

Dissociated, not good, persons can do impersonal evil. Persons who have become personae, masks; persons who have permitted themselves to be reduced to social functions, alienated, bureaucratized; persons who can kill out of abstract strategy, but who are out of touch with their own capacities to express and transcend hostility, persons who obey orders in societies where the civilizing process

> has become hyper-rationalized. ... It is dissociated persons doing impersonal, and therefore potentially boundless, evil who are the threat in modern civilization—they are the irresponsible.[157]

The violence of our society includes the breakdown of our universalized schizophrenic reality. It includes the mass murderers, the killing sprees, gang violence, workplace shootings, domestic violence, racist and xenophobic attacks, parents killing their children, cops killing unarmed individuals, and acts of "homegrown" terrorism. It includes crimes that spread from endemic poverty and as an outcome of addictions. It includes those who kill to reclaim their social power and those who must kill in self-defense.

To compare the murder rate of Detroit and nomadic foragers in the Kalahari, our programmers will readily pat themselves on the back for achieving stasis, so any improvement on the numbers looks good.

There is no replication; there is no equation for the weight of egalitarianism within this. There is no weight put on circumstance, no need for further reflection beyond the sheer numbers of dead bodies. There is no thought put into the prospects for resolution and reconciliation, for the ability to have a dispute end in ritualistic celebration rather than funerals.

There is no responsibility in any of this.

But there is deception.

The state creates an entire form of violence that has no precedent in a society without strangers: structuralized, systemic violence.

A life mired in unending, and often unseen, war.

Economic power, a historical creation upon which all social power is built, "is based on the ability to restrict access to key productive resources or consumptive goods."[158] This is the production that begins when gardens or fields are planted, when animals are bred in captivity, and when storehouses are filled.

The economy originates when the self-reliant nomadic forager is forced into social dependence rather than choosing social life.

Like all change, things happen slowly. Perhaps even imperceptibly.

Yet by the time the state appears, there is no question: social hierarchy and stratification are implicit. The side effect of authority is poverty. And "the world's poor are the chief victims of structural violence – a violence which has thus far defied the analysis of many seeking to understand the nature and distribution of extreme suffering."[159]

The supposed benefits of civilization, the triumphs of Progress, have never been even handed. Not even close.

And despite the stories spun by domesticators, priests and programmers, it can't be. If domestication requires conquest, civilization is the epitome of it. Literally everything that we touch within civilization is soaked in blood. Down to the finest details; the sugar in your cup, the rare earth metals in your cellphone battery, your "sustainably sourced" organic palm shortening; everything that we touch in the civilized world is produced on a global scale and distributed through the technological infrastructure that consumes resources at an unprecedented rate.

The reason that nomadic foragers and horticulturalists are being imposed upon is because of us. Because of our civilization and its unrelenting need for perpetual growth. Nothing is sacred. Nothing is left untouched.

So when we begin to proselytize about the supposed virtues of our "improving conditions," it is a continued act of colonization to disregard that the rising homicide rates that accompany contact with stateless societies are a part of our own homicide rates. At this point, we are no longer disconnected, we just perceive ourselves to be because that is the lie that we are told.

It is the definition of irony that this globalized civilization is the most violent force in the history of this planet, one that if left unchecked could result in the extinction of humanity itself in less than a hundred years,[160] while promoting itself as the bastion of peace and prosperity.

This bravado is the malicious internalization of the Otherization that arises with sedentism and domestication: we remove ourselves from responsibility and consequence. We raise flags over the mass graves of the conquered and massacred. There is no shortage of examples of the level of brutality implicit in the building of Modernity. We can dissociate from the death tolls, the destroyed forests, the displaced populations, the slavery, the power of coercion and domination, the diseased and polluted habitats, dead rivers, dying oceans, and, everywhere, the crude spills, the toxic leaching, the carcinogenic spraying, and the looming unknown present of abrupt climate change with increasingly violent weather patterns.

As our social and ecological circumstances worsen, we too turn towards our own variations of witchcraft and sorcery accusations. The refugees of war-torn Syria, a result of the intersection of climate change and fragile geo-politics, become targets themselves as they are suspected of perpetuating the very terrorism that they are risking their lives to flee. One murdering religion turns on the others. We have caliphates and drone strikes. We have the pathologically fragmented perpetuators of military occupations emboldened with the power of a badge in increasingly militarized police forces.

As the semblance of climate stability withers, we turn further and further inwards. We get lost within the narcissistic sea of the Self, enshrined in social media and technology. We increasingly fragment our world, looking for outcasts to blame for our worsening condition so that we don't have to face the insurmountable whole of our condition: so that we don't have to face the reality of a globalized civilization that has far surpassed its peak.

We are harvesting our diminishing returns at the cost of each other's lives, our own future, and any sense of ecological sanity or hope. Technology allows us to get hyper-focused on singular events long enough to feed the overwhelming sense of mutually assured destruction.

But the thoughts don't stay. Eyes on our devices, we refresh daily with a new tragedy.

As the Jívaro can only retain two *arutam* souls, but can accumulate their power infinitely, we become cumulative rage.

As cell phones increase the ability to quickly record and disperse videos documenting the way that police systemically target black men, we become the filters for seeing the reality of brute force in real time. In true form, the reaction to these increasingly visible displays of brute force is met with a further raising of flags, restating allegiance to the ideology of the state: *they* must have done something wrong. Force, meted out by the state, is always justified. For those buying the merits of civilization, they can be presented with counter-evidence to the false confidence eschewed by Pinker and his kind, but they can't recognize it.

This comes back to the domestication process: that internalization of both the group identity and the need to counter the ecological imbalance of sedentary life. Headmen can call upon the group to band together to fight an externalized source of tension. Chiefs can pull together an army.

But kings, like presidents, can coerce them.

And with the Law at their hands, they can use them against anyone who tries to stand in their way.

Perhaps those who seek authority are not unlike /Twi. The ability to kill on mass scale, to order the death of thousands, if not millions, from afar takes a certain kind of psychotic personality. The very person that most likely was never checked by parents and other children in a *bopi* kind of environment.

Perhaps those individuals would kill in any society, regardless of their upbringing and any attempt to resolve or dissolve conflicts before they mounted. It's nearly impossible for us to say, as nearly every person alive, even within recent memory, has not been a stranger to civilization and its systemic violence in one form or another. But we have unquestionable evidence that even if those personalities had existed, a society without strangers created coping mechanisms for dealing with them when they get out of hand.

Civilization, on the other hand, has found ways to empower them.

You have this constant current throughout the history of civilization of patterns of behavior that are unusually vicious, even for societies with militaries; that is societies where there are not only specialists in killing, but specialists in strategizing mass killing and technocrats dedicating their life to increasing the ability to kill more efficiently.

At the outposts of civilization, you have systemic empowerment of unhinged psychotics like King Leopold II of Belgium who built an empire of terror in the Congo on the fortunes of rubber.[161] A man who took hands and feet of slaves for not meeting his imposed rubber quotas and killed with absolute indifference to foster his own power. He became the influence for the character of Kurtz, an ivory trader, in Joseph Conrad's *Hearts of Darkness*. His source of power became interchangeable because this bloodthirsty king of the frontier story arises again and again throughout the history of civilization.

We have child sacrificing Mayan kings and the decapitating soldiers of the Caliphate, like the Old World crusaders or New World colonials. And they are all a part of the ongoing expansion of the civilization that we inhabit.

Technology scales carnage. Though some acts might be more brutal than others, it is only because they can be. Warfare, within Modernity, can "be waged by technicians." While politicians are quick to rile up public support for their killing, the needs of civilization are of a more rational sort: to protect resources, to maintain order, to advance territory, and to eliminate potential threats.

As Stanley Diamond points out, this kind of violence may be even more frightening by its inhuman and methodical nature:

absolutely modern, up-to-date war, lacking in ritual, lead by technicians, in a kind of rationalized madness, does not require hate, or rather, I should say, the open and direct expression of hostility. Such a war between antagonists at more or less equivalent levels of civilized development, would be, of course, obliterating, but if there were survivors, it would leave, I believe a heritage of hate at the commission of dissociated evil *that staggers the emotional imagination.*[162]

Drone strikes may typify this kind of behavior, but warfare, as purely the realm of technicians, has not come. Soldiers are embedded within the pride of nationalism and tasked with its defense. But like the rest of us, they are stuck within the consequences of insurmountable tensions and the feeling of subjugation implicit in the state.

All of us, as we have clearly all seen, are equally capable of breaking. "Caged creatures show much aberrant behavior," Paul Shepard writes, "including psychopathic fits of bloody carnage, and many of the same psychotic symptoms as humans in our developed nations."[163] And with the technology of civilization, the death count increases. Exponentially.

So while the kind of psychotic murderer that we've empowered with technology and given authority through politics may have existed at any point in our nomadic forager past, there were social mechanisms to cope with them. They risked being shunned or exiled. They had to know their potential victims and face their kin.

They weren't given more authority.

They weren't given justifications.

They weren't rewarded with more efficient killing technology.

And if all else failed, they faced the unrelenting spears and arrows of an egalitarian society capable of handling them.

Cultures of Resistance

> *All the movements of the left and right are functionally the same inasmuch as they all participate in a larger, more general movement toward the destruction of the human species. Whether people stay confined within certain obsolete strategies and forms, or whether they submit to the mechanisms of technology—either way the result is the same.*
> - Jacques Camatte, *This World We Must Leave*[164]

So what do we do about this? How do we respond to a globalized civilization and its implicit violence?

This is no simple question and there are no simple answers. But we have plenty to work with.

For me, the question of conflict resolution is both empowering in terms of how societies can function without the law and in exposing the fragility of domestication. The state is built upon technology, and that is neither a small feat nor a minor footnote in the history of civilization and systemic violence. As we see every day, when people stand up to power, they face the blunt force of its physical brutality. The law serves it well to lock away potential threats.

But it is fragile in the sense that it works because we are trained to ignore even the potential to deal with each other without the inclusion of state infrastructures; that is, without prisons and without police.

The state is strong if we continue to see resistance only on civilization's terms: limited by the law and by the ownership of violence. If you focus on the source of that power, technology, or to be more specific for our current world, electricity, then things look very different.

In order to understand and undermine civilization on that level, we have to go back to the beginning: why do primal anarchistic societies function? The answer is community. Namely egalitarian communities built on the foundation of flux and fluidity.

For us, I'm talking about building *communities of resistance*.

As I have argued elsewhere and repeatedly, the success of indigenous resistance, in contrast to revolutionary movements, lie within the strength of communities.[165] Revolutions are fought for ideologies; they are fought to correct the wrongs of the State and the want to reshape the enlightened future society upon the failures of the existing empires.

Needless to say, even when they are successful, it's hard to argue that they're more appealing.

Radicals and extremists, in many ways, simply mimic the form of religious death cults, most notably, in our times, ISIS. The vision of the Caliphate and the righteousness of the martyr need no real world actualization. In offering the promise of life after living, the martyr is the ultimate ideologue. By the time they are able to be disappointed about the future that wasn't awaiting them, it's too late to matter.

Being untethered by the existing world, the relentless nihilism of indiscriminate murder sadly draws a new kind of allure. Terrorism grants an escape from the consequences of being dispossessed by the domestication process. It gives vindication to ending an unfulfilling life. A justification that serves as the only difference between the two technologically infused archetypes of Modernity: the suicide bomber and the mass shooter.

We get to this point because we believe the domesticator's innate lie: authority lies within the law and the power of authority lies in its monopolization of violence. So long as violence remains reified, so long as violence becomes and remains a *thing*, it has allure. It becomes the tool of liberation just as much as the functional force of conquest.

If the end goal of revolution, true to its innately political nature, is the conquest of authority, then time is always working against it. The Soviets who fought in the Russian Revolution might have had the numbers to take on tanks and cannons. I suspect they wouldn't have fared quite as well against drones.

Nor would we.

But it is the *demystification of violence* that creates the potential to erode the sanctity of authority and to understand, much like egalitarian nomadic foragers, that there are ways to mitigate and dissolve tension without violence. In a world of billions of people, it is vital to recognize that it is not the lives of individuals that seal our fate, but the technology that grants individuals the power to wield authority and coerce systemic violence. It is the domestication process that keeps us in line and keeps us from viewing civilization as a failed attempt at creating a biological organism and acting upon it.

In the words of John Bodley, "Civilizations are artificial cultural constructions, not biological organisms, and they would be poor biological performers if we insisted on considering them as organisms."[166] Civilizations are not alive, but they are parasitic. They demand the wholesale consumption of entire ecosystems, of the devouring of their wild hosts.

Civilizations may not be biological organisms, but their existence demands that they act like one.

So they can die like them.

So they have died like biological organisms.

Like its forbearers, this civilization too will die.

The decaying infrastructure of its technological reign crosses the span of nations and oceans. The precision of its war machine and logistics both lie in the precision of satellites and cell phone towers, neither of which is impervious to destruction, intentional or not. The earth decimating ability of power stations can be undone by storms as well as sabotage. The perpetuation of its growth is dependent upon agricultural production as its primary crops continue to be threatened and tainted by climate instability. Its need for an unrelenting stream of finite resources remains undeterred.

Its bloated and overwhelmed rendition of a biological organism, unlike its ever-growing harness of militaristic force, is exceptionally fragile and vulnerable.

Humanity has survived millions of years of evolution by embracing fluidity and flexibility.

There is no reason to believe that our biology can't outlast the synthetic one of the state.

Holding the line at the Standing Rock DAPL camp.

Our resistance, like our potential to survive the collapse of this civilization, lies in grounding.

It lies in reclaiming the refusal of authority that was innate in societies without a state. It lies within the heart of primal anarchy: by returning to the world of face-to-face existence. It lies in connecting with the resistance against civilization that the communities of wildness have always taken part in. It lies in viewing the world in terms of ecosystems rather than the separated and programmed world of the state.

Domestication is a process. It needs to constantly adapt to the channeling of our needs as social animals into the authority of domesticated societies, but it can never be complete. We are captives, caged animals in a cell comprised of technological gadgetry on one end and the blunt force of the police on the other.

We may be unfit to match their force, but we may not need to.

When we resist authority in our own lives by handling our own conflicts without outside intrusion, we can get a glimpse of what we are capable of. In fostering self-sufficiency, we undermine the state's hegemony of dependence upon stagnancy. In fighting against the circumstances that make inequality possible, as opposed to fighting for equality in the eyes of the law, we embolden ourselves within community.

Considering the ways that civilization has bastardized any notion of what "community" might mean, it is easy for my intents to be overlooked here. Community, as I use the term, carries no reflection of the pacifist, hippie want for communal living. Like the horticulturalists, liberals seek to create situations where "we all must get along"—only they've removed the internalized "safety valves" of external warfare.

Such delusions can lead to the other extreme of mystified violence: ideological pacifism. The epitome of violence externalized. A false sense of security in believing that if you don't respond to the violence of the state in kind, that your rights under the law will be respected.

This stems from the notion of community as a thing of ease: supplanting the dynamic tension of the wild with the well-massaged sense of arrogant removal implicit in a placid view of *nature*. That center of communal life amongst nomadic foragers revolves around singing, dancing, playing and, overall, joy, comes at the recognition and confrontation with the potential and likely unpleasant aspects of being a living creature.

As we've seen, this can be far from traumatic. But it requires openness, honesty, and, above all else, an ability to handle circumstances as they arise: as individuals, as a community.

That means dealing with internal tensions and external ones.

That means being able to take on civilization directly.

There have been individuals and groups that have sought to co-opt the fury of indigenous resistance while refusing the connectivity implicit within them. They have sought to adopt the rage of grounded peoples without the grounding and pair it with the displaced, reified violence that we have been impregnated with.

To understand indigenous resistance, you have to understand that it is inseparable from the world of native peoples. It is when their communities are assaulted that they can respond in kind.

It is here that it is almost tragic that more indigenous societies weren't as warring as they were made out to be. The Huaorani were able to keep Westerners at bay by spearing the first missionaries that attempted to contact them to death. Having been subjected to the attempts to raid for slaves by the Malays and Burmese, "shipwrecked mariners and the members of landing parties seeking to replenish water supplies were often killed by the Andamanese."[167]

It is telling that most nomadic foragers lacked the experience to be openly hostile to colonizers. The result of which has been nothing short of tragic. And that tragedy is still on going.

It is possible that the act of rebuilding communities, which, much like rewilding, will take place over generations, will be able to incorporate this reality into their mythos. The resistance to and refusal of civilization may become the central stories told around the hunting campfires of our descendants.

Against all odds, this has happened before.

James Kaywaykla lived from 1877 to 1963. He was a part of the Warm Springs Apache and grew up during the most violent period of their history. In his words, "Until I was about ten years old I did not know that people died except by violence."[168]

As horticulturalists who reintegrated with the horse to become mounted hunter-gatherers, the Apache were no strangers to warfare. They had an established pattern of raiding and warfare prior to colonization and a reputation for being particularly effective warriors.[169] However, they weren't prepared for the wholesale onslaught of the Europeans who intentionally sought to decimate the entire ecosystem to destroy the inhabitants of this New World. This led to a familiar rise of inter-tribal warfare, but quickly escalated.

A series of back-and-forth battles between the Chiricahua Apache and the intruding whites peaked in 1863. Mangas Colorado, among the most respected of chiefs and father-in-law to Cochise, came to a colonizer's encampment under a truce agreement that, to his surprise resulted in his arrest upon arrival. Considered an instigator of hostilities, the officers didn't respond in kind. After torturing him alive, *they shot him six times through the head and torso. His body was rifled for souvenirs, while his corpse was later scalped and dismembered, the massive head being cut off and boiled down to a skull in a big pot.*

This incident shook the Chiricahua and led to a decade of war with whites.

And it didn't fare particularly well for the whites. Between 1862 and 1871, the US Army spent $38 million on a campaign of elimination that resulted in 100 Apache men, women and children being killed. But in that time, the Apache killed 5,000 whites.[170]

Having the knowledge, skill, and grounding of a hunter-gatherer paid off. Proficiency and skill with a bow-and-arrow certainly were crucial, but ecological knowledge is helpful. The whites, they knew, never learned to dig for water in the dry desert. They would drink "a spring dry, leaving only mud for the soldiers" who would often die of thirst. Or they would poison aboveground pools of water for the soldiers to drink.[171]

Kaywaykla was born during this war. He saw all of it and his story tells about Nana, Victorio, Lozen, Juh, and Geronimo; their battles, victories and executions. But what is most inspiring about his retelling of this period of exceptional violence and forced settlement is not the warfare, but the importance of what Chiricahua life, even amidst genocidal conquest, means.

It is our dissociation that allows us to split the violence, to uphold the heroism of violence against civilization, from the essence of Apache identity and culture. It is by understanding and respecting the essential nature of that identity and community, to know its place and how it tied them to the land giving unflinching purpose to their resistance that we stand to learn the real lessons here.

Against all odds of survival, the Apache fought.

And while many died, others survived and continued that struggle.

Against all odds, this is happening now.

As I write this, the most diverse gathering of Native Americans in the history of the occupied Americas is taking place at Standing Rock where the Hunkpapa Lakota and Yanktonai Dakota stand their ground against pipelines carrying hydraulically-fractured natural gas seeking to destroy the remnants of their home.

This is the latest among a series of indigenous resistances to energy extraction in North America that includes the Unist'ot'en, the Madii Lii and Lax U'u'la among others.[172] The strength of these camps is their communal nature: the establishment of camp, the invigoration of traditional cultures, and the indisputable tie to the resistance of their parents and ancestors.

This is not about politics: in contrast to the efforts to confront the law on its own terms I have to borrow a phrase from Iyuskin American Horse of Standing Rock: "We are protectors, not protestors."[173]

Communities integrated to the wild, integrated with the vast web of ecosystems, cannot dissociate from their actions and responsibilities. The ability to become anonymous or to escape consequence is something they have the fortune of not knowing.

And in their grounding, idleness ceases to be an option. Resistance becomes reality.

Fate ceases to be an ideological or moral abstract.

Strangers fade from existence.

Trained from an early age to understand the dynamic tension of life, these communities and the individuals that they are comprised of are capable of confrontation.

In embracing the complexity and complications of life, in being prepared and ready to take on its challenges, the wild communities can also dance and sing in its joy.

They can find peace within its potential violence and not live in fear of it.

And in embracing that tension, in creating and fostering our own wildness and self-reliance, in refusing the authority of the state and the myths of domestication, we may one day dance and sing upon the rusting remains of this empire.

Endnotes

1 Richard B Lee, *The !Kung San*. London: Cambridge UP, 1979. Pg 399.
2 This story was told to Richard Lee and printed in Lee, 1979. Pgs 394-395.
3 Nancy Scheper-Hughes and Philippe Bourgois, 'Introduction: Making Sense of Violence' in Scheper-Hughes & Bourgois (eds), *Violence in War and Peace*. Malden, MA: Blackwell, 2004. Pg 2.
4 For more on this topic, see my essay 'To Speak of Wildness' in *Black and Green Review* no 2.
5 Tamarack Song, *Becoming Nature*. Bear & Co, 2016.
6 Steven Pinker, *The Better Angels of our Nature*. New York: Penguin, 2011. Pg 1.
7 Frans de Waal, *The Age of Empathy*. New York: Three Rivers Press, 2009. Pg 10.
8 Richard Dawkins, *The Selfish Gene*. Oxford: Oxford UP, 1979. Pg 3.
9 Jane Goodall, *The Chimpanzees at Gombe*. Belknap Press, 1986.
10 R Brian Ferguson, 'Ten Points on War' in Alisse Waterston, *An Anthropology of War*. New York: Berghahn, 2008.
11 Frans de Waal, 'Foreword' in Fry (ed) *War, Peace and Human Nature*. Oxford: Oxford UP, 2013. Pg xi.
12 Smithsonian Museum of Natural History, 'Taung Child': http://humanorigins.si.edu/evidence/human-fossils/fossils/taung-child
13 Ibid. Pg xii.
14 Peter Verbeek, 'An Ethological Perspective on War and Peace' in Fry, 2013. Pg 56.
15 Ibid. Pg xiii. See also Marc Bekoff and Jessica Pierce, *Wild Justice*. Chicago: University of Chicago Press, 2009.
16 Verbeek, 2013. Pgs 66 & 67.
17 Joseph Birdsell, 'Some Predictions for the Pliestocene Based on Equilibrium Systems among Recent Hunter-Gatherers' in Lee and DeVore (eds), *Man the Hunter*. New York: Aldine de Gruyter, 1968. Pg 235.
18 John Bodley, *The Power of Scale*. Armonk, NY: ME Sharpe, 2003. Pgs 87-91.
19 Ibid, pg 55.
20 Thomas Malthus, *An Essay on the Principle of Population*. New York: Penguin, 1983 [Orig. 1798].
21 Bernard Sellato, *Nomads of the Borneo Rainforest*. Honolulu: University of Hawai'i Press, 1994. Pg 143.
22 James Woodburn, 'Stability and Flexibility in Hadza Residential Groupings' in Lee and DeVore, 1968. Pg 105.
23 https://en.wikipedia.org/wiki/List_of_urban_areas_by_population
24 Elizabeth Marshall Thomas, *The Old Way*. New York: Sarah Crichton Books, 2006. Pg 230
25 Ibid, Pgs 225-227.
26 Pinker 2011, Pg 54.
27 Lee, 1979. Pg 401.
28 Mark Cocker, *Rivers of Blood, Rivers of Gold*. New York: Grove, 1998. Pg 344.
29 Thomas, 2006, Pg 227.
30 Lee, 1979. Pg 389.
31 Ibid, pg 395.
32 Thomas, 2006. Pg 228.
33 Ibid, pg 229.
34 Ibid.
35 Lee, 1979. Pg 371.
36 Ibid, pg 372.
37 Richard Lee, *The Dobe Ju/'hoansi: third edition*. St Davis, CA: Wadsworth, 2003. Pg 114.
38 Victoria Katherine Burbank, *Fighting Women*. Berkeley: University of California Press, 1994.

39 For more on this, see my essay, 'Hooked on a Feeling' in *Black and Green Review* no 3. Spring 2016.
40 Carleton Coon, *The Hunting Peoples*. New York: Lyons, 1971. Pg 238.
41 Frank Marlowe, *The Hadza: Hunter-Gatherers of Tanzania*. Berkeley: University of California Press, 2010. Pg 141.
42 Kirk Endicott & Karen Endicott, *The Headman was a Woman: The Gender Egalitarian Batek of Malaysia*. Long Grove, IL: Waveland, 2008. Pg 66.
43 Csilla Dallos, *From Equality to Inequality*. Toronto: University of Toronto Press, 2011. Pg 132.
44 Brian Morris, *Forest Traders: A Socio-Economic Study of the Hill Pandaram*. New Jersey: Athlone Press, 1982. Pgs 160-161.
45 Jana Fortier, *Kings of the Forest*. Honolulu: University of Hawai'i Press, 2009. Pg 97.
46 Coon, 1971. Pg 240.
47 Marlowe, 2010. Pg 141.
48 Thomas, 2006. Pg 230. For more of this, see 'Hooked on a Feeling'.
49 Dallos, 2011. Pg 135.
50 Fry, 2013. Pg 11.
51 Ibid.
52 Douglas Fry, *The Human Potential for* Peace. New York: Oxford University Press, 2006, Pg 22.
53 David Dye, 'Trends in Cooperation and Conflict in Native Eastern North America' in Fry, 2013. Pgs 133-134.
54 Ibid, pg 136.
55 Turnbull, ' The Importance of Flux in Two Hunting Societies' in Lee and Devore, 1968. Pg 135.
56 Woodburn, 1968. Pg 105.
57 Tim Ingold, 'Notes on the Foraging Mode of Production' in Ingold, Riches and Woodburn (eds), *Hunters and Gatherers: Volume 1*. Oxford: Berg, 1988. Pg 278.
58 Nurit Bird-David, 'Studying Children in "Hunter-Gatherer" Societies" in Hewlett & Lamb (eds), *Hunter-Gatherer Childhoods*. New Brunswick, NJ: Transaction, 2005. Pg 96.
59 This is a huge topic that I will be following up in later works. For more see Hewlett & Lamb, 2005, Barry Hewlett, *Intimate Fathers: The Nature and Context of Aka Pygmy Paternal Infant Care*. Ann Arbor, MI: University of Michigan Press, 1993, Barry Hewlett (ed), *Father-Child Relations*. New Brunswick, NJ: Transaction, 1992, and Jean Liedloff, *The Continuum Concept*. Cambridge, MA: Perseus, 1985.
60 Bird-David, 2005. Pg 97.
61 Paul Shepard, *Nature and Madness*. San Francisco: Sierra Club, 1982.
62 Bird-David, 2005. Pg 101.
63 Melvin Konner, 'Hunter-Gatherer Infancy and Childhood: The !Kung and Others' in Hewlett & Lamb, 2005. Pg 29.
64 Jean Peterson, *The Ecology of Social Boundaries: Agta Foragers of the Philippines*. Urbana, IL: University of Illinois Press, 1978. Pg 16.
65 Morris, 1982. Pg 147.
66 Colin Turnbull, *The Human Cycle*. Simon and Schuster: New York, 1983. Pgs 42-45.
67 Colin Turnbull, 'The Ritualization of Potential Conflict Among the Mbuti' in Leacock and Lee, *Politics and History in Band Society*. Cambridge UP: London, 1982. Pg 142.
68 Endicott & Endicott, 2008. Pg 117.
69 Turnbull, 1983. Pg 47.
70 Hugh Brody, *The Other Side of Eden*. Pgs 57-58.
71 Turnbull, 1983. Pgs 47 & 45.
72 'What Makes Indians Laugh' in Pierre Clastres, *Society Against the State*. Brooklyn: Zone, 1989.
73 O. Yu. Artemova, 'Monopolisation of knowledge, social inequality and egalitarianism'.

Hunter Gatherer Research. Volume 2, Issue 1. 2016.
74 Dallos, 2011. Pg 168.
75 Richard Lee, 'Eating Christmas in the Kalahari.' *Natural History.* December 1969: 60-64.
76 Ibid.
77 Michele Ruth Gamburd, *The Kitchen Spoon's Handle*. Ithaca: Cornell University Press, 2000. Pg 111.
78 An example of this is Koji Sonoda, 'Give me the Meat, the Child Said.' *Hunter Gatherer Research.* Volume 2, Issue 1. 2016.
79 Ingold, 1988. Pg 283.
80 Tim Ingold, 'On the Social Relations of the Hunter-Gatherer Band' in Lee and Daly, *The Cambridge Encyclopedia of Hunters and Gatherers.* Cambridge UP: Cambridge, 1999. Pg 401.
81 Clastres, 1989. Pg 205.
82 Marvin Harris, *Cannibals and Kings.* New York: Vintage, 1977. Pg 7.
83 Martin Fried, *Evolution of Political Society.* New York: McGraw-Hill, 1967. Pgs 109, 186, 185, & 229.
84 Harris, 1977. Pg 50.
85 Marshall Sahlins, *Culture in Practice.* New York: Zone Books, 2000. Pg 78.
86 Fried, 1967. Pg 133.
87 Clastres, 1989. Pg 46
88 Neil Whitehead, 'Tribes Make States and States Make Tribes' in R. Brian Ferguson and Neil Whitehead, *War in the Tribal Zone.* Santa Fe: School of American Research Press, 1992. Pg. 129.
89 Harris, 1977. Pg 51.
90 R Brian Ferguson, 'Pinker's List: Exaggerating Prehistoric War Mortality' in Douglas Fry (ed), *War, Peace, and Human Nature.* Oxford: Oxford UP, 2013. Pg 126.
91 Fry, 2013. Pg 7.
92 Ibid. Pg 11.
93 Dallos, 2011. Pg 97.
94 Coon, 1971. Pg 262.
95 R Brian Ferguson, 'Introduction: Studying War' in Ferguson (ed), *Warfare, Culture, and Environment.* Orlando: Academic Press, Inc, 1984. Pg 5.
96 Harris, 1977. Pgs 51-52.
97 Andrew Vayda, 'Hypotheses About Functions of War' in Fried, Harris and Murphy (eds), *War: The Anthropology of Armed Conflict and Aggression.* Garden City, NY: The Natural History Press, 1968. Pgs 88-89.
98 Raymond Kelly, *Warless Societies and the Origins of War.* Ann Arbor, MI: University of Michigan Press, 2000. Pgs 3-6.
99 Andrew Vayda, *Warfare in Ecological Perspective.* New York: Plenum Press, 1976. Pg 2.
100 Douglas Fry, *Beyond War: The Human Potential for Peace.* New York: Oxford University Press, 2007. Pg 73.
101 Roy Rappaport, *Pigs for the Ancestors: Ritual in the Ecology of a New Guinea People.* Prospect Heights, IL: Waveland, 2000 [1984]. Pgs 57-58.
102 Marvin Harris, *Cows, Pigs, Wars, and Witches.* New York: Vintage, 1989 [1974]. Pg 48.
103 Rappaport, 2000. Pg 110.
104 Peter Wilson, *The Domestication of the Human Species.* New Haven, CT: Yale University Press, 1988. Pg 146.
105 Alexander Alland, 'War and Disease: An Anthropological Perspective' in Fried, Harris and Murphy, 1968. Pg 65.
106 Rappaport, 2000. Pg 19.
107 This process is detailed in Rappaport, 2000 and Vayda, 1976.
108 Scheper-Hughes and Bourgois, 2004, Pg 1.
109 Sylvia Fisher Carrasco, *Peru: A Chronicle of Deception.* Copenhagen: IWGIA, 2010. Pg

15.
110 Michael Harner, *The Jívaro: People of the Sacred Waterfalls*. Garden City, NY: Anchor Books, 1973. Pg 111.
111 Ibid. Pg 80.
112 Harris, 1977. Pgs 50-51.
113 Harner, 1973. Pg 135.
114 Ibid. Pg 141.
115 Ibid. Pgs 143-147.
116 Ibid. Pg 147.
117 Daniel Steel, 'Trade Goods and Jívaro Warfare: The Shuar 1850–1957, and the Achuar, 1940–1978.' *Ethnohistory*, Volume 46, Number 4. Fall 1999 and Jane Bennett Ross, 'Effects of Contact on Revenge Hostilities among the Achuarä Jívaro' in Ferguson, 1984.
118 See R Brian Ferguson, 'A Savage Encounter: Western Contact and the Yanomami War Complex' in Ferguson and Whitehead, 1992; R Brian Ferguson, *Yanomami Warfare*. Santa Fe: SAR Press, 1995; and Patrick Tierney, *Darkness in El Dorado*. New York: WW Norton, 2000.
119 See Eric Wolf, *Europe and the People Without History*. University of California Press, 1997 and Francis Jennings, *The Ambiguous Iroquois Empire*. New York: WW Norton, 1990.
120 Harner, 1973. Pg 201.
121 Ibid. Pg 118.
122 Sadly, I'm not kidding: http://www.realshrunkenheads.com/
123 Harner, 1973. Pg 88.
124 Ibid. Pgs 89-93.
125 Yolanda Murphy and Robert Murphy, *Women of the Forest*. New York: Columbia University Press, 2004 [1984]. Pg 111.
126 Ibid. Pg 106.
127 Fry, 2007. Pg 80.
128 Kelly, 2000. Pg 68.
129 Shepard, 1982. Pg 113.
130 Victoria Bekiempis, 'Nearly 1 in 5 Americans Suffer Mental Illness'. *Newsweek*. 2/28/14. Accessed on September 26, 2016: http://www.newsweek.com/nearly-1-5-americans-suffer-mental-illness-each-year-230608
131 Christopher Ingraham, 'Our Infant Mortality Rate is a National Embarrassment'. *Washington Post*, 9/29/14. Accessed on September 26, 2016: https://www.washingtonpost.com/news/wonk/wp/2014/09/29/our-infant-mortality-rate-is-a-national-embarrassment/
132 Endicott and Endicott, 2008. Pg 114.
133 Bird-David, 2005. Pg 97.
134 Konner, 2005. Pg 20.
135 Endicott and Endicott, 2008. Pg 114.
136 Percentage figured using the following data: 'A Visual Guide: Abortion in America' CNN http://www.cnn.com/2016/06/27/health/abortion-in-america-charts-and-graphs-trnd/ 2012 Abortions: 699,202 and 'Births: Final Data for 2012' National Vital Statistics Report http://www.cdc.gov/nchs/data/nvsr/nvsr62/nvsr62_09.pdf. A total of 3,952,841 births were registered in the United States in 2012. 15.03% of total pregnancies (births plus abortions).
137 Peterson, 1978. Pg 10.
138 Kelly, 2000. Pg 37.
139 Center for Disease Control, 'Leading Causes of Death'. 2015. Accessed on September 26, 2016: http://www.cdc.gov/nchs/fastats/leading-causes-of-death.htm
140 Shepard, 1982. Pg 113.
141 'Facts about PTSD' Accessed on September 26, 2016: http://psychcentral.com/lib/facts-about-ptsd/
142 Peter Wilson, 1988. Pg 183.

143 Stanley Diamond, *In Search of the Primitive*. New Brunswick, NJ: Transaction, 1987. Pg 229.
144 Ibid. Pg 17.
145 Timothy Earle, *How Chiefs Come to Power*. Stanford, CA: Stanford University Press, 1997. Pg 106.
146 'I can't breathe': Eric Garner put in Chokehold by NYPD officer – video, *The Guardian*. https://www.theguardian.com/us-news/video/2014/dec/04/i-cant-breathe-eric-garner-chokehold-death-video
147 Timothy Earle, *Bronze Age Economics*. Boulder, CO: Westview Press, 2002. Pg 55.
148 Ibid. Pgs 43-44.
149 Kelly, 2000. Pg 101.
150 Harris, 1977. Pg 55.
151 Kelly, 2000. Pgs 7, 44-45.
152 Diamond, 1974. Pg 270.
153 Harold Barclay, *People Without Government: An Anthropology of Anarchy*. London: Kahn & Averill, 1990. Pgs 24-25.
154 Ibid. Pg 32.
155 Paul Shepard, *The Tender Carnivore and the Sacred Game*. Athens, GA: University of Georgia Press, 1998. Pg 123.
156 Jeff Zeleny, 'Accepting Peace Prize, Obama Offers 'Hard Truth'. *New York Times*, 12/10/2009. http://www.nytimes.com/2009/12/11/world/europe/11prexy.html
157 Stanley Diamond, 'War and the Dissociated Personality' in Harris, Fried and Murphy, 1968. Pgs 187-188.
158 Earle, 1997. Pg 7.
159 Paul Farmer, 'On Suffering and Structural Violence' in Scheper-Hughes and Bourgois, 2004. Pg 288.
160 Jonathan O'Callaghan, 'Will Your Child Witness the End of Humanity?' Daily Mail, June 19, 2015: http://www.dailymail.co.uk/sciencetech/article-3131160/Will-child-witness-end-humanity-Mankind-extinct-100-years-climate-change-warns-expert.html
161 See Adam Hochschild, *King Leopold's Ghost*. Boston: Mariner, 1999 and Sven Lindqvist, *Exterminate all the Brutes*. New Society, 1996.
162 Diamond, 1968. Pg 187.
163 Shepard, 1998. Pgs 215-216.
164 Jacques Camatte, *This World We Must Leave and Other Essays*. Brooklyn: Autonomedia, 1995. Pg 95.
165 See 'Revolt of the Savages' and 'The Failure of Revolution' in Tucker, 2010.
166 Bodley, 2003. Pg 65.
167 Kelly, 2000. Pg 81.
168 Eve Ball, *In the Days of Victorio*. Tucson: University of Arizona Press, 2003 [1970]. Pg xiii.
169 Keith Basso, *Western Apache Raiding & Warfare*. Tucson: University of Arizona Press, 1998 [1971].
170 Cocker, 1998. Pg 216.
171 David Roberts, *Once They Moved Like the Wind*. New York: Touchstone, 1994. Pg 180.
172 See 'Wild Resistance, Insurgent Subsistence' in *Black and Green Review* no 3.
173 Iyuskin American Horse, 'We are Protectors, Not Protestors.' *The Guardian*. 8/18/2016. Accessed at https://www.theguardian.com/us-news/2016/aug/18/north-dakota-pipeline-activists-bakken-oil-fields

DISCUSSION

Hummingbird. Photo by Yank.

Response

Dear Black and Green Review,
John Zerzan sent me a copy of issue 2. It was a fine work & I feel compelled to send along a letter of comment. I know you don't have a letters column, so I don't know how interested you are in receiving such things, but here goes anyway.

Zerzan's "Not So Close Encounters" makes some fine points on alienation, but I question how easily these could be related to autism. John seems to have forgotten a point made by antipsychiatry, not only does society drive people crazy, but it also pathologizes behavior that was previously considered, if not normal, just eccentric. At times this draws more people into a reign of therapeutic control. John has done some fine writing on just this subject in the past, such as the antipsychiatry material he included in *Future Primitive*. I find it questionable whether there is an increase in autism as more people are drawn into a label of high functioning autism.

In "To Speak of Wildness" by Kevin Tucker, I would it is a very good decision to focus on the concept of wildness over that of wilderness. This is the focus of verb over noun, a resistance to reification. This prevents the dogmatic and ideological usage of terms like nature, wilderness, and primitive by authoritarian vanguardists, like Deep Green Resistance.

This also prevents the use of theory to reinforce civilization, or at least resists the usage so often this usage. So often the idea that nature is socially constructed is used to defend civilization, by stating that there is no essential natural state. We shouldn't allow them their initial assumption in this argument. This idea of wildness helps us to have agency and distances our views from silly folks who believe in some pure state.

I found "Stone Tools and Symbolic Thought" by Cliff Hayes to be really problematic. Am I missing something? This seems like a dead end. He begs the question "could the linear process of shaping a rock into a preconceived form be the first step towards symbolic thought?" Under this conception we had already fallen by the time our ancestors were homo erectus. If this argument is true, then why even bother? We could never improve our situation or successfully resist civilization. I tend to think the basis of a critique of technology must be a critique of division of labor to be relevant.

Luckily this is followed by Zerzan's "News from Prehistory", which does a great job countering these errors without even knowing it was doing so. John shows that humans could accomplish amazing things without civilization. Noting that these earliest stone tools are 3.3 million years old, John discredits Hayes point. A fantastic piece by Zerzan.

"Subjects Object!" by Tucker goes a long way towards developing a working critique of language. The critique of language is a big interest of mine and probably the area I find hardest to put into application. Tucker points out a crucial component, that the term language refers to a great multitude of things. His focus on grammar might be the means of getting us out of this rut. The rigid reification of grammar might be the key to how language controls, and looking at the Piraha will probably help to find a way out. If nothing else their communication while "lacking the kind of rigid grammar rules" has a lot to teach us.

As a side note, Chomsky is not considered the father of modern linguistics, except by people who were his students and leftist ideologues who don't understand linguistics. Interesting to learn his linguistic theories have been useful to the development of AI, since that venture long ago proved a failure. Since AI has not been able to emulate consciousness, it has shifted focus towards a very limited concept based on instrumentally and accomplishing specific tasks. This in turn has probably weakened and limited our concept of what human consciousness is.

Tamarack Song's comments on the failure of the primitive skill movement relates to a greater recuperation of the concept of DIY towards a very limited instrumentality, the sort that produces good commodities to sell on Etsy and other such websites.

I think Steve Kirk's review of Nicholas Carr's *The Glass Cage* was a bit hard on Carr, characterizing him as "a pro-technology stance with an anti-technology argument". This is a problem for a few reasons. At times it makes sense to try to preserve what we had in older technology, since the only other option is a trajectory into the transhuman hive. It can make sense to try to fortify ourselves until we come

137

Response

up with another option. Also, in the paperback edition of *The Shallows* Carr includes a new afterwards, in which he calls for revolution against computers, presenting the example of how in the 60s draft resistors literally destroyed computers.

Anyways, thank you for the fine publication and please keep up the good work.
Take care & live well,
Jason Rodgers
Albany, NY

Cliff Responds:

Yes, my question was open ended on purpose to elicit a response from other editors on the topic of stone tools and the development of language/symbolic thought. This is a theory that has been gaining popularity in the sciences recently.

There is a difference between symbolic thought and symbolic culture which is something the editorial staff discussed internally. I believe this was covered in 'Written in Stone' by Four Legged Human, 'Subjects Object!' by Kevin, and yes, John also provided further insight in 'News from Prehistory.' My piece was meant as a starting point, largely built off my reading of DeLanda's book Philosophy & Simulation: The Emergence of Synthetic Reason, *not a completed tightly knit argument showing that language, symbolic thought, agriculture, civilization flow organically from the process of making stone tools. I think that is what might be missing in the reading of the piece. I didn't intend for it to be a dead end, but rather an opportunity to address this burgeoning theory on the link between stone tools and language.*

The dialog continues if anyone is interested:

Morgan, T. J. H. et al. 'Experimental evidence for the coevolution of hominin tool-making teaching and language.' *Nat. Commun.* 6:6029 doi: 10.1038/ncomms7029 (2015).

Stout, Dietrich, and Thierry Chaminade. 'Stone Tools, Language and the Brain in Human Evolution.' *Philosophical Transactions of the Royal Society B: Biological Sciences* 367.1585 (2012): 75–87. PMC. Web. 2 Aug. 2016.

FREQUENTLY MADE ASSERTIONS
AN ANARCHO-PRIMITIVIST FAQ, OF SORTS
KEVIN TUCKER

Note: this is a preview of the "FAQ" section of Roots: A Field Guide to Anarcho-Primitivism *which is coming soon (and long overdue) from Black and Green Press.*

In any primer, a Frequently Asked Questions (FAQ) section is always helpful.

An anarcho-primitivist (AP) one is certainly no exception. The problem is that when I was pulling this together, and even when I had it open for suggestions, I didn't really get a single question. As the whipping child of nearly all tangents of anarchism, it's easy to see that AP is rarely, if ever, given the benefit of the doubt. We get tired presumptions where earnest questions typically arise.

So, in kind, I'm having to be more specific: these are responses to frequently made assertions about anarcho-primitivism. Our clarifications always have to fight uphill battles. Hopefully this will help get us over that hurdle a little further, but I'm not holding my breath.

It would be impossible to cover all the assertions, but after hearing these *ad nauseum* for the better part of two decades, these are some of the most common ones.

Enjoy.

ASSERTION:
Anarcho-primitivists are against horticultural societies.

This highlights the difference between ideology and critique.

A critique has grey areas and in-betweens. Ideology does not. In talking about the origins of domestication and about its consequences, primarily with horticultural and delayed return hunter-gatherer societies, it is my belief that we can get a better understanding of how domestication works.

Domestication is the apparatus. It is the means by which civilization continues to move forward both inwards and outwards. But domestication is about the origins of civilization, not whether it exists or not. There are plenty of societies with domestication, but without civilization. One goal of the AP critique is to explore those instances to understand how civilization does and can work.

For the most part, horticultural societies are technically anarchistic. They have no state or state-level organization. They are, more or less, without government. They are also largely closer to sustainability than anything that involves agriculture ever could hope to be. Slash-and-burn horticulturalists can get as much as 70% or more of their caloric intake from hunting and gathering and are prone to trekking or nomadism. Even well documented horticulturalists like the Yanomami have only recently turned more towards a horticultural lifestyle as a response to constantly impending colonization, conquering, and ecological decimation.

Horticultural societies, by and large, are far from the problem. These are societies that are struggling and demand our support if you are against civilization. They lie at the forefront of the impasse between economy and ecology, and that's a bloody battlefield. In no way, shape or form is any of my hatred of civilization aimed at them.

Being a critique means being critical. If we chose to understand civilization and how domestication makes it possible, it means using all of the tools at our disposal to understand it. If we were to simply say, "civilization is here and not there" and that was it, we wouldn't be getting very far. And we owe it to ourselves, each other and the earth to be honest about the world that lies before us.

Given that we have so far to go from our current modernized reality, it makes more sense to me that we focus our attention towards the most egalitarian ways of life that have existed if we wish to talk about any kind of future. Pre-history is replete with times where horticultural societies have passed the tipping point and their future lied in returning to a nomadic hunter-gatherer way of life.

Horticultural societies can exist for long periods of time. But that survival is not without social consequence. By understanding the consequences, we understand how societies have responded to domestication in social, ecological, and spiritual/religious terms. It is at that early point that we can most clearly see the domestication process at work.

Our solidarity lies first and foremost with those who are facing down the onslaught of civilization. Our critiques lie without the framework of finding an exit strategy that is the most plausible, flexible, and accommodating.

I see no reason why it should run short of promoting the most egalitarian way of life that we have ever known.

ASSERTION:
Given the chance, agrarian civilizations would have lasted.

There is often an idea that civilization just hasn't been "done right" yet. That's historically naive. Civilizations have been rising and falling from the beginning of this unfortunate era. Carrying capacity, as it turns out, is an ecological reality that can't be negotiated.

We've seen this play out time and time again. By all means, this is that "chance." The only difference that ever existed with agrarian societies is a matter of scale, but none have passed the test. Now this globalized, modernized civilization is going through the motions.

ASSERTION:
It is not our place to critique indigenous societies.

Those of us in the First World are indisputably the most complicit in the onslaught of civilization. As I type these words on a computer, as you read them in a book, the balance of all life is in the details. We live in a globalized, hyper-technological clusterfuck of a civilization.

And within that framework indigenous societies of all types are resisting the very modernity that we partake in. From that vantage point, an anarcho-primitivist narrative of the rise of domestication, one that takes into account some of the more brutal aspects of even non-state societies, can look excessive. This is the flip side of arguments about cherry picking anthropological data; ironically, we get hit on both sides. In short, there are activists who think that digging into the details of indigenous societies is airing dirty laundry and counter-productive, even "colonial."

There are a lot of issues here, so it's hard to unpack them all.

So let's start with the idea of "indigenous societies." The perspective, that "indigenous societies" are categorically contrary to civilization, is simply false. *Indigenous*, as a term, is not a particularly helpful starting point. In technical terms, it's about cultural geography, not proximity with the Earth. It is certainly not about bio-centric or animistic worldviews. But among the Left and liberals, "indigenous" has become interchangeable with a romanticism surrounding an impossibly unified idea of native societies.

The point at which a society stops being "indigenous" is when it aggressively colonizes other areas: when a society has outgrown its proximity. That isn't particularly helpful. All civilizations start out as "indigenous." And plenty of them never truly stopped being "indigenous." They may have not had the impact that our civilization has, but that really comes down to scale.

Anarcho-primitivists aren't against civilization solely because of its scale. We see patterns of repetition amongst all civilizations, even within the domestication process in non-state societies. Where an anarcho-primitivist effectively draws their lines is up to them, but in terms of the overall critique, the details are important: whether they are critique or simply documentation. If we are being honest, then drawing parameters about what is off limits or not is falling into ideological blinders and romanticizing an arbitrary grouping of peoples regardless of how they interacted with the world.

There are indigenous societies that I have unending solidarity for. That isn't something reserved for immediate-return hunter-gatherers. Speaking honestly about the consequences of domestication doesn't mean that I think all delayed-return societies are on par with this civilization. But to go too far the other way means overlooking some pretty atrocious realities: immediately that brings to mind societies where patriarchy is enforced through ritualized gang-rape, child sacrifice, and slavery. There are indigenous societies that do all of those things.

Across the Mississippi River from where I grew up are the remains of the Cahokia, a civilization that collapsed roughly two centuries before Europeans set foot on what is now the United States and Mexico. At its peak, this city-state hosted roughly 40,000 inhabitants. They built mounds and temples; they denuded the forests and took part in massive trade networks that spanned North and South America. Women and children were sacrificed. The hierarchy was absolute and rigid. And the civilization collapsed on itself after denuding the land for miles.

The Cahokia were an indigenous society. They warred with other stateless indigenous societies, abducting women and children, killing men.

Had I been alive there and then, I would have fought them. I wouldn't have felt some kind of rose-colored liberal sympathy for this society solely because they had remained localized. They never faced the massive army of the Europeans and their weaponry, unlike other indigenous civilizations throughout the world. This isn't a justification for the onslaught that would follow for those societies, but it is equally ridiculous to think that other smaller-scale and far more sustainable societies that were terrorized by these civilizations should be lumped into the same category and given the same treatment and respect.

I am against civilization. All of them. I can be as guilty as anyone of using the term "indigenous" too loosely, but I certainly won't use it carte blanche to pretend that locality gives any insight into how a society exists and interacts with the world around it.

Which brings me to the other side of this: the idea that talking honestly about indigenous societies is in some way just "airing dirty laundry."

Even in cases far from the Cahokia, there are those in the liberal and Left who want to impose their own morality, their own colonial guilt. To speak honestly about the cultures of any "indigenous society" is simply opening the door for speaking negatively of them. Speaking about warfare or the use of intoxicants by shamans or slavery is to effectively kick the dispossessed while they are down.

This is simply another form of pedantic colonialism. Either these societies do what they do because they didn't know better or because the practices were somehow innately different than how our own civilization does them. Again, what we're really talking about is scale.

The problem is that our civilization exists because we are able to displace and disassociate ourselves from the consequences and reality of our day-to-day lives. We can pretend that we don't have blood on our hands or that our consumption doesn't force children into mines and sweatshops or bolster corporate, political or religious sociopaths and prop up warlords and fascists. We operate under a veneer of naivety. It allows us to remain unaccountable for our complicity, so we can simply pretend to distance ourselves from aspects of our culture that we find ugly.

Our privilege is to hide our shame. Even to ignore it completely.

But even those that should know better are just conscious enough of their barely-repressed guilt that they are willing to impose it, paternalistically, onto other societies. And that is absolutely insulting.

Horticultural societies and hunter-collector societies engage in and uphold warrior ethos because war is a social response to ecological pressures when a society pushes its carrying capacity. Removed from the balance afforded by nomadic hunter-gatherer life, the externalization of conflict, the need for group cohesiveness, along with the creation of territory and a need to defend it become a part of life.

I say this without judgment. No doubt, as an anarchist, I certainly have a preference for the egalitarianism of nomadic foragers, but these cultural realities are a response, and a fairly apt one at that, to shifting circumstances.

The thing about it is that these aspects of the culture that arise: the role of the Big Man or Chief, the Shaman or Priest, and the rise of Man the Warrior, aren't hidden artifacts uncovered by shifty Western anthropologists looking to tarnish these cultures. These are central and vital aspects of what it means to live within these societies.

If a horticultural or sedentary hunter-collector culture is seeking to hide their embrace of the warrior or socio-religious authority central to their cultures, it's typically because their first and prolonged contact have been with missionaries who target them specifically. Granted, liberals would probably encourage the same suppression to save face.

The reality is, this "dirty laundry" is not a secret: it is a pivotal part of cultural identity. It is not an act of colonialism to speak of it, but it is to pretend that these aspects of their society don't exist.

And these aspects exist within an overarching narrative: these are responses to domestication and shifting socio-ecological relationships. It is hard to see not only why they should be considered off limits, but also why anyone would want to ignore them. If you want to support these societies, then it should behoove you to know more about them, not to simply impose Western, civilized values on where to turn a blind eye.

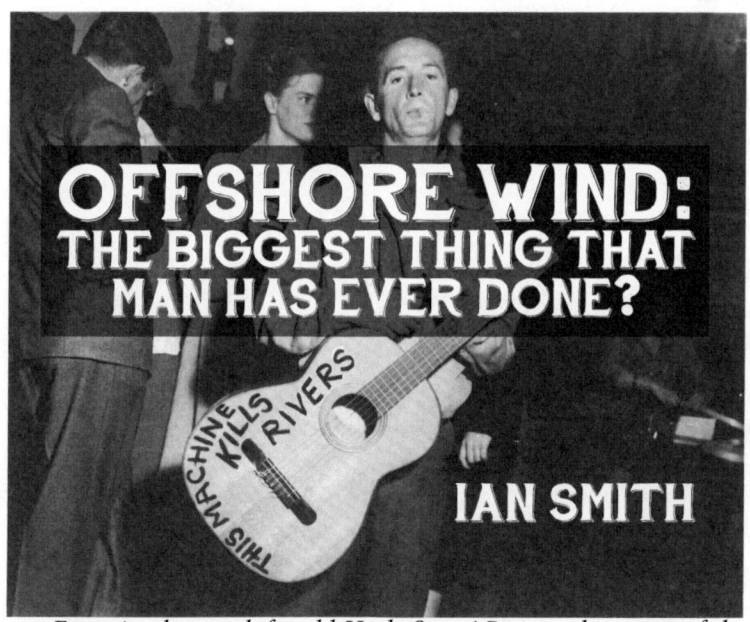

OFFSHORE WIND: THE BIGGEST THING THAT MAN HAS EVER DONE?

IAN SMITH

Factories that work for old Uncle Sam / Run on the power of the Grand Coulee Dam
            -Woody Guthrie, *"Song of the Grand Coulee Dam"*

Seventy-five years ago, folk singer Woody Guthrie signed a contract to write songs for the federal government. The recently created Bonneville Power Administration (BPA) needed to generate enthusiasm and support for massive hydroelectric dams on the Columbia River most notably for the Grand Coulee Dam. The Roosevelt administration envisioned the dams providing cheap electricity and irrigating farm land—creating *"green pastures of plenty from dry desert ground"* as Guthrie would put it.

To complete this assignment, Guthrie traveled through the Pacific Northwest along the Columbia River Gorge and wrote 26 songs in a month's time. Some of the songs were destined to be amongst his most well known such as "Pastures of Plenty," "Biggest Thing That Man Has Ever Done," and "Roll On, Columbia"; these are songs that would enter the folk music canon and the American psyche.

With the benefit of hindsight, Guthrie's zealous support for the Grand Coulee Dam project has been the subject of some debate and much scrutiny: defended by some and condemned by others. In his recently released book *26 Songs in 30 Days*, Greg Vandy writes:

By today's thinking, it can be difficult to understand why a folksinger

> like Woody Guthrie, who proved willing to walk away from good money based on principles before, so vociferously endorsed a project like the Grand Coulee Dam. It killed salmon, took away tribal land, and powered war industries—all factors well understood by Guthrie at the time.[1]

But the explanation for Guthrie's support is quite simple. The project aligned incredibly well with his leftist politics. As Vandy explains, from Guthrie's perspective "the dams were the answer to the ills of his time and the path forward for his people."[2] In short, "the dam project was [Guthrie's] idea of democratic socialism realized."[3] It was capital-p Progress.

We never arrived at Guthrie's intended destination. Indeed, in *A River Lost: The Life and Death of the Columbia River*, Blaine Harden writes:

> The river was killed...and was reborn as plumbing. The place where this fateful murder and curious resurrection took place was up the Columbia at the Grand Coulee Dam.[4]

Flash Forward to the Present

Last August, a private company, Deepwater Wind (not to be confused with Deepwater Horizon), completed construction of the nation's first offshore wind farm—the Block Island Wind Farm—off the coast of Rhode Island. It's scheduled to begin operating before the end of the year. The news was received with great enthusiasm amongst many environmentalists, liberals, and leftists.

Like the Grand Coulee Dam, it's a massive project. The surface area of each individual blade is roughly equivalent to the surface area of a football field and the turbines themselves penetrate 200 feet into the sea floor. The turbines are nearly four miles offshore and stand 260 feet tall.[5] There are only five turbines but this is widely considered a test run for much bigger operations.

Writing about wind power generally 350.org founder Bill McKibben has said: "We need a new aesthetic for the 21st century—one that looks at a turbine blade spinning as a sign that we're finally getting our act together. I can't think of anything lovelier than the breeze made visible."[6]

Regarding Block Island Wind Farm specifically, the Sierra Club enthusiastically explained: "Block Island isn't just an offshore wind farm, it's also a starting gun...the success at Block Island proves that investment in offshore wind is viable."[7]

A column in Grist states: "The potential for offshore wind power is enormous. The Department of Energy thinks offshore wind could one day deliver twice as much electricity as Americans used to keep the grid stable last year."[8]

The *New York Times* editorial board published an op-ed titled "The Unlimited Power of Ocean Winds."[9]

Unlimited power! To listen to the hype, it seems offshore wind could be the biggest thing man has ever done.

While not as lyrical as Guthrie, the Department of Energy explains that "offshore wind technologies...can capture wind resources."[10] The technology is introduced and sold as a way to combat global climate change and quickly becomes about "unlimited power" and capturing resources. It's the very same process that transformed the Columbia River from a wild, living river into mere plumbing. Instead of commanding humanity's respect it now takes humanity's commands. It became something to be harnessed just as there is now talk of harnessing the wind.

Guthrie's song "Grand Coulee Dam" makes the point explicit:
Roll along Columbia, you can ramble to the sea /
But river while you're rambling, you can do some work for me.

Endnotes

1 Greg Vandy, *26 Songs in 30 Days: Woody Guthrie's Columbia Rivers Songs and the Planned Promised Land in the Pacific Northwest* (Seattle: Sasquatch Books, 2016), 74.
2 Ibid, 76.
3 Ibid, 89.
4 Blaine Harden, *A River Lost: The Life and Death of the Columbia River* (New York: W.W. Norton & Company, 1996), 75.
5 Brendan Cole, "The US is Finally Getting its First Offshore Wind Farm," *WIRED* July (2016) https://www.wired.com/2016/07/us-finally-getting-first-offshore-wind-farm/
6 http://www.windustrious.org/champions2/bill-mckibben
7 Mark Kresowik, "Construction Complete on America's First Offshore Wind Farm," Aug. 23 (2016) http://www.sierraclub.org/compass/2016/08/construction-complete-americas-first-offshore-wind-farm
8 Heather Smith, "Offshore Wind is Finally—Finally!--Coming to the US. Here's What You Need to Know," Sept. 28 (2016) http://grist.org/business-technology/offshore-wind-is-finally-finally-coming-to-the-u-s-heres-what-you-need-to-know/
9 "The Unlimited Power of Wind," *The New York Times* Aug. 27, 2016 http://www.nytimes.com/2016/08/28/opinion/the-unlimited-power-of-ocean-winds.html
10 http://energy.gov/eere/wind/offshore-wind-research-and-development

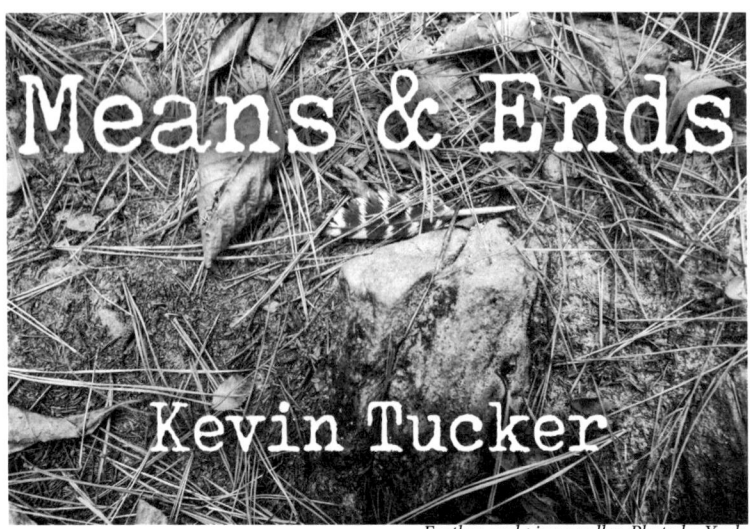

Feather and pine needles. Photo by Yank.

Resilience.

This is what has permitted humans a place in our world. It may be the defining trait of *Homo sapiens*. We adapt. Ice ages, rising temperatures, changed climates, evolving terrain: for better or for worse, we are exceptionally adaptive beings. And for nearly the entirety of our time on this Earth, there was no reason to believe that it was anything but for the better.

And yet the very thing that allowed us to live through ice ages, to navigate the oceans in boats built with stone tools, to master fire, is the very thing that permits us such leniency in diet as to find a way to continue sustaining on fast food. It allows us to continue the natural and necessary internal functioning the body of a nomadic hunter-gatherer requires while it spends an average of over 10 hours per day staring at screens. It allows us to celebrate the creation of technologies that may prolong our existence long enough to witness the catastrophe that awaits us.

The catastrophe that civilization has initiated.

Against all odds, against all likelihood, in a wave of horrid and vile extinction events, we are still here. We are still killing. Through our active or inactive participation, we remain spectators of a world in the decline of our own making. And we get to enjoy the delusion of pretending that it isn't even happening or that it doesn't even matter.

We have scientists within NASA proclaiming the probability of human extinction and we don't blink an eye. But why would we? How do you fathom the very real potential for human extinction, the immediate and aggressive alteration and shattering of ecological feedback loops and just erasing the possibility of seeing any kind of stability in weather patterns again?

To put it mildly, our circumstances were unforeseeable on an evolutionary timeline.

Our sea faring nomadic hunter-gatherer ancestors utilizing stone tipped spears and arrows hadn't evolved to dominate the world, to create a circumstance where the actions and choices of the individual could impact all life the world over. Like many other species, our minds could grasp and work around the use of tools.

But that was not true for technology. Technology, driven by its need for complexity, organization, labor and social hierarchies, created and fostered a divorce between action and consequence. Foolishly our adaptive, resilient bodies stuck along for the ride.

The core principle of technology, echoed infinitely through technological society, is that control is possible, that it is in our hands. It is that belief that made civilization possible. That belief carried civilizations across the Earth, maiming, raping, pillaging, decimating, and dismembering every step of the way. That belief blinded the power hungry, the elites, the priests from being able to see that while the consequences of civilization were very real, their belief in control was not.

Our belief in control is not.

Resiliency may be the defining trait of humanity, but uncertainty is the defining trait of our future.

We do not know what will happen. We don't know the consequences of our actions, of our technology, of its social and ecological warpaths: we have ideas, but we don't know how civilization will fall apart. All we know is that it will fall apart.

That it *is* falling apart.

It is this reality that has allowed the more individualistic among us to decry any notions of rewilding as fantastical. It is this reality that has allowed the more optimistic among us to cling to the hopes of permaculture as lifeboats for the coming storm. In an honest assessment of our circumstances, it's hard to not teeter-totter between those two opposing sides. Both reflect some hope for the necessity of control: for our ability to persevere at the helm.

It can be just as easy to look around and fall in line with the nihilistic embrace of hopelessness. But this itself is another type of control: nihilism dissolves into a belief that control is mine to do away with.

All of this is about varying degrees of control. About the maintenance or shifting of power: another reiteration of the mythos of technology. Faced with sheer and unrelenting uncertainty, any and all of these reactions are logical.

The problem is that *logical* is what got us into this mess.

I am a proponent of rewilding. I am a proponent of resisting civilization and domestication. I cannot and will not distinguish those approaches as separate. If we are to fight civilization, we must learn to give up our hopes for control, we must give in to uncertainty, to root our lives and our resistance into the struggle, the pain and the loss felt by all wild beings. To embrace our wildness is to trust in our own resiliency.

It is through building and immersing into the communities of wildness that we find our strength. That we become strategic in learning to target the elements of control that technology requires to perpetuate itself.

This is illogical, but intentionally so. And it takes work.

The domestication process requires constant upkeep.

Civilization is so counter-intuitive to who we are that we have to be trained and retrained constantly to ignore our instincts. Unable to defeat the wild urges within us, domesticators have learned to redirect those needs and wants. We are sustained at barely functioning levels and encouraged to indulge our quest for self-worth. We become workers, consumers, and spectators.

But we also break.

For the most part, medications and other stimulants/supplements keep pulling us back in. For many, that break is violence. Random or misdirected violence underscores the day-to-day reality of Modernity: spoken, thought or enacted, each of us is boiling over in a pit of rage and confusion or subdued by complicity and hopelessness. So much so that when we do wake up to the reality that we face, we struggle to overcome these hurdles in opening our vision of what can be done.

And so we default, we back slide. I'm not here to point fingers, I'm no less guilty of this than anyone, but no one ever said breaking the domestication cycle would be easy. It's ironic how rough it can be learning to listen to our own intuition again.

This brings us back to the unthinkable uncertainty that lies ahead and one particularly difficult part of the pathway ahead: land projects.

I want to be clear that largely speaking I have nothing against land projects. Considering the primary alternatives are renting and living in cities, it's not a hard argument to say that any element of self-sufficiency and, ideally, lesser impact living isn't a better alternative. If you can bolster wildness on that land by creating refuges then all the better.

Search and rescue boat in a post-hurricane flooded creek. Photo by Yank.

There are arguments against owning property. As a landowner myself, I'm only more familiar with them. There are compelling arguments against being in situations where you are paying land taxes or buying leases from national agencies, all of which are completely valid. But in practical terms, they can often be the same kind of problems that we're stuck with in all aspects of life until civilization is gone.

Fortunately that time is coming.

Which brings me to my point on the matter: the problem that I see with land projects is that they can become an oasis for logical thought. With homesteading, with off-grid living, with the influx and rise of survivalist projects; land projects can slide back into that realm of control where we want to hold on to the delusion that civilization has given us.

That delusion is the idea that self-sufficiency in off-grid living is resiliency.

What we have seen throughout history is that it most definitely isn't.

Now it is easy to say that my steadfast insistence upon focusing on nomadic immediate-return hunter-gatherer life is simply ideological.

Some have even accused me of moralism. I see it as pragmatic. But that pragmatism comes with benefits.

The reality is that nomadic immediate-return hunter-gatherer life is our most ancestral, primordial and instinctual way of being. This is how we, as humans, have evolved. Our senses, movements, sight, and intuition arise from this mode of subsistence. And it is the community that arises from it that has created and bolstered our resiliency. It has allowed us to move. To switch gears when hunting or foraging while a particular species of fauna or flora was in ebb and flow. It has given us the chance to respond to long-term and short-term ecological change.

And I believe that this is also our best chance for surviving the current and on-coming ecological crisis.

The problem with land projects is that they are, by and large, fixed. Sedentary. Permaculturalists have set out to create *food-forests* (a very civilized projection) that are meant to sustain communities with or without civilization. They can be far more diverse and far more resilient than gardens, certainly far more ecologically sane than farms. They may be more set to withstand the unprecedented cycles of heat and freezing, of drought and flooding that this destabilized climate may bring, but it is far more likely that they won't.

What we are currently seeing in the world is the new era of refugees. *Climate* refugees are now joining the ranks of *political* and *economic* refugees. As Story Teller discussed in *Black and Green Review* no 3, *grid* refugees are likely to arise. While Syrians have become the face of climate refugees, we overlook those who have and will continue to lose their homes to rampant and unchecked wildfires as they blaze through the boreal forests and the parched regions throughout the entirety of western North America. It is likely that the fuel being added to the fire by overwhelmed and hastily repurposed pipelines that are flooded with natural gases and fracking supply lines or as the number of train derailments continues to escalate carrying that thick, heavy crude from tar sands will cause those wildfires to spread into central and eastern North America forcing evacuations.

This is our certainty: instability will feed abrupt and unpredictable change.

Land projects are not fail-safes.

In times of uncertainty, the very sense of self-sufficiency that they have sought to offer is the very thing that could make them targets from dislodged survivalists (current or future) or it could weaken the potential of any community on them to prepare for the coming era of refugees: the new nomadism of a world of shifting climates.

For me, this all comes down to a question of means and ends.

Is the purpose of a land project to create self-sufficient communities through off-grid, smaller-scale living, possibly even emulating horticulture? If so, it may do well. It may thrive. I don't doubt that life there would be infinitely more fulfilling than edging out a living and trying to stay sane through any other civilized "options".

Or is the purpose of the land project a means of fostering community, rebuilding ties, creating a basin for rewilding? Is the land project the ends or the means? This may be a simple question, but it's a framework and perception that can be a threshold for our own resiliency.

On the ground, it may not even look any different.

Seeing a land project as a place to build community capable of nomadism doesn't mean that the land itself shouldn't be respected or that the return of wild beings and fauna shouldn't be a priority. The purpose of rooting is that we should be respecting and partaking with the wild community and helping it heal and regrow regardless of what may lie ahead for us.

That is another part of the uncertainty: we have to realize that having trained and rooted all the resilient, nomadic hunter-gatherer parts of our bodies and minds doesn't give us any more certainty that we are equipped or given a free pass to weather the coming storms. It certainly helps. But we don't know what is coming ahead; we just know that it is coming.

It is easy to see this as a cop-out, as a chance to give in to nihilistic urges and shrug off any effort as idealistic play. But that's the thing about community, the part that gets lost when we allow our understandings to be based in the all-loving trap of a hippie or liberal commune or to maintain that it is a relic of sub/urban neighborhoods: building community isn't easy.

It is not a coincidence that the immediate-return hunter-gatherer communities that were based on nomadism were also the most egalitarian societies to have ever existed. That is the added benefit of embracing the coming nomadism and the direction of building land projects around movement instead of stagnancy. When we break down those antiquated notions of community and start to really understand resiliency through movement, even just the ability to trek, to understand what it can be like to live without civilization or how to build a society without state infrastructure, then we begin to really root ourselves in our own animality. We build self-sufficiency that transcends place and circumstance.

The truth is that we don't always get along.

Nature isn't a passive reality; it's just a bandage term we apply to the wilderness we see around us. *Wildness* is an active reality; we ignore it because the domestication process has taught us to. But wildness is within us and surrounds us. And it impacts us just as we impact and interact with it.

Nothing about this is to imply notions of perfection or angelic life ways where we magically co-exist with everything.

That simply isn't what is going to happen.

Wildness, to borrow a term from Tamarack Song, is a state of *dynamic tension*. It requires awareness, grounding, perception, intuition, and, above all, a readiness to move and react abruptly at any time.

This may sound overwhelming, but that's because we look at it as outsiders. We don't recognize the stimulation overload and complete lack of empathy that Modernity provides. We are deadened to the world by technology, numb to our need to constantly assess and respond to the massive killing machines surrounding us, such as cars. We are deadened to each other as we are drowned in sheer numbers of equally wounded, damaged and breaking people all around us. Even if we hate the State we can get too used to the presence of overarching structures that corral some of the violent among us while bolstering and empowering others.

Rewilding is not surrender to the world: rewilding is embracing it. It's about becoming an active participant rather than a spectator or passive participant. It means undoing the delusions that make domestication possible. The delusions that permit civilizations to exist.

When we open our awareness, when we learn to walk through wild communities and to hear their warnings and communication, we begin to see the cracks in the Empire of civilization more clearly. We see the weak points that an anti-ecological system holds and how delusions serve to bridge the gaps.

And we feel it.

We feel the pain that is inflicted. We feel the loss that comes with feeding civilization, especially a hyper-modern technological one. We see the weakness in its infrastructure and its philosophical underpinning. We awaken our own empathy to that unthinkable, unquantifiable pain and loss in the context of community and we build a platform for resistance in our own resiliency.

And we learn to stop relying on someone or something else to take care of our problems for us.

We learn to act without mediation.

None of this is easy. None of this is simple. None of us have allowed ourselves to really get there.

But if we are willing to make that perceptional change, to learn to embrace the coming age of nomadism, to see beyond ourselves and to empower ourselves through taking part in something much larger and more magnificent than our own lives, then we have the world to gain from it.

And this is where land projects can focus.

I interviewed Andrew Badenoch of *Feralculture* in *Black and Green Review* no 1 to discuss the idea of land projects being built around *nodes*. The idea that he has pushed and now others have been pursuing is to build up networks of smaller properties that embrace the nomadic spirit. Nodes can have a particular draw to them: a better spot for hunting, a better spot for fishing, a better spot for foraging berries, nuts, tubers, or whatever. Embracing the original means of conflict resolution: they give a network for individuals or families to disperse and move.

A large enough network also gives the ability to explore and become accustomed to different bioregions. It allows us to become familiar with different climates and to understand their challenges and promises. It gives us the chance to meet others seeking the same, to build connections with them.

The community we will be building now, if we walk this path, is a disjointed one. It spans large spaces and focuses of ebb and flow, but it is an innately different conception of land projects than that of homesteading, even if homesteads remain a part of the larger network. What it can offer is a slow shift back to our nomadic minds: to become rooted in places so we can think, act and move as will likely be necessary to both prepare for the shifting climate on the horizon and to actively take part in the fracturing of civilization's infrastructure.

We have a lot of work to do in terms of undoing domestication in our own lives, but we can foster circumstances that will help us take larger steps. Ones that bring us further into that dynamic tension without leaving us feeling lost and isolated there. Moves that can undo the survivalist mentality that life within civilization requires.

And it is a process.

We will likely continue to live between two worlds: of wildness and of civilization, until the end. We have to get over notions of puritanism. Of thinking that we will shed all civilization from our lives so long as it continues existing. Saving ourselves from civilization means nothing so long as civilization continues to pull itself along and destroy the potential for all life.

We get no guarantees. We have no certainties here.

But we have no certainties anywhere beyond one: uncertainty is here. Uncertainty is growing more erratic as it gains speed.

Is our end to continue to survive: to hold on to some semblance of civilized normality through turbulence? Or is our end to move beyond domestication entirely? This won't happen quickly. It likely will take generations. We simply don't know.

But that is all the more reason to embrace uncertainty rather than to give in. We are participants in this reality whether we chose to acknowledge that or not. But we can embrace our wildness. We can become resilient again.

We can rebuild communities of sustenance: communities of resistance.

We have seen the world we want to live in and it is struggling. It is resisting and striving to outlast civilization. It exists within us and around us.

And it is worth fighting for.

Post-hurricane flooding hubris debris. Photo by Yank.

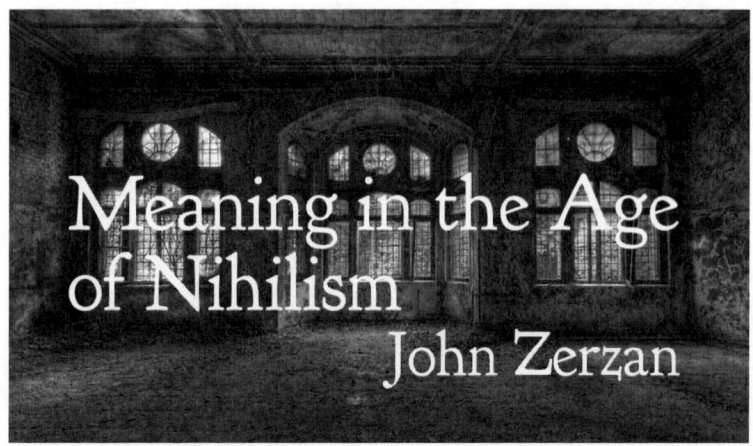

Meaning in the Age of Nihilism
John Zerzan

In 2000 I wrote a few hundred words on "The Age of Nihilism." Some years later that descriptive title is far more apt than before. Like a poison gas settling down over a battlefield, nihilism has, at least for the moment, begun to cloak or threaten so much of contemporary life and thought.

The old "meaning of life" question seems to have a new urgency, unless it's too late to explore it. Adorno provides a stunning response to the meaning of life/point of living query: "A life that has any point would not need to inquire about it. The question puts the point to flight."[1]

A pointless life is a relatively new phenomenon. Terry Eagleton poses the meaning-of-life question in the context of 19th century British literature, observing that a shift occurred in about 1870. Before that date, writers like Jane Austen and William Thackeray rarely referred to it, whereas after 1870 Thomas Hardy, Joseph Conrad, and others addressed it with some urgency.[2] Unsurprisingly, this cultural turning point coincides with the decisive ascendancy of industrial life in England (a worldwide first). At base, today's meaninglessness is a function of machine existence. Viktor Frankl, referring to the individual as "a being in search of meaning," goes on to note that "today his search is unsatisfied and thus constitutes the pathology of our age."[3]

A contagious nihilism accompanies the crisis all around us. The absence of meaning and value is seen in rising suicide rates, epidemic addictions, suicide bombings, and rampage shootings, and so much else in the landscape of no community. Because social life is based on the meaning it provides for its participants, social life itself is visibly waning.

Albert Camus famously opens *The Myth of Sisyphus* with the question of suicide: whether life is worth living. Many have the means to live, but no meaning to live for. The columnist David Brooks cites this example: "We ask students to work harder and harder while providing them with less and less of an idea of how they might find a purpose in all that work."[4]

Freedom is a struggle for meaning which is itself a dynamic force, according to William James, Viktor Frankl, and others. The drive to find or create meaning and value is a perpetual task, and at the heart of every human endeavor. In a mainly non-alienated world, this effort was possibly far less needed, compared with our civilization, where experience is de-grounded. We no longer feel at home in this massified, mediated world. We talk so much about meaning because meaninglessness is far advanced into all our lives. Yet it's very hard to confront. A common response is nervous laughter at Woody Allenish jokes or Monty Python's *The Meaning of Life*.

The meaning of life is meaning, but just where do we find that? All this varies hugely on the individual level. Women and men may see their own lives very differently from the inside. What we value can change at various points in our lives. Millions of self-actualization books and videos are sold; some check out Quality of Life approaches, or flock to hear the vague nostrums of the Dalai Lama. The approved idea is that the meaning of life is primarily an individual or personal affair––a severely limited, failed orientation.

Philosophy centers on the question of meaning; but this, too, has failed. As countless philosophical works attest, many if not most philosophers conflate the question of meaning with a close study of language and how it works.[5] During the past century, it has been generally acknowledged that meaning can't be considered apart from language; meaning is widely viewed as essentially a linguistic phenomenon. Meaning can only be approached and encompassed by means of one's (preferred) semantic theory; this method reduces philosophy to questions of signification, such as, how can we be sure what a given sentence says?

Philosophers such as Gottlob Frege, Michael Dummett, and Ludwig Wittgenstein dealt with meaning only in a narrow, formal sense, suggesting that we abandon it as misleading and study instead the way language is used. But Jan Zwicky, also a philosopher (and poet), avers that Wittgenstein never abandoned "the intuition that deep matters of value in some way fall outside the scope of language."[6] She goes on to say that "a significant part of the meaning of words rests in wordlessness."[7]

Language itself is value-laden; grammar calls the tune in fundamental ways, as I've discussed elsewhere.[8] Whatever can be represented can be controlled. Poet Stéphane Mallarmé responds to this constraint exquisitely: "Meaning is a second silence deep within silence; it is the negation of the world's status as a thing. This ever unspoken meaning which would disappear if one ever attempted to speak it...."[9] This unspoken, lived meaning defies reification and language games. Foucault was wrong: not all life is built around language.

Life takes place in this world, not on a page or a screen. It isn't fully possible to live the right life in a wrong world, even if we assert that the meaning of life is a life of meaning. In this destructively disenchanted context, some of us find meaning in commitment to a project, a goal of liberated life. Studies and surveys continually point to the obvious, that those who lack meaning tend to be less happy with every aspect of their lives.[10] Meaning has a physical aspect. There is a healing force there.

It is also valid to realize that meanings must be sought and found by each of us, in an active engagement with life. Relationship is the greatest single source of well-being, and the key to overcoming nihilism. Love and friendship are likely the most powerful motivators to do anything at all. Life cannot be without meaning to anyone who loves. Conversely, the nihilist does not change diapers.

It's said that the meaning of it all is to be found in moments. I think of how a stranger's smile can light up my day. To mean is to be present, present to the moments, transparent to presence. The recognition of what is important for its own sake. Meaning is irreducible. *All* of this is the meaning.

This is not the right world and everyone knows it. There is a longing, a need, and as Adorno has it, "the need in thinking is what makes us think." And this "need is what we think from, even where we disdain, wishful thinking."[11] Mark Rowlands puts it well: "Any satisfying account of the meaning of life must be capable of redeeming life."[12]

Endnotes
1 Theodor W. Adorno, *Negative Dialectics* (New York: Continuum, 1973), p. 377.
2 Terry Eagleton, *The Meaning of Life* (New York: Oxford University Press, 2007), p. 34.
3 Quoted in Dennis Ford, *The Search for Meaning* (Berkeley: University of California Press, 2007), p. 12.
4 David Brooks, "Inside Student Radicalism," *The New York Times*, May 27, 2016, p. A21.
5 e.g. Stephen R. Schiffer, *Meaning* (Oxford: Clarendon Press, 1972); Ruth Garrett Millikan, *Varieties of Meaning* (Cambridge, MA: The MIT Press, 2004); Stefano Predelli, *Meaning Without Truth* (New York: Oxford University Press, 2013); Vincent Descombes, *The Institu-*

tions of Meaning (Cambridge, MA: Harvard University Press, 2014).
6 Jan Zwicky, *Lyric Philosophy* (Toronto: University of Toronto Press, 1992), thesis 118.
7 *Ibid.*, thesis 261.
8 "Language: Origin and Meaning," in John Zerzan, *Elements of Refusal* (Columbia, MO: C.A.L. Press, 1999); "Too Marvelous for Words," in Zerzan, *Twilight of the Machines* (Port Townsend, WA: Feral House, 2008).
9 Quoted in Peter Schwenger, "The Apocalyptic Book," Mark Dery, ed., *Flame Wars* (Durham, NC: Duke University Press, 1994), p. 64.
10 e.g. J.L. Freedman, *Happy People* (New York: Harcourt Brace Jovanovich, 1978).
11 Adorno, *op.cit.*, p. 408.
12 Mark Rowlands, *Running with the Pack* (New York: Pegasus Books, 2013), p. 100.

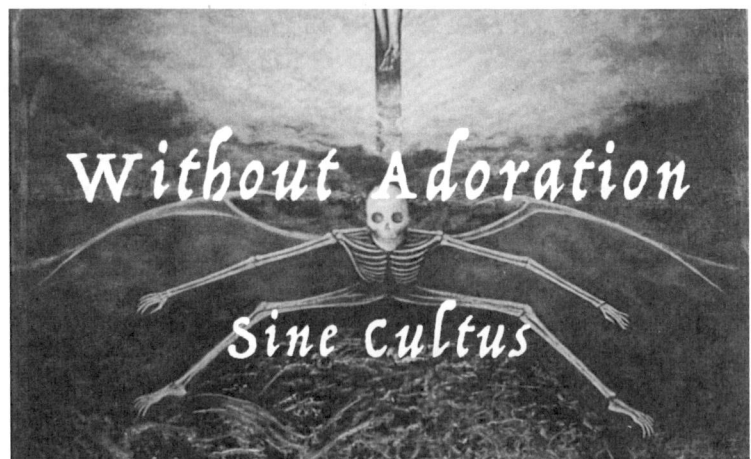

Questioning what nihilism is or isn't opens oneself up to being battered by opinions. Everyone has an opinion on what nihilism is, what it isn't and how one can use, or ignore, whatever it has to offer. Contrary to a popular folktale told in anarchist circles, nihilism did not originate in Russia in the mid-19th century. However, perhaps for those mining the 19th century as the origin and pinnacle of anarchistic though and theory, it is useful to believe such fairy tales.

In this brief essay, it will be suggested that the roots of nihilism and nihilistic thought extend further into civilized history and are heavily indebted to the theological tradition. As such, nihilism should be approached without adoration. The techniques of skepticism and negative theology can be seen as laying the groundwork for what has become modern day nihilism. Whether the reader makes the aesthetic choice to engage the roots of nihilism as presented in this essay is up to them and depends upon their own intellectual integrity. As any nihilist could recite: all values are baseless and nothing can be known or communicated.[1] The nihilist is a dutiful servant to the belief in meaninglessness complimented by an attendant doctrine of extreme skepticism. As within the theological tradition: the deeper one's devotion, the deeper one's convictions.

There are two major influences upon the nihilism of today. One being the Greek school of skepticism and the other being the apophatic, or negative, theology.

From the skeptics, the modern day nihilist has inherited the operating principle of questioning all phenomena of experience. This forms the basis of their analytic excursions. The nihilistic experience of life is one that is doused in doubt. Never one to accept another's interpretation of phenomena, the skeptic must experience and interpret on their own before any form of communicated experience would affirm, or conflict with, their own experience. However, the skeptic is too optimistic for the nihilist in this regard. Even a skeptic provides an opportunity for knowledge to be gained (an understanding) and for the communication of that knowledge (a shared understanding). This is too much for the nihilist whose allegiance is with meaninglessness. The proper nihilist would recognize that any meaning being offered is false, whether that comes from their own thoughts or in transmission from others. To the nihilist, wherever meaning is posited, there is a lie. Whereas the skeptic may believe there is a limit to knowledge, the nihilist believes there is no knowledge to limit.

The skeptic may also develop a system for evaluating experiential data in order to classify certain types of knowledge. This is another pitfall to be avoided by nihilists. If nothing can be known or communicated, then surely any methodology in servitude to knowledge generation and classification is a mistake. The nihilist has adopted the extreme skeptical position of "question everything," but they have abandoned the skeptics thirst to provide answers. As such, nihilists provide no answers because doing so would entail speaking from a position of knowledge. When one has renounced the possibility of anything being known or communicated, one has renounced the ability to answer. The nihilist will push for any and all meanings or answers to be destroyed. When viewed like this, it hardly seems instructive to ask questions at all. If a devotion to meaninglessness is the core nihilistic desire, then what is truly desired is that no questions be asked. If the nihilist decides a priori that meaning doesn't exist, then wouldn't asking questions be a spurious act?

If the nihilist is well-educated regarding skepticism, then they would understand that asking questions is not a way to further nihilistic thought. The path forward for nihilistic thought is not questions, but rather statements of negation. It is not the task of the nihilist to ask questions and elicit answers. This is already against their devotion to meaninglessness. Their devotion is to embrace meaninglessness and seek paths leading to the affirmation of meaninglessness. In seeking out these paths to meaninglessness, the nihilist speaks in terms of negation and it is in this act that they are heavily indebted to the apophatic theological tradition – negative theology.

Negative theology is an attempt to describe God by what God is not.[2] It is by the same technique that nihilism tries to define life by what life is not. Specifically, life is not defined by meaning attributed to it by humanity. This is very similar to negative theologians pointing to what God is not as a way to promote the idea that God is unknowable by the human mind. God lies beyond our abilities for expression. Nihilism follows a similar path. When one reads something like this - "Meaning is found in approaching the void rather than in the false knowledge of what is on the other side of it"[3] - this is clearly echoing the techniques of negative theologians. It seems closely related to this type of statement - "The purpose of Negative Theology is to gain a glimpse of God (divinity) by articulating what God is not (apophasis), rather than by describing what God is."[4]

One can clearly see a nihilistic value based choice coming from the following description of "Nihilist Anarchism":

...*a frame of reference to begin to impact the world can be based on one of two options. Either shrink the world that you desire to understand and touch or assert yourself onto a world gone mad in such a way as to transform scale.*[5]

By presenting only two choices for Nihilist Anarchism, the author has clearly laid down the rails for a moral choice. However, it is not clear why these two choices are the only two choices presented. A possible justification for these two choices is that the author has decided for the reader that these two choices are the only morally adequate responses to a world that doesn't suit one's needs... and that is clearly a moral response to an experience of the world.

Another expression of this moral response comes from the current nihilist anarchist oral tradition which is exemplified by the statement that "anarcho-nihilism simply means one doesn't believe that revolution is desirable or possible."

If this is the case, then perhaps the anarcho-nihilist actually desires the existence of civilization/society because without it the aesthetic choice of not believing in revolution, or the possibility of any other mode of human life, evaporates. This robs the anarcho-nihilist of a core belief. Without a civilization/society to provide the possibility of something to revolt against, one would be forced into a different mode of life outside the concept of "revolution." Outside of civilization/society, the anarcho-nihilist has no operating principle.

Nihilism is indebted to negative theology for providing it a mechanism of action based on the negation and destruction of what it feels is oppressing it. At base, nihilism is the ultimate play of victimization. It needs an oppressor as fuel. The nihilist needs to be subjugated and repressed in order to bring about its values of negate and destroy. Yes, it is driven by clear values and morals, just as negative theologians. It is here that the anarcho-nihilist finds value and an attendant moral compass by attacking whatever is felt to be enabling that victimization.

So it is that nihilism appears to be a peculiar form of negative theology. For instance, one can transform this phrase:

Those who espouse **Negative theology**, *therefore, claim that it is better to avoid making affirmations about* **God** *in order to prevent placing* **God** *in a «cage of concepts,» which may limit human understanding of* **God** *and «become a type of intellectual idolatry.»*[6]

Into this phrase:

Those who espouse **Nihilism**, *therefore, claim that it is better to avoid making affirmations about* **Life** *in order to prevent placing* **Life** *in a «cage of concepts,» which may limit human understanding of* **Life** *and «become a type of intellectual idolatry.»*

Nihilism certainly has value as an exercise to evaluate what it means to live. This is how Kierkegaard, Nietzsche and Camus, to name a few, treated their contemplation of nihilism. However, the point being made here isn't to uphold nihilism as a clear alternative to the theological tradition. It was to expose nihilism as being indebted to negative theology for its methodology.

As such, it doesn't escape any Christian or theological paradigm as many so-called nihilists hope. It is embedded within the same history and can't escape being "value-free," as it pretends to do. By taking up the avoidance of discussing "what life is," it is operating upon a grounding, or framing, that sees life as meaningless. By framing life in terms of what it isn't, nihilism declares itself a valuable perspective that instructs one to what life could potentially be. It's not this, it's not that... and because life is "not this nor that," nihilism is saying that those perspectives which do see life as "this or that" are restricting what life could be. And that is quite clearly a moral judgement on what life is.

Endnotes
1 http://www.iep.utm.edu/nihilism/
2 http://www.theopedia.com/negative-theology
3 http://theanarchistlibrary.org/library/aragorn-anarchy-and-nihilism-consequences
4 http://www.newworldencyclopedia.org/entry/Negative_Theology_(Apophatic_Theology)
5 http://theanarchistlibrary.org/library/aragorn-anarchy-and-nihilism-consequences
6 http://www.newworldencyclopedia.org/entry/Negative_Theology_(Apophatic_Theology)

Morality is a long-standing target of anarchists. And for good reason, like ideology, the stagnancy of such definitive codes of conduct can hinder an anarchistic existence. And who would be doing the enforcing?

But let's just clarify our terms. I'm using a pretty straightforward definition of *morality* here:

a particular system of values and principles of conduct concerning the distinction between right and wrong or good and bad behavior.

Obviously it can get more nuanced, but let's focus here.

Anarcho-primitivists are often subject to attempted refutation over our "moralistic claims" by asserting that "civilization is wrong." Here we get into some details: morals are "a particular system of values and principles of conduct," be it of an individual or society; morals ought to be guidelines, not ideals. To that end, if "civilization is wrong" is a moral grounding, I think that's a pretty good principle to live by.

But it isn't quite that simple.

If "civilization is wrong" was a "code of conduct" then anyone who knows it in their bones would be a hypocrite were they to partake in civilization. Considering the reality that we are all faced with, *leaving civilization* is just another delusion granted by the supposed freedoms given by the State. We are not here by choice: we just believe we are. If you need evidence of that, take a closer look at the circumstances surrounding indigenous societies worldwide as their lands are infringed upon by civilization.

Hypocrisy is an easy insult to launch. It is soothing to believe that an anarcho-primitivist using a computer means that domestication isn't a problem. That misses the point of the anarcho-primitivist critique, or any critique for that matter, entirely. The hope of anarcho-primitivists is often, not surprisingly, to live without civilization. Our reality, however, is that while civilization exists any hope to live by a moral code of based on *non-civilized existence* is impossible to enact.

The point of anarcho-primitivism is that we intended to show just how "civilization is wrong," how it got here and what can be done about it. Ideally the end point could be to reach a point where not being civilized was a possible code of conduct. But when or if you get to that place, what's the point of the moral code?

The problem here is a merging of want and will. And that's really something only civilized people can do.

Civilization doesn't exist in a vacuum. You can't turn it off and on. No one has ever nor will ever create a civilization by themselves. So it's not like there will be a day when there's an immediate return hunter-gatherer society in the future living by a moral code against civilization threatened because "fucking Frank turned on his nuclear power plant. Again."

Civilization only works systemically. It functions because of technology: be it in the form of organized labor or in the form of tools built using a division of labor to reinforce the hierarchy that requires the use of such tools. Hunter-gatherer and horticulturalist societies, the only functioning anarchist societies to have existed (also the only functional human societies to exist), didn't require a moral code.

Values? Yes, they have those. Elaborate mythos prohibiting the circumstantial consumption or use of certain plants or meats? Yes, they have those as well. But these are functioning, living relics of trial-and-error. Essential for survival is hardly in the same category as the arcane, self-serving religious rites. In fact, the only universal among non-civilized societies regards incest. A fairly simple "don't do it" that was tellingly only ever disregarded by the very moralistic civilized gentry.

Everything else is prone to circumstance. Even "thou shall not kill" is granted a good bit of leniency in these societies. There are reasons why someone would kill beyond war or vengeance, so overwhelmingly avoiding that outcome isn't the same as ideologically or morally prohibiting it.

Is that alone qualification for *moralism*? I think that is a fairly hard argument to make.

The reason that morality arises is that it's a social contract for a society of strangers. How you should or should not interact with others. It is necessary because domesticated life *and its subsequent technologies* create the first time in society where a universal code of conduct would be necessary because technology makes it possible for the impact of one person's decisions or life systemically spread beyond their reach.

Short of killing or direct violence, a hunter-gatherer with stone tools is hardly capable of creating a situation that other hunter-gatherers couldn't just walk away from. If Barack Obama wanted to wipe out enemies using drones flying beyond the field of sight and killing untold people, there only needs to be a moral code surrounding that if he had the capability of doing it.

Technology is the great enabler. It offsets the playing field. It exists by perpetuating unethical and anti-social/ecological circumstances.

The problem isn't that there is a missing moral code regarding technology: it's that technology exists at all. And this is where the nuance lies: the goal of anarcho-primitivists isn't to create a new morality; it's to undermine and eliminate the society where moral codes are necessary to the functioning of domesticated peoples.

There is a goal here and it is based on objective reality: civilization is here and it needs to be attacked. Technology creates situations beyond our reach and beyond our potential to comprehend the consequences. It allows us to act with a perceived impunity and distance from the outcomes of our actions.

We don't need to create a new ethos that has us put down or limit our interactions with technology; we need to render technology useless. That's a large enough target in its own right. And it doesn't leave a lot of need to articulate the possible mythos of a potential future primitive society where moralism is unnecessary: a society where the playing field is leveled again.

FIELD NOTES FROM THE PRIMAL WAR

Copperhead. Photo by Yank.

True Crime Case Files: Shutting Down the Tar Sands Pipelines

Where: 4 Locations
When: October 11, 2016

In the early morning hours of October 11, 2016, a group of five activists took part in an important act of direct action. Armed with bolt cutters, they cut their way into the enclosures for the following pipelines: Enbridge Line 4 and 67 in Leonard, Minnesota; TransCanada's Keystone pipeline in Walhalla, North Dakota; Spectra Energy's Express pipeline in Coal Banks Landing, Montana; and Kinder-Morgan's Trans-Mountain pipeline, Anacortes, Washington.[1]

Once they were in, they cut the chains on the manual overrides on each pipeline, shut the valves and then relocked the shut offs. This act shut off the flow of *all* tar sands crude into the United States from Alberta, Canada.

All of it.

The direct action was well documented and public. The five activ-

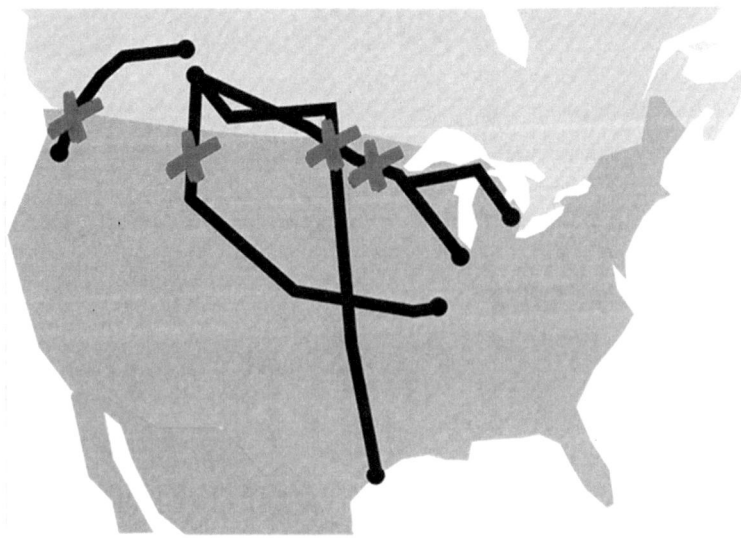

ists, aged 50-64, were all arrested immediately along with four other crew members. A statement was issued that the action was in solidarity with the protector camp at Standing Rock and a fairly lofty letter to President Barack Obama.[2] Their demands were as follows:
1. Invoke the National Emergencies Act and continue the shutdown of the tar sands pipelines we have initiated;
2. Immediately begin a process for federal closure of all US coal and tar sands oil extraction, and;
3. Put before Congress a plan for a national mobilization to transfer US energy use from fossil fuels to renewable energy sources, maintain and expand natural carbon sinks, and undertake a US-led and financed global campaign to meet the 1.5°C international target.[3]

Now, I would think that none of our readers would be shocked to hear that Obama did none of these things. I would trust the activists involved anticipated that outcome as well.

Nonetheless, the action was a solid one. Effective? Doubtful.

But it did shine a light on one thing in particular: if so inclined, *one could manually shut down pipelines.*

That's pretty interesting to hear.

Now, if you follow this feature in *Black and Green Review*, then you should be familiar with acts of sabotage against pipelines, historically speaking. There are many ways that people have tried attacking these structures before they are constructed. In most regards, once the pipeline is there, it might be too late.

However, what we are learning here is that a pipeline, even in the ground and in use, is not impervious to sabotage. Particularly, it's not immune to sabotage that doesn't require blowing or bleeding the line.

Thanks to our friends at the Sierra Club, we know that automatic pipeline monitoring systems only go off when the line is pumping more than 2% less than usual.[4] How quick and accurate they might be for shut offs is hard to say. What we do know is that, in this case, the intent of the direct action was to have it known and, with that understanding, the activists involved would be arrested. In fact, the activists gave the corporations a 15-minute heads up prior to their actions. At least two of the activists simply waited for the authorities to show up.[5]

Hilariously enough, that's got industry talking heads in a tailspin. David Holt, president of the Consumer Energy Alliance (CEA), the "leading national consumer advocate on energy issues," issued a statement in response to the action:

> *The steps taken by these individuals to sabotage pipelines – in addition to the threats, intimidation, and cyber-bullying tactics they are using – clearly show that their agenda has nothing to do with protecting the environment and everything to do with shutting down the American economy and hurting everyday Americans, families, small business, and our economic way of life...*[6]

The idea of America's energy corporations and consortiums feeling the brunt of "cyber-bullying" aside, this raises an interesting hypothetical question: are the pipelines, in particular, really this vulnerable? More broadly speaking, is the American economy this fragile?

Naturally there's a lot of bravado and chest pumping here with a dash of victimization. But there's still some truth. In 2011, energy (in the form of utilities and mining) made up 4% of America's GDP. That might not sound like a lot, but it's just under half of the percentage of state and federal government's GDP combined.

It's also a bit misleading. In 2013, three of the top four US corporations by revenue were energy related. That is a list that includes Exxon Mobil, Chevron, and Conoco Phillips.[7] When it comes to energy, time is most certainly money. Considering that the Enbridge pipeline alone carries an average of 1.4 million barrels of crude daily, any slowing or stopping of that flow quickly adds up.

Holt is inadvertently showing his cards. While the energy industry is a behemoth, it is not on sturdy ground. If minor acts of symbolic sabotage threaten such a beast, it's clear that more clandestine counterparts could wield far more significant results. Had the participants opted for more permanent ways of locking down the manual shut offs instead of use chains and locks it could have posed far more damage to the system.

What keeps people like Holt up at night though is that the activists, out of an untold number of options, specifically chose these locations. There are hundreds of thousands of miles of pipelines throughout the United States. And they all have regular manual safety valves. What protects them? From what we can gather, simply a chain link fence and, seemingly often, a locked chain around the valves. These things are everywhere that pipelines run.

For these activists, it seems to have taken effort to get arrested and they did it for a reason.

With the genie out of the bottle, it seems unlikely that others would do the same.

Endnotes

1 http://www.democracynow.org/2016/10/11/breaking_activists_reportedly_shut_down_five
2 http://www.shutitdown.today/oct11
3 http://www.shutitdown.today/dearobama
4 http://www.huffingtonpost.com/entry/dakota-access-pipeline-protests-water_us_57d85a51e4b0aa4b722d12b1?section=&
5 http://www.reuters.com/article/us-usa-canada-pipeline-activists-idUSKCN12D2R7
6 http://consumerenergyalliance.org/2016/10/cea-issues-statement-extremists-manual-shutdown-pipelines/
7 https://en.wikipedia.org/wiki/Economy_of_the_United_States

Tar sand mines in Alberta. Hell on Earth.

shut down the dakota access pipeline: standing with standing rock

Since we started working on this issue, we've been keeping a close eye on the Sacred Stone Camp as they shut down construction on the Dakota Access Pipeline. That camp started on April 1, 2016 and as we go to print, the tensions have only mounted.

The Dakota Access Pipeline is a 1,134 mile underground pipeline being built by Energy Transfer Partners. It will transport crude from the Bakken formations in North Dakota to transfer stations in Illinois. The section in question is where the pipeline crosses the Standing Rock Reservation, home of the Hunkpapa Lakota and Yanktonai Dakota, crossing sacred lands and burial grounds, ones bulldozed by ETP without consequence despite federal holding orders. This is the site where the pipeline crosses the Missouri River: the driving force behind the central message of the "water protectors": *Mni Wiconi*, "water is life" in Lakota.

Much has happened since April. The Sacred Stone Camp has grown, leading to a second camp hosting thousands of supporters and protectors. Media attention has been scant, unable to compete with a dumpster fire of an election. But the more things change, the more they stay the same. The lifeblood of civilization is resource-dependency. Being finite in nature, resources run dry. And in the wake of their abuse lie collapsed civilizations. As we have discussed elsewhere in this issue ('Ecology of a Bubble'), the Bakken formation that this pipeline originates at is not far from peaking.

This pipeline, like all others, will be its own ecological disaster. One that has been dissociated from reality as media have portrayed the protectors as simply defending "their water." As though, a spill on the Missouri River, the longest river in the U.S., would magically not impact anyone else.

What has been inspiring is the Camp with its steadfast and total resistance to the pipeline. This has drawn together a wider collective of Native American tribes than any event since the colonization of this continent.

What has been sobering is the awful familiarity with the response to the camps. We've seen ETP alongside pigs from all over the nation being drawn in and constantly keeping the camps in a state of unrelenting tension and terror. Lights on all night, militarized cops standing on the front lines, armed, badgeless, and just eager to fight. Sound cannons, tear gas, smoke grenades, concussion grenades, and constant surveillance, all of it.

In a nod to the kind of terror used by the State, private security firms have unleashed attack dogs on protectors. In a nod to the present, cops have used Facebook check-ins to identity participants. Individuals have been arrested, strip searched and left in dog cages or in prisons without food or charges. The press has been directly targeted, with one filmmaker currently stuck with 3 felony charges, a potential 45 year prison sentence.

The looming threat of violence consume the camps. Live streaming videos have shown the eagerness of pigs to swing at protectors and natives. Videos emerge of police creating violent confrontations and blaming protectors. They sprayed the camps with water in sub-freezing temperatures and wounded water protectors with "non-lethal" rounds while simultaneously claiming that they didn't.

This is old and new colonialism with all the hallmarks of modernity, the constant flow of live streams exposing the lies of the State, even when they try to cut bandwidths. Yet it has the absolute stench of the decaying corpse of colonizers. And the familiarity for native peoples is apparent. Yet they continue to hold their ground.

Without irony, the Army Corps declared on the day after Thanksgiving that the camps would be cleared by December 5th. The camps have staked their ground and are refusing to leave.

The situation remains tense and continues to worsen. How it unfolds remains to be seen, but there is no question: this is what communities of resistance can do. When the water, the very essence of life is under threat, grounded people have shown, repeatedly, that they are not afraid to do what many of us would not: to stand against the armed state and hold their ground.

It is our comfort and complicity that keeps us from standing up. Without grounding, we stand for nothing. It is all water, all life, that the extraction and distribution of resources that threatens. It is our world that is under attack. When we recognize that, we will fight because our lives depend on it.

Mni Wiconi.

Stemming the Tide
Cliff Hayes

The launch of Smarter Planet was not merely the announcement of a new strategy, but an assertion of a new world view.

Amid the global economic crisis of 2008, IBM began a conversation with the world about the promise of a smarter planet and a new strategic agenda for progress and growth.

As the internet grew, so did technology-driven enterprise needs and a truly global workforce. Computational power was being infused into things no one had thought of as computers: phones, cars, roads, power lines, waterways and food crates. A trillion connected and intelligent things were becoming a system of systems — an "internet of things" — and producing oceans of raw data.[1]

This system of systems that we find littering the orbit of the Earth, its environment and down to our immediate surroundings and bodies, is more than just the marketing campaign of a large multi-national tech-based corporation. It certainly has roots going deeper than the 2008 global economic crisis, but as it stands today, it is a system that the majority of civilized humanity has come to depend upon for existence.

Much of the promotional material for such a new world view is centered around the concept of interconnectedness. The promise being that the humans on disparate ends of the unifying system will now be connected, and remain connected, in ways not possible without the development of this so-called smarter planet. Of course, the connection is physically carried out by various apparatus of technology, not humans, and there is a definite qualitative difference between these types of connection. The human connection is reduced to symbolic representations that the technological apparatus can disseminate. As such, those representations of all physical existence become amplified, literally and figuratively, in their importance to such a civilization that depends on them. The message of IBM's "new world view" is clear enough - if you can't tread in the "oceans of raw data," then be prepared to drown.

Those of us unwilling to have life defined by the ability to navigate these digital oceans have other ideas, though. On either side of the stormy seas of technology lies an existence not engulfed by our ephemeral technological aspirations. There are various actors in bringing about such an existence and not all of them are human. In fact, a formidable opponent to the life-blood of such systems, electricity, is the largest benefactor of all life on Earth: the sun.

Geomagnetic Storms and the Carrington Event

Geomagnetic storms are disturbances in Earth's magnetic field that often occur when coronal mass ejection (CME) or a persistent high speed solar wind stream sweeps past Earth causing the magnetic field to become unsettled for an extended period of time.[2] CME is described as "a giant cloud of solar plasma drenched with magnetic field lines that are blown away from the Sun during strong, long-duration solar flares and filament eruptions."[3] The effects of such storms on systems dependent on a steady and stable flow of electrons are not hard to imagine. One such event that came in modern times was the Carrington Event of 1859.

On September 2, 1859, one of the largest recorded geomagnetic storms hit the Earth's atmosphere and wreaked havoc on the communication technology of the day - the cutting edge telegraph system. The system "shorted out in the United States and Europe, igniting widespread fires."[4] Telegraph operators experienced electric shocks, telegraph pylons sparked and the aurora generated by the storm was seen at locations near the equator, which is extremely rare.[5] This geomagnetic storm of 1859 became known as the Carrington Event based on the solar flare that was observed and recorded by the English amateur astronomer Richard C. Carrington just before noon on the previous day.

Earth's magnetic field can protect the surface of the planet from smaller solar storms (they are categorized similar to Hurricane strengths),[6] but the storm in 1859 overwhelmed Earth's magnetic field and penetrated to the surface of the planet. In 1989, there was a similar solar storm that caused a nine-hour power outage across Quebec, Canada.[7] The 1859 Carrington Event was reported to be three times as strong as the 1989 storm that wiped out power in Quebec.[8] If a storm as strong as the Carrington Event were to happen today, it could be a crippling blow to communications systems worldwide that may take multiple years of recovery and, according to U.S. Homeland Security Committee, "could pose the risk of the largest natural disaster that could affect the United States."[9]

In 2012, another strong solar storm was observed, however this time it came from a section of the Sun that wasn't pointed directly at the Earth. Our technology was spared the onslaught. "If it had hit, we would still be picking up the pieces," reported Daniel Baker of the University of Colorado back in 2014.[10]

The solar storm of 2012 wasn't widely covered in the press and it actually took two more near misses before these events started reaching a wider audience. In March 2014, Michael Snyder published his article, "After Several Near Misses, Experts Warn the Next Carrington Event Will Plunge Us Back Into The Dark Ages," where he wrote:

Most people have absolutely no idea that the Earth barely missed being fried by a massive [Electromagnetic Pulse] burst from the sun in 2012, in 2013 and just last month. If any of those storms would have directly hit us, the result would have been catastrophic. Electrical transformers would have burst into flames, power grids would have gone down and much of our technology would have been fried. In essence, life as we know it would have ceased to exist – at least for a time. These kinds of solar storms have hit the Earth many times before, and experts tell us that it is inevitable that it will happen again.[11]

Previously in December of 2012, Snyder had warned of the devastation that geomagnetic storms could unleash on our smarter planet:

A single gigantic electromagnetic pulse over the central United States could potentially fry most of the electronics from coast to coast if it was powerful enough. This could occur in a couple of different ways. If a powerful nuclear weapon was exploded at a high enough altitude, it could produce an electromagnetic pulse powerful enough to knock out electronics all over the country. Alternatively, a massive solar storm could potentially cause a similar phenomenon to happen just about anywhere on the planet without much warning. Of course not all EMP events are created equal. An electromagnetic pulse can range from a minor inconvenience to a civilization-killing event. It just depends on how powerful it is. But in the worst case scenario, we could be facing a situation where our electrical grids have been fried, there is no heat for our homes, our computers don't work, the Internet does not work, our cell phones do not work, there are no more banking records, nobody can use credit cards anymore, hospitals are unable to function, nobody can pump gas, and supermarkets cannot operate because there is no power and no refrigeration. Basically, we would witness the complete and total collapse of the economy. According to a government commission that looked into these things, approximately two-thirds of the U.S. population would die from starvation, disease and societal chaos within one year of a massive EMP attack. It would be a disaster unlike anything we have ever seen before in U.S. history.[12]

Clearly, the administrators of the technological era have taken notice of the potential for destruction that these geomagnetic storms have and they've responded.

The UK government announced plans to fund a new space-weather forecasting service in 2013.[13] This was intended to serve as a backup to the US based Space Weather Prediction Center, a laboratory and service center for the US National Weather Service which itself is part of the larger National Oceanic and Atmospheric Administration (NOAA).[14] And in September 2016, NOAA announced that they were going to start releasing more accurate forecasts of electromagnetic storms based on a more sophisticated prediction model. In part, this model was to be informed by a NOAA satellite positioned 1.6 million kilometers away from the surface of Earth, known as DSCOVR.[15] The new NOAA model will incorporate three models that describe the solar atmosphere through interplanetary space and into the Earth's magnetic realm. One model describing the Earth's entire magnetosphere, another describing the inner magnetosphere and a third model for electrical activity in the upper atmosphere.[16]

As it has been with the history of technological developments, the problems of one form of technological innovation have to be ameliorated through the development of more technology. The vulnerability of techno-addicted life is exposed by its dependence on a stable and steady flow of electricity. If the flow of electricity is affected by events beyond the control of current technology, then the rush is on to create the technology to control those events. Or at least, the rush is on to create yet another ocean of raw data about those events. With the raw data, technocrats can craft a plan of action to minimize the damage to those technological systems of our creation.

So, what about that aforementioned "system of systems" comprised of a trillion interconnected machines? Perhaps it won't take an external event, such as a geomagnetic storm, to bring the system to a grinding halt. Perhaps it can come from an internal manipulation of the system itself.

Powerline in a snow storm. Photo by Yank.

The Internet of Vulnerable Things

The Internet of Things (IoT) is a system of components that traditionally lacked computational power or a means to communicate with each other. The IoT is the result of a push to build computational power into technological devices and enable them to communicate with users, and each other, through the internet. There are many "smart devices" out there filling up that ocean of raw data, but being smart and connected doesn't make the IoT safe from being deceived and manipulated. In fact, being smart and connected might just be IoT's biggest vulnerability.

On September 20th, 2016, the largest distributed denial-of-service (DDoS) attack was launched against KrebsOnSecurity.com. Engineers at Akamai, a content delivery network service provider who protect the Krebs site from digital attacks, reported that the attack was nearly twice as large as any other attack they had seen and was among the biggest assaults the Internet has ever witnessed.[17] What made the attack so large was the bandwidth of the attack directed at Krebs. It reached 620 Gbps (gigabits per second). The interesting thing here is the way it was carried out:

> There are some indications that this attack was launched with the help of a botnet that has enslaved a large number of hacked so-called "Internet of Things," (IoT) devices — routers, IP cameras and digital video recorders (DVRs) that are exposed to the Internet and protected with weak or hard-coded passwords.
> Each botnet spreads to new hosts by scanning for vulnerable devices in order to install the malware. Two primary models for scanning exist. The first instructs bots to port scan for telnet servers and attempts to brute force the username and password to gain access to the device. The other model, which is becoming increasingly common, uses external scanners to find and harvest new bots, in some cases scanning from the [botnet control] servers themselves. The latter model adds a wide variety of infection methods, including brute forcing login credentials on SSH servers and exploiting known security weaknesses in other services.

In this way, one doesn't need to personally own the hardware and the pipe to the internet big enough to flood it. This method is something like a "zombie army" of IoT devices that are manipulated into blasting data back into the system. The result is a targeted attack from, as IBM states, "a trillion connected and intelligent things."

On October 1st, 2016, the following was published on the KrebsOnSecurity blog:

> The source code that powers the "Internet of Things" (IoT) botnet responsible for launching the historically large distributed denial-of-service (DDoS) attack against KrebsOnSecurity last month has been publicly released, virtually guaranteeing that the Internet will soon be flooded with attacks from many new botnets powered by insecure routers, IP cameras, digital video recorders and other easily hackable devices.
> The leak of the source code was announced Friday on the English-language hacking community Hackforums. The malware, dubbed "Mirai," spreads to vulnerable devices by continuously scanning the Internet for IoT systems protected by factory default or hard-coded usernames and passwords.
> Vulnerable devices are then seeded with malicious software that turns them into "bots," forcing them to report to a central control server that can be used as a staging ground for launching powerful DDoS attacks designed to knock Web sites offline.[18]

But even before this announcement was made on Krebs's site, the Mirai botnet was implicated in another attack that more than doubled the size of the Krebs attack.

On September 23, 2016, OVH, the France-based Internet Service Provider, was blasted by the same Mirai botnet that hit Krebs. This time to the tune of 1.5Tbps (terabits per second), as tweeted by the founder of OVH, Octave Klaba.[19] His tweet reported, "This botnet with 145607 cameras/dvr (1-30Mbps per IP) is able to send >1.5Tbps DDoS." To quote Dave Larson, chief technology officer at security form Corero, "The tools and devices used to execute the attacks are readily available to just about anyone; combining this with almost complete anonymity creates a recipe to break the internet."[20]

Within a month of OVH being targeted, the hacking collective calling itself New World Hackers claimed to be behind a large-scale attack using the Mirai botnet code that targeted Dyn, a Domain Name System (DNS) provider.[21] The attack occurred on October 21, 2016 and came in three waves roughly at 7am, noon and 6pm. Dave Allen, the general counsel at Dyn, reported that "tens of millions of internet addresses" were being used to blast internet traffic at the company's servers.[22] Dyn is a company that provides internet infrastructure services to large, popular sites including Amazon.com, BBC, Fox News, PayPal, Reddit, Starbucks, Twitter, Visa, Wired and Yelp.[23] Clearly the attacks were coordinated and their target strategically chosen. The IoT devices strung together in such a botnet are at a disadvantage when it comes to security because they are unable to run standard security software intended for commercial operating systems. IoT devices are certainly aiding in the rise of DDoS attacks as evidenced by a report from Verisign that shows a 75% increase year over year in the frequency of such attacks.[24]

Devices built to be controlled over the internet are beginning to proliferate. Business Insider reported, back in 2014, that by 2019 that "the Internet of Things" would be the largest device market in the world – "…more than double the size of the smartphone, PC, tablet, connected car and the wearable market *combined*."[25] Clearly, many users of these products leave the default security settings in place, meaning the units are open to being easily manipulated. Many devices are put into service without much thought to their configuration. Plug'n'play for the user is also making it plug'n'play for the hacker. While the Mirai botnet targeted consumer equipment and non-infrastructure websites and systems, the ramifications of a spreading

IoT changes when industrial and business devices enter the picture. The National Security Agency's Tailored Access Operations chief, Rob Joyce, recently said a large-scale attack on more critical infrastructure "…is something that keeps me up at night."[26]

Sweet Dreams of the NSA

Rob Joyce leads a team that is purported to be the best-resourced group of hackers in the world. They operate to infiltrate computer networks to gather foreign intelligence and they also probe the U.S. government networks to improve their security.[27] In a presentation at the January 2016 Enigma conference in San Francisco, Joyce said he considered IoT as a major boon when his team needs to attack a target. He singled out heating and cooling systems as examples of internet-connected devices that offer national-level hackers a route into organizations that computer network administrators often overlook.

The above quote where Joyce revealed what keeps him up at night was specifically related to SCADA security. SCADA stands for "Supervisory Control and Data Acquisition" which is a system for remote monitoring and control that operates with coded signals over communication channels, typically using one communication channel per remote session.[28] It isn't just Joyce who acknowledges SCADA security as a source of sleep deprivation. Nicholas Weaver, a computer researcher at the International Computer Science Institute in Berkeley, California, was quoted as saying, "I don't do SCADA research because I like to sleep at night."[29] However, those who do look into SCADA security find evidence of groups looking to infiltrate industrial systems and exploit their vulnerabilities.

At the Black Hat Conference of 2013 in Las Vegas, Kyle Wilhoit, a researcher with security company Trend Micro, gave a talk on what happened when he set up a dummy water control system that could be accessed via the internet. In his talk, he discussed how a Word document hiding malicious software was used to gain full access to his U.S. based decoy system, or "honeypot." The attack was carried out, allegedly, by a Chinese based hacking group known as Comment Crew, or APT1, and it illustrated the point that there are hacking groups out there that target infrastructure systems. Wilhoit pointed out that between March and June in 2013, 12 honeypots were deployed in 8 different countries and they had attracted 74 international attacks. 10 of the 74 attacks were sophisticated enough that they took complete control of a dummy control system. Wilhoit reported that, while his findings were based on his decoy systems, "these attacks are happening [to real systems] and the engineers likely don't know."[30]

In October, 2012, U.S. defense secretary, Leon Panetta, warned that successful attacks have been made on computer control systems of American electricity and water plants, as well as transportation systems. While the details were light in Panetta's report, it prompted a response from Chris Blask, founder and CEO of ICS Cybersecurity, where he said, "Stability and reliability are more important than anything – you have to keep the lights on."[31] Because we "have to keep the lights on," these power and water systems are running on older hardware and software that simply works. As such, systems remain unpatched and vulnerable to known security issues. Also, since some of these systems are located in remote areas, companies, contractors and employees have pushed for remote access to these systems. Thus exposing them to infiltration via the internet.

Roy Campbell, who researches the security of critical-infrastructure systems at the University of Illinois at Urbana-Champaign, reported that the pattern of connections between different parts of the electrical grid can create weak spots that would make it relatively easy for a hacker to bring down a wide area, "If you can isolate a power station, for example, it can be difficult to turn it back on because you need power to do that."[32]

More topics to keep the NSA up at night are discussed at the Black Hat Conference every year. I'm sure they're listening very closely and building up their defenses, but with the expansion of

IoT being so rapid and the network being so dispersed, it would be difficult for them to protect all of it, all of the time. Some demonstrations of hacking attacks covered at the conference in 2013 were:

* Spraying the audience with water from a replica water plant component forced to over-pressurize
* Showing how wireless sensors commonly used to monitor temperatures and pressures of oil pipelines and other industrial equipment can be made to give false readings that trick automatic controllers or human operators into taking damaging action
* Detailing of flaws in wireless technology used in 50 million energy meters across Europe that make it possible to spy on home or corporate energy use and even impose blackouts
* Exploiting a protocol called Dbus that has been used to control industrial equipment since the 1970s and is still in wide use today on devices often connected directly to the internet

It's been reported that the incentive to update or patch these security flaws is low because current law doesn't hold energy operators or the manufacturers of control systems liable for the consequences of poor security, such as damage from an explosion or lengthy power outage.[33] So, maybe while the NSA is losing sleep over the possibility of infrastructure hacking attempts causing damage, the private companies don't feel the same pressure because they aren't exposed to monetary damages resulting from the failures of their systems.

One final note here related to the sweet dreams of the NSA. In his spare time, HD Moore, decided to carry out a personal census of every device on the internet. Moore's census involved sending simple, automated messages to each of the 3.7 billion IP addresses assigned to devices connected to the internet around the world. Not even Google has publicly attempted such a census. The result of Moore's census was that many of the 310 million IPs that responded were vulnerable to well-known flaws, or configured in a way that would let anyone take control of them. Moore was quoted as saying, "There [are] some fundamental problems with how we use the Internet today. We're sitting on mountains of new vulnerabilities."[34]

Cutting the Cords

So while the IoT appears vulnerable to celestial and digital attacks, how does it stand up to some good old fashioned and therapeutic physical destruction? The good news is that even though the smarter planet invents a virtual layer for programmers to manipulate in the confines of cyberspace, it has to run on physically existing hardware. And that hardware is certainly available to physical attacks.

In April, 2016, Verizon reported that its equipment was sabotaged in the wake of a strike by its unionized workers. Fiber optic cabling was sliced at facilities in New Jersey, Pennsylvania and New York, which cut services to customers that included police and fire departments. A Verizon spokesperson reported that during a normal year, they might experience 5 or 6 deliberate cable cuts, but since the strike started, the number of suspected deliberate cable cuts rose to 49.[35] If only humans could recognize the damage done by and for technology extends far beyond their paycheck…

Announced in July, 2015, the FBI began investigating at least 11 physical attacks on high-capacity Internet cables in the northern California. One such attack, which took place near Sacramento, was carried out by the perpetrators breaking into an underground vault and cutting three fiber-optic cables belonging to Internet service providers. In April 2009, underground fiber-optic cables were cut at four sites, knocking out landlines, cell phones and Internet Service for tens of thousands in Santa Clara, Santa Cruz and San Benito counties. Similarly, in Arizona, underground fiber-optic cables were sliced in early 2015 which resulted in tens of thousands of residents being cut off from the Internet. In response, JJ Thompson, CEO of Rook Security said, "When it's situations that are scattered all in one geography, that raises the possibility that they are testing out capabilities, response times and impact. That is a security person's nightmare." Yes, and by the same token, what a nightmare our technological dependence has become! To turn FBI Special Agent Greg Wuthrich's words around about carrying out attacks on technological infrastructure would be appropriate, "We definitely need the public's assistance."[36]

In March, 2015, USA Today published an article entitled, "Bracing for a big power grid attack: One is too many." In this article, it was revealed that the U.S. power grid is hit by cyber or physical attacks about once every four days. While many of the attacks are small-scale, the analysis carried out by USA Today on federal energy records lists some important facts:

* Transformers and other critical equipment sit in plain sight, often only protected by chain-link fencing and a few security cameras
* Suspects have never been identified in connection with many of the 300-plus attacks on electrical infrastructure since 2011
* In 2011, an intruder gained access to a critical hydro-electric converter station in Vermont by smashing a lock on a door. In 2013, a gunman fired multiple shots at a gas turbine power plant along the Missouri-Kansas border. Also in 2013, four bullets fired from a highway struck a power substation outside Colorado Springs. No suspects were apprehended in any of these incidents.
* The power grid is susceptible to cascading outage due to the reliance on a small number of critical substations and other physical equipment

And here's a rundown of the "seven bullets theory" from John Axelrod, a former energy security regulator from a presentation at a 2013 security conference in Louisville. He describes how a mass outage could be triggered by a physical attack targeting key pieces of equipment:

> *The Eastern power grid is highly interconnected and relies on rolling power between different utilities, he said, according to a video of the presentation.*
>
> *"If you know where to disable certain transformers, you can cause enough frequency and voltage fluctuation in order to disable the grid and cause cascading outages," said Axelrod, who now heads the power and utilities information security practice at Ernst & Young. "You can pick up a hunting rifle at your local sporting goods store ... and go do what you need to do."*[37]

Sometimes the system doesn't even need any external push,

though. It regularly generates failures of its own. In March, 2016, Lockheed Martin faced months of delivery delays for the first six of eight GPS III satellites when it was discovered that small cracks in ceramic capacitors supplied to them by Harris Corporation were causing failures. Apparently, Lockheed has had so much trouble delivering a working system to the customer, the United States Air Force, that the Air Force was considering opening the troubled program up to multibillion-dollar competition. However, it's not only the satellite project that is weighed down with technical problems, the ground based system to communicate with those satellites being built by Raytheon is running five years late. The system itself appears to hobble along running on technology it can barely produce well enough to keep up the charade.

John Zerzan has been cataloging the manufacturing defects and recalls from various industries for years on his weekly radio show, *Anarchy Radio*. One could, and I believe I have on previous shows, point out how entropy continually conspires against the aims of technology to dissolve its systems of control and force. Entropy, in simple terms, is the measure of energy of a system that is unavailable for doing useful work.[38] Somewhat of a loaded definition with the phrase of "useful work," the point is clear enough that the laws ascribed to nature by science end with all the sound and fury of technological innovation leading to a slow decay away from the order it attempts to impose. As such, entropy can describe, in general, the trajectory of technological systems and components – they will eventually fail to meet their desired operating specifications.

Keeping all this in mind, I suppose one could say the system will eventually cut its own cords, but with a little determination and help, those cords could be severed more readily.

Endnotes

1 https://www.ibm.com/smarterplanet/us/en/
2 http://www.northernlighthouse.ca/geomagnetic-storms/
3 https://www.spaceweatherlive.com/en/help/what-is-a-coronal-mass-ejection-cme
4 http://www.space.com/7224-150-years-worst-solar-storm.html
5 https://en.wikipedia.org/wiki/Solar_storm_of_1859
6 http://www.northernlighthouse.ca/geomagnetic-storms/
7 https://en.wikipedia.org/wiki/March_1989_geomagnetic_storm
8 http://www.space.com/7224-150-years-worst-solar-storm.html
9 https://www.dhs.gov/xlibrary/assets/rma-geomagnetic-storms.pdf
10 https://science.nasa.gov/science-news/science-at-nasa/2014/23jul_superstorm/
11 http://thetruthwins.com/archives/after-several-near-misses-experts-warn-the-next-carrington-event-will-plunge-us-back-into-the-dark-ages
12 http://theeconomiccollapseblog.com/archives/a-massive-electromagnetic-pulse-could-

collapse-the-economy-in-a-single-moment
13 http://www.nature.com/news/uk-bolsters-defences-against-crippling-solar-storms-1.14432
14 https://en.wikipedia.org/wiki/Space_Weather_Prediction_Center
15 http://www.nesdis.noaa.gov/DSCOVR/
16 http://www.nature.com/news/us-sharpens-surveillance-of-crippling-solar-storms-1.20630
17 https://krebsonsecurity.com/2016/09/krebsonsecurity-hit-with-record-ddos/
18 https://krebsonsecurity.com/2016/10/source-code-for-iot-botnet-mirai-released/
19 http://www.bbc.com/news/technology-37504719
20 ibid
21 http://www.oregonlive.com/business/index.ssf/2016/10/cyberattack_disrupts_websites.html
22 http://www.nytimes.com/2016/10/22/business/internet-problems-attack.html
23 https://en.wikipedia.org/wiki/October_2016_Dyn_cyberattack
And from their own website, https://dyn.com/about/, they describe themselves as – "a cloud-based Internet Performance Management (IPM) company that provides unrivaled visibility and control into cloud and public Internet resources. Dyn's platform monitors, controls and optimizes applications and infrastructure through Data, Analytics, and Traffic Steering, ensuring traffic gets delivered faster, safer, and more reliably than ever."
24 https://www.nab.org/cybersecurity/Verisign-report-ddos-trends-Q22016.pdf
25 http://uk.businessinsider.com/how-the-internet-of-things-market-will-grow-2014-10?r=US&IR=T
26 https://www.technologyreview.com/s/546251/nsa-hacking-chief-internet-of-things-security-keeps-me-up-at-night/
27 ibid
28 https://en.wikipedia.org/wiki/SCADA
29 https://www.technologyreview.com/s/546251/nsa-hacking-chief-internet-of-things-security-keeps-me-up-at-night/
30 https://www.technologyreview.com/s/517786/chinese-hacking-team-caught-taking-over-decoy-water-plant/
31 https://www.technologyreview.com/s/429611/old-fashioned-control-systems-make-us-power-grids-water-plants-a-hacking-target/
32 ibid
33 https://www.technologyreview.com/s/517731/hacking-industrial-systems-turns-out-to-be-easy/
34 https://www.technologyreview.com/s/514066/what-happened-when-one-man-pinged-the-whole-internet/
35 http://www.foxnews.com/tech/2016/04/28/verizon-claims-sabotage-on-network-and-cables.html
36 http://www.usatoday.com/story/tech/2015/06/30/california-internet-outage/29521335/
37 http://www.usatoday.com/story/news/2015/03/24/power-grid-physical-and-cyber-attacks-concern-security-experts/24892471/
38 https://en.wikipedia.org/wiki/Entropy

The Ecology of a Bubble

Kevin Tucker

I have heard the sound of the Earth screaming. I have felt its heat, its burning. And it will forever be etched into my soul.

The sound was terrifying. It sounded like a thousand children screaming as their bodies were consumed by fire, or at least how I imagine that would sound. In a way that is how it looked too: a ball of flame shooting straight up into the sky. It was mesmerizing and terrifying in the way that only fire can lock you in. On this cloudy night, the flame reflected into the clouds, illuminating the sky as though it was an entire city fighting the darkness of night.

But this was no city.

We saw the reflection of the flames from miles away. Tracked it down winding roads. Tracing its path along an otherwise quiet night. We didn't know what it was, but it had to be seen. It drew us in.

And we found it: the eerie sight of a quiet suburban home in a rural landscape with a ray of burning fire screaming and tearing its way through the sky, reflecting off the slowly melting plastic siding of the house. The flames were literally burning the veneer off of the unsustainable and unattainable mythos of a quaint life in complicity.

The police were equal parts mesmerized and distracted while attempting to divert the other voyeurs of catastrophe. But we were all lost in the sight. The sound. The feeling. All of us except the representatives of the natural gas drillers who operated this well, who sought to bury this other worldly spectacle without context. They said nothing. There was nothing to see here.

But this was just the beginning.

This was my first experience with hydraulic fracturing, fracking as it is now known. At that point, none of us knew what it was nor what was coming. Before everything was recorded and uploaded in real time, this event had neither name nor precedence. This sight, this hydraulic fracturing natural gas well, blown, burning and screaming, was our new present: a glimpse of the future to come.

A vicious and violent end to the era of cheap energy.

Fracking is not the first economic bubble within the span of the Modernity, but it may be one of the quickest. Fracking, like its contemporaries in tar sands mining and mountain top removal, are trailblazers in terms of ecological devastation. The damage being done here is swift and, at times, endemic. But beyond that these methods of extraction, hailed as the second coming of fossil fueled exuberance, work only as long as the price of crude stays impossibly high.

The problem is that crude oil did jump to impossibly high prices during the 2000s.

At the beginning of the millennium, a barrel of crude hovered in the low- to mid-$30 range. But then the entire Middle East erupts again under the force of Western militaries. By late 2004, the price of crude surpasses an average price of $60 per barrel, ending a nearly two decade long glut in oil prices. Three years later and $100 per barrel became the new norm.[1]

Just as attention was turning slightly back towards looking at Peak Oil, opportunism came knocking.

And in 2005, opportunity came in the form of legislation. Former Halliburton CEO and overall dark lord Dick Cheney was sitting Vice President who oversaw exemptions to the Clean Water Act by way of the Energy Policy Act of 2005. This opened what was called the 'Halliburton Loophole', which meant that the chemical concoction required by natural gas drillers to drill deep oil wells could remain proprietary and exempt from regulation.[2]

How Fracking Works

The response of oil industry mouthpieces has remained steadfast that, much like human-induced climate change, peak energy is not a concern. The reason? Massive swaths of untapped fossil fuels that technology was going to magically open to bolster civilization. The reality is that all of these potential reserves were known of, but they were largely inaccessible.

At least they were inaccessible in a profitable manner.

Fracking is an exceptionally intensive process of energy extraction. Natural gas within shale formations is far from the concentrated pools of crude that conventional oil extractors bore into. It lies far deeper and needs coaxing to be captured. Never having intended on being used to fuel an ecocidal civilization, it was out of reach.

Sadly the history of civilization is driven by sociopaths with infrastructure and technology to feed the needs of growth in any sadistic manner. In 1947, a group of these earth-plundering profiteers decided they could try to work out the disorganized natural gas from rock formations by drilling deeper, setting off an explosion to crack shale formations and flooding the wells with a mixture of chemicals and water until the gas found its way back to their well sites.

Even more sadly, it worked. Halliburton drilled the first commercial wells during the following decade.

From this start, the rest of the millennium is fairly quiet. The larger shale plays were deeper and the technology wasn't there to really maximize this method of extraction for mass production.

And this brings us back to that pivotal moment in 2005.

For fracking to be effective, it needs to drill deeper, blow wells more aggressively, and operations have to be amplified exponentially. As a venture, it is as economically costly as it is ecologically. Wells that are fracked are pumped with a sandy mixture of water and a cocktail of up to 200 chemicals that flood the natural gas out of complex rock formations and strata back towards the well. The fracturing is the explosions and high pressure flooding that cracks through layers and any other natural boundary far beneath the soil to extract the gas.

Because of the depth of the extraction, wells dig through layers upon layers of strata. They blow through underground water reservoirs and, quite often, the fracking blows into them. If you are unfamiliar with the process, it shouldn't be hard to imagine what happens if you decide to set off some fireworks underneath a glass of water. That is essentially what is happening here.

Not an assuring picture.

Ecologically speaking, this is an absolute assault on the earth. It is a rupturing of ecosystems in untold means. And it is absolutely sickening.

But we'll get back to that.

Capitalists have no values other than to make money. The programmers and architects of civilization, particularly in this hyper-technological late era, uphold that single virtue above all else. If fracking didn't make money, they wouldn't do it. That is their sole barrier. Laws and regulations, like politicians, can easily be bought.

And when a barrel of gas broke the $60 mark and then shot up past the $100 mark, everything was back on the table. This is how a

bubble works. There is no long term planning or thought, it is a blood thirsty and cannibalistic gorge. Nothing else mattered.
Make moves, make them fast and you will make money.
And some people did just that.

Before ramming his natural gas-powered Chevy Tahoe headfirst into an underpass at 78 miles per hour, former Chesapeake Energy CEO Aubrey McClendon was the poster child of the natural gas bubble. Prior to bursting into flames literally, he was known for his explosively reckless business savvy. He co-founded Chesapeake Energy Corporation in 1989 to focus on unconventional gas extraction during what was otherwise a pretty lengthy lull from that first experimental well in 1947 and what was to come.

And he got his payout.

By the time the fracking bubble really got underway he was dubbed the "Reckless Billionaire". That's a fairly apt title. And for it, he was among the highest paid CEOs of 2008.[3]

The bold extravagance of McClendon's life should have been proof of how much money was to be had from the supposed "Saudi Arabia of natural gas" that the talking heads of the gas industry, such as McClendon and T. Bone Pickens, boasted that the US could be. Those myths have been greatly deflated, so I won't focus on them here.[4]

But if any of that was true, this wouldn't be the story of a bubble.

McClendon made his fortune the same way that the heads of Enron did: elaborate Ponzi schemes. Natural gas rights come from landowners when they're fortunate enough to have secured them. Chesapeake, like every other natural gas venture (and there are plenty of them), largely didn't buy land; they bought the mineral rights and wrote overwhelming contracts granting full access to them. Savvy and wide-smiling salespeople, who were willing to parrot the dreams of wealth and prosperity that sold the bounty of drilling locally, procured those contracts. Even energy independence was used as a sales pitch despite interest in exporting liquefied natural gas.

As hard as it can be to sympathize with landowners willing to sign over their mineral rights, the context is one we're all familiar with: the American Dream. This is the dream of making it and of winning the lottery: the dream of winning the capitalist game. If the person who is willing to write you a check tells you what you want to hear and down plays the risky new technological innovation they are going to be using on your home, then there are grounds for suspending disbelief and indulging. Besides, if you didn't sign, the horizontal well they drill next door can get under your property anyways, might as well join the winning team, right?

The number of companies out there drilling and securing leases has been unprecedented. Each of the companies maintain levels of fragmentation to add to the smoke and mirrors of the Ponzi scheme. No one is really sure of who is doing what. Without state and federal regulation, little pressure was applied to do otherwise.

And without knowing how badly this would play out, more moving parts meant less focus.

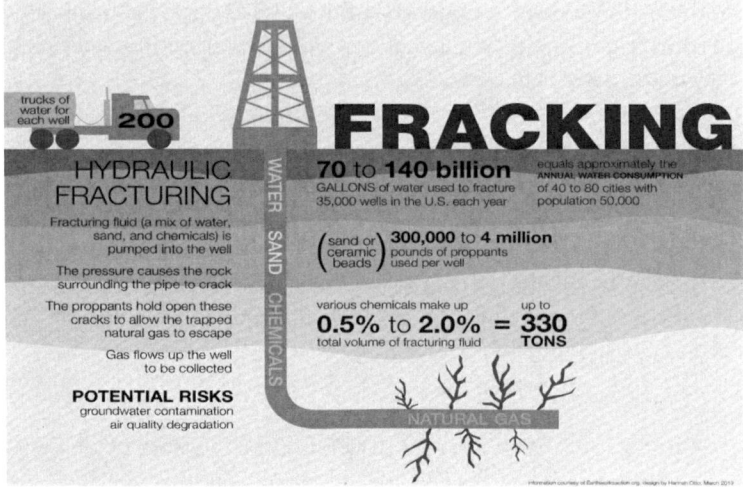

The executives knew what they were doing. This was a smash and grab operation. The quantities and qualities of shale plays were greatly overestimated. The production was massively exaggerated, being based off of the best production numbers from the early days of the most strategically placed well heads in a shale formation. Then landowners were gloriously bathed in what amounted to a fraction of the price tag that lease buyers sold to investors.

On paper, so long as crude prices stayed high, fracking was a numbers game. A numbers game sold to investors so that McClendon and scum like him could fill that third "trophy wine" cellar and buy his sixteenth antique boat.[5] In reality those numbers didn't add up. As Peak Oil analyst Richard Heinberg points out, fracking is impossibly costly:

> *Hiring personnel, renting the drilling rig, paying for the lease, hiring trucks—all of this is expensive. By the time you turn on the tap, you probably will have invested $10 to $20 million in your well pad—*

which, if you've been drilling for gas, may produce only $6 to $15 million worth of product over its lifetime at today's prices.[6]

And it caught up to McClendon too.

His risky business practices didn't earn him a lot of support within the company he co-founded, leading him to step down as CEO on April 1, 2013. True to form, he started a new natural gas drilling corporation the very next day, just down the street from Chesapeake's headquarters.

What really did him in was the shady economics he used to falsely prop up the natural gas industry. In June of 2014 crude was still striding high at over $105 per barrel. But the conventional industry shifted back.

The price of crude plummeted.[7]

By January of 2016, a barrel of crude had dropped below $30 per gallon. McClendon's personal fortune was halved in the process. Accelerating his drive towards self-implosion was his indictment on March 1, 2016 by a Federal Grand Jury on charges of rigging the bidding process for oil and natural gas leases which was a violation of antitrust laws. Having destroyed the land was fine, but crossing other capitalists is a federal offense.

Having hit a wall figuratively, he did what any power-hungry narcissist would do and ran into a wall literally the next day.

Having used his rise to power and prestige as the poster child of the fracking bubble and its potential for exploitation he unwittingly became the martyr for this very brief era. Unfortunately, this isn't a cautionary tale. At this point it is quickly becoming history, but the daily reality of it is the one we are left in.

And that's where things get scary.

How Fracking Actually Works

"It just ruined everything."

At 80 years of age, Shirley Eakins of Avella, Pennsylvania is an unlikely figurehead against fracking. And that's because she isn't one. She is a victim of it.

Her story is one that has quickly become common in Pennsylvania, just as it had in North Dakota, Oklahoma, Texas, Wyoming, Arkansas, Colorado and Louisiana. Just as it is becoming common in Ohio, Kentucky, and West Virginia. In 2009, Atlas Energy began fracking up the road from the Eakins. And that is when things went sour. They started getting rashes and moles after showering. The water became slimy and no longer usable.

Between 2007 and 2016, 2,800 complaints had been filed over water violations caused by fracking in Pennsylvania alone. Ever the puppets, the Department of Environmental Protection claimed only 279 were linked directly to fracking.

In 2012, a couple living a hundred miles to the north started getting sand coming through their showerhead with high levels of iron, manganese and chlorides.[8] Elsewhere videos started showing up on the news and online with people lighting the water from their tap on fire.[9] Livestock and pets started getting sick and dying.[10]

The well sites and derricks set up to frack a well are impressive. Towering above the landscape, the derricks are intensive work sites. Crews work around the clock and the lights never shut off until the well is up and running, usually off at least one permanent diesel fueled generator.

The expenses of setting up a well come down to this. The clearing and preparation of a well site is possibly the smallest part of the operation, even when land is graded to leave open the massive clearing necessary to get a well blown.

And a well may be fracked as many as twenty times before the gas begins to flow.

This is no simple equation.

A single well site may require up to 8 million gallons of water. Additionally upwards of 40,000 gallons of chemicals may be used in the fracking process. That's 40,000 gallons of a chemical mixture that has been found to span over 1,000 chemical products and 650 individual chemicals. A group of doctors isolated at least 59 of those chemicals, finding that 67% were harmful to humans.[11]

Transporting those chemicals breaks down to upwards of 2,000 tanker truck trips *per frack*. Where those used chemicals are transported is always a spot of contention. Often the water and chemical mixture is left to air out in open pits at the well sites, but most of it never comes back out. 60-80% of it is never retrieved.[12] Some of it is claimed to be recycled through additional fracking sites, but a lot of it is injected back down into the fractured shale formations through deep well injection sites.[13]

The process of blowing wells is about as precise as you can imagine.

The intended goal is to dig deep into the shale formation, then drill horizontally, setting off a series of explosions to flood the water-chemical concoction into. As terrestrial beings, our knowledge about this depth of the earth is subject to the whims of the same scientists who think setting off explosions down there to flood with toxins is a good idea.

Having been living in Pennsylvania, the first earthquake I experienced stood out fairly prominently. The sound, amplified through the rolling mountains, was enormous. Almost overwhelming anything that was felt. It was such a foreign experience that I was barely able to register what had happened. Not true the second time. Nor the third.

What was as clear as could be was the relationship between blowing wells and earthquakes. But no one was willing to talk about it. At that point, few even really knew what was going on despite the fact that the link between fracking and earthquakes was acknowledged in the UK in 2011.[14]

But this is quantifiable.

Oklahoma, where the fracking boom has picked up steam only more recently, was forced to issue a government statement about the indisputable creation of a new norm of constant quaking. That doesn't mean they had to be honest about it. In fact, their intentional wording is almost hilariously bad:

...we know that the recent rise in earthquakes cannot be entirely attributed to natural causes. Seismologists have documented the relationship between wastewater disposal and triggered seismic activity.

That's laughable because the situation is truly dire. Earlier on in the boom, in 2013, there were 109 earthquakes in the state. That number grew exponentially to 585 in 2014 and a staggering 907 in 2015.[15]

The entire fracking industry is standing on shaking grounds.

The Ecology of Fracking

The consequences of this process don't end at the fracturing.

A well isn't simply fracked and that is it. The entire structure of the industry is built around the overreaching Halliburton Loophole. Get in, get your funds, drill, and bleed it dry. There is no thought here. The company that created the loophole to push aside oversight (not that it would have done anything) is the same company that is selling the equipment, tools and technology to blow the wells and keep them pumping.

No one in the industry seems to have thought it was worth thinking beyond getting their fortunes set. And why would they? To them, the earth is dead. Anything beyond the sacred Self is sacrilegious unless they're giving stump speeches on the virtue of "creating jobs" or maximizing the earth that their created God has given us to plunder.

It's the same story that colonizers, kings and priests have always told to those willing to believe they will get their reward through playing along.

The imprecise blowing of wells leads to a series of unknowns.

There is no long term example or study here on how water is impacted by fracking: just a litany of excuses for how fracking isn't to blame for declining water quality in proximity to new wells.

True to the nature of a bubble, what we do know is that the hastily created wells and infrastructure weren't built to last.

Not only is there little to no thought put into the actual process of fracking, there is no long term thought or action on how to operate the wells. The *Wall Street Journal* found that "industry studies clearly show that five to seven per cent of all new oil and gas wells leak. As wells age, the percentage of leakers can increase to a startling 30 or 50 per cent." Fracking wells are the worst offenders, the fracturing process itself often leading to cross contaminating wells increasing the likely catastrophic spread of fracking compounds even before leaks may occur.[16]

Virtually every stage of the process is prone to failure.

Methane leaks that have resulted in explosive faucets are due to sealant failures on the well lines or eruptions into wells during the fracking process. Sand coming out of showerheads comes from fracking compounds flooding wells and reservoirs. This is easy to say, but it's almost impossible to absorb.

The reality behind these numbers is grim and we can only psychologically cope with it by biting the industry perspective and believe that a contaminated or leaking well is an isolated and containable or solvable issue.

But they aren't.

This is the new norm of life within the shale basins. Even without having property you live on or near being fracked can't isolate you from the devastation that comes with the process. And we only become aware of its span when it is too late.

Not surprisingly, the earth is far more complex than the industry geologists would like to believe it is. Underground water is far more connected than they would like to believe or than they are willing to acknowledge. Such is the fractured and specialized perspective that a scientific mentality is only capable of understanding. But multiple wells and reservoirs (surface level or underground) are often subject to a litany of wells surrounding them.

If we believe the industry numbers, statistically if twenty wells surround one water source, one will leak. If we use our brains or eyes, we acknowledge that means the entire body of water is at risk.

Reality is a bit more depressing than that.

In Pennsylvania alone, of its 9,794 wells, there had been 5,790 violations.[17] Makes that terrifying industry number of "five to seven percent" seem almost palatable.

At this point, there can be absolutely no question about the industry talking points. There can be no question about the motives behind the Reckless Billionaires.

This is a full on assault on the earth. On all of those who live in these areas: those who breathe the air or drink the water. Any being that walks through the clearings, burning their feet on the residual chemicals that settle in lawns and into streams.

This is far larger than any kind of "not in my backyard" issue.

This isn't just about showerheads and faucets, those are just the indicators we become aware of. The ecological consequences here are devastating. I saw this as the Allegheny National Forest turned into a parking lot of well sites. I saw the forest being reduced to the scenery between clearings, as roadless areas suddenly were crossed with crude roads. As the core of the forest turned into a roadside, reducing the areas for deep forest dwellers to exist. Eliminating the breeding grounds for birds. Increasing the disturbed soil where fast growing invasive species would suffocate the existing ecology.

This is an amplification of the omnicide that civilization carries: a technologically assisted ability to push further beyond the bounds of ecocide. Even putting the roads aside, the ecological toll of running a single well site is strong enough to risk *up to thirty acres per well.*[18]

Animals wander or fall into the open wastewater pits, suffocating on its fumes and contents, or withering away from direct exposure if they make it out. A single leaked well into a river in Ohio in 2014 resulted in the death of 70,000 fish and other aquatic life.[19] The water for fracking a well is often pumped directly from creeks, streams and rivers, isolating populations and resulting in die offs. Methane released into streams and rivers suffocates fish. The immediate and constant rise of sound and light pollution in remote areas has proven fatal to the more ecologically sensitive species that sought those spaces out.[20]

While natural gas and the methane released from its drilling may be colorless, odorless and non-toxic, they are also explosive and highly flammable. But for all living beings in proximity to the well-heads, they are exposed to a number of other chemicals: hydrogen sulfide, ethane, propane, butane, pentane, benzene, and other hydrocarbons, among others.[21] For species and places already feeling the pressure of logging and subsequent road construction, all of this just adds to the impact on all wild beings, just as it does humans.

This is the reality for all beings that are stuck with this legacy, this persistent wound.

We are stuck with this mess. They are stuck with this mess.

And then it explodes.

When the Bubble Explodes

When the fracking bubble burst, it carried a toxic stew of exposed lies, outrage, destroyed regions, wrecked lives, and all the maladies of an economic free-for-all.

Like fracking fluid, all of this was inevitably going to come to the surface. The dangers had slowly been more and more apparent. The payoff was quickly revealing itself as an overstatement and after years of having to truck in supplemental water for cooking, cleaning and showering those who were convinced to sign away their mineral rights were getting fed up.

In southwestern PA, the area I considered home, that bubble fully burst into flames on April 29, 2016.

On that day, there was a blowout on Spectre Energy's 36" Texas Eastern pipeline. The resident of the home where the blast occurred suffered extensive internal and external burning, but watched his home burn as flames eclipsed the tree line. And it drew a crowd. The blast was so strong that my own family members had windows rattling over three miles away. They felt the blast up to eight miles away.

This was hardly the first blowout or victim, far from it. But what was particularly telling about this incident is that while the blast happened at 8:30 AM, Spectre had "declared force majeure at midday."[22]

Force majeure. Legally speaking, "an act of God." This means that a company can remove itself from all liability for damages and, often, cleanup, because, well, it couldn't have been *their* fault.

And this is where we are left off.

For anyone opposed to fracking and civilization itself, there should be reason to celebrate when a bubble like this bursts. Every single well site or proposed pipeline that doesn't happen is just that much more of the earth and of wildness that stands a better chance of surviving the collapse of civilization.

In every sense, that is a great thing.

However, it's also a complicated kind of joy. The problem with an energy bubble isn't that it will end quickly—that is the only upside. The downside of it is that the profiteers and architects of these schemes move very quickly. All of those jobs that politicians and corporate heads were talking about came through; often bringing a bolster in crime, alcoholism, drug use, and rape with them. And then they're gone. The micro-economy they created and politicians used, that's gone too.[23]

Everything else is here to stay.

Frantically assembled, horribly executed, and with zero foresight into the future, what they did remains. And it will continue to erode, decay, leak into the water supply, and explode violently.

This is the new reality that we've inherited. One that has come to fruition faster than the fracking boom started.

What happened is that when those high crude prices crashed, they shut down the economic argument for fracking very quickly. The money stopped flowing and all the proposed wells were dropped. That is great news.

As of February 2016, the drilling rig count in the US fell to 571, the lowest count in the last century. During the fracking peak of 2012 there were over 2,000. Over the last year, 35 rigs were shut down in Pennsylvania alone.[24] Cabot Oil and Gas cut its 2016 budget 58% from 2015. A restructuring firm purchased Chesapeake Energy only further fueling rumors of bankruptcy.[25]

North Dakota, home of the Bakken shale play (one of the largest in the US), had its largest production decline in April of 2016 dropping down 70,000 barrels per day. The number of drilling rigs went down to 28 rigs in the state. That is compared to 27 in July of 2005, before the boom, and the all time high of 218 in 2012.[26]

Immediately that translates to pulling proposed rigs off the table, bringing pipeline projects into question and keeping assured long-term damage away from these areas. The light pollution, the deforestation, the increased traffic, the chemicals, spilled intentionally or not, are not going into these areas.

But on the flipside, the brevity of this bubble and seeing how quickly it has accelerated and withdrawn highlights the dangers it leaves behind.

Explosions are nothing new.

In June of 2016, an oil worker was killed and two others injured during an explosion at a well operated by a subsidiary of ExxonMobil.[27] This kind of accident is something that is par for the course. But what stood out more was when a Pennsylvania oil worker died after being engulfed as flames consumed the backhoe he was operating.[28] It's hard to sympathize with oil workers, but what he struck was something that is far more telling about the nature of how fracking companies work: he hit an unmarked, unregistered "gathering line".

Gathering lines are lines that take gas from the wellhead to a larger transmission line or processing facility.[29]

And they are unregulated.[30]

The oil worker who hit a line with a backhoe hit an unmarked, unregulated line. An unregulated line that is totally legal, carrying extremely volatile and explosive gases. The corporations, their subsidies, and anyone who could foster up the money to have a drilling rig set up could run their gathering line and bury it without having to mark it.

So long as natural gas is being extracted in these areas, it remains likely that people, animals, or anything will continue to unknowingly strike them. And then they explode.

These lines could be anywhere within the shale regions.

But the explosion threat hardly ends there. What stands out far more are the explosions like the one in New Alexandria, PA: pipeline explosions. In December 2012 the Sissonville gas pipeline exploded in West Virginia producing a massive and intense flame that destroyed three houses and melted a chunk of Interstate 77.

Pipeline explosions, unlike gathering lines, can happen anywhere gases or crude are transferred through, meaning they can happen hundreds of miles away from shale plays. Most of the pipelines that are currently being used were built for smaller amounts of natural gas for years, but are just one more part of the aging infrastructure that the frack boom sought to use against any and all logic. The Sissonville pipeline was a 20" gas pipe that failed, in the words of the NTSB, because of "severe wall thinning caused by external corrosion."[31]

It is possible to catch a leak before it explodes, but even where high tech methods of detecting leaks are used, they typically fail. When leaks are discovered at all, prior to explosions or blowouts, it's typically by locals.[32] For the most part, the supposed "high tech" detection hardly happens. Detection software typically only goes off when a line drops over 2% in total production.[33] Any size oil spill is an ecological catastrophe, but when lines are pumping around a half-million barrels per day, 2% of that is a nightmare. For the most part, old pipelines are just repurposed without renovation.

Kinder Morgan's Tennessee Gas Pipeline is currently set to transport liquefied natural gas from Ohio and Pennsylvania to Louisiana and Texas. This pipeline seeks to repurpose an older pipeline and its use requires reversing the flow. Flow reversal in pipelines was found to be the reason for 20,000 barrel and 5,000 barrel crude spills in North Dakota and Arkansas, respectively, in 2013. The pipeline that Tennessee Gas seeks to repurpose and reflow includes 343 miles that were installed in the 1940s and over 1,000 miles installed before 1970.[34]

And this is what we are left with: a quick bubble that has filled and covered the earth in a pit of toxins, cut roads through isolated areas, destroyed the water reservoir, resulted directly in fish kills, threatens sensitive and threatened species, while leaving the landscape scoured, wounded and crossed with pipelines and gathering lines that are ticking time bombs.

Like all of civilization, it is only once it is too late that we even stop to wonder if it was worth it.

Like all of civilization, it wasn't worth it.

It isn't worth it.

This is the new landscape that arises and the fragile ecology of a culture that no longer considers itself a part of the ecology while systemically destroying it in new and ferocious ways.

This isn't a cautionary situation. This isn't just the canary in the coalmine of a flaunted new energy revolution.

This is happening. This is going on now and the *only* reason that it was reigned in, en masse, is that the economics of the situation shifted against it. It is the cutthroat nature of the energy monoliths that permitted the price of crude to drop and sink their supposed alternatives. That move, we can be assured, is temporary.

A result of this is feeling like an ecological exile of the place that I love: the Monongahela Valley into the Appalachian Mountains. I have lost family because of the fracking. Many of them once took the bait on the sales pitches, but when their neighbor's houses start blowing up, their moods shifted. When I went to New Alexandria the week after the Spectre pipeline explosion (entry into the area was under strict control by the company that destroyed it), many of the one-time supporters were out for blood.

That should be reassuring. In some ways it is. When civilization starts taking out your water, your home; just attacks your entire life, you should be angry. And they are. Some have started putting the pieces together, but many are just defeated.

What can I do?

What can anyone do against this?

Those questions feel like defeat. I can't even say them enthusiastically, but I don't ask them rhetorically. The problem is that this isn't just an analogy for what civilization does, for what technology has permitted: this is the problem.

And it remains the problem.

I maintain hope, against all logic, that these regions will heal in time.

The Monongahela River valley hosted over 1,000 smokestacks at the turn of the 20th Century that would have felt equally impossible to recover from. It has made some improvements, but so long as these wounds continue to be inflicted it doesn't stand much of a chance. Having fractured the strata of the earth and then pumped it full of toxins that will surely find their way to the groundwater (where they haven't already) is a problem that will span generations.

Perhaps even longer than that.

The stay of execution that the downturn in fracking has seen over the last year remains a threat, but perhaps the bigger threat is what may come on the next round. What horrid thing are technocrats and programmers working on now? I see the areas that I love after having been fracked, I have seen water that can no longer be touched, wild beings that have been caught in the consequences of all of this and wonder if it can get worse. But when you look to the history of civilization, you quickly realize that is the kind of question that doesn't end well.

It is easy to look at this and to give up.

But I can't. I won't.

There is no safety in submitting to despair, of giving in to the rampant individualism of civilization and just try to make the most of our own lives. That is the hard part about grounding, about getting a sense of place and belonging: you can't just turn your back and pretend that it isn't happening, no matter how grotesque the sight becomes.

The future of our ignored ecology demands that we don't allow it to remain obscured by pathological distancing through economics, philosophy, theorizing or posturing. The distinctions we make between our way of surviving and the ability for wildness to continue existing are arbitrary, but they are constantly reinforced. As participants in our own demise, as those who want to stop the wounds, giving in to the despair simply isn't an option.

I mourn for loss. I will mourn as more family and wildness succumb to the cancer that fracking has created.

But that mourning does nothing for them.

This is our problem. It cannot be ignored. We have to be prepared for both our future of living in wounded places and dealing with the remnants of a decayed and decaying infrastructure: even beyond the final stage of civilization collapsing.

It will mean nothing to wait for that moment to speak honestly about what is happening, why it is happening and to act with foresight instead of sulking into despair in hindsight. Hope alone isn't enough.

This earth, our home, is worth fighting for.

Endnotes
1 http://www.macrotrends.net/1369/crude-oil-price-history-chart
2 Richard Heinberg, *Snake Oil: How Fracking's False Promise of Plenty Imperils our Future.*

Santa Rosa, CA: Post Carbon Institute, 2013. Pg 39.
3 http://heavy.com/news/2016/03/aubrey-mcclendon-net-worth-home-homes-oklahoma-thunder-salary-income-wife-billionaire-aep-mansion/
4 Heinberg's *Snake Oil* is the shortest and sweetest summation of all of this. I highly recommend it.
5 http://www.reuters.com/article/us-chesapeake-mcclendon-profile-idUS-BRE8560IB20120607
6 Heinberg, 2013. Pg 44.
7 For more on this, see the 'Over a Barrel' interview with Richard Heinberg and 'Fieldwork in the End Times' interview in *Black and Green Review* no 3.
8 http://www.huffingtonpost.com/entry/pennsylvania-fracking-water_us_576b7a76e4b-0c0252e786d5e
9 See http://www.newsweek.com/fracking-wells-tainting-drinking-water-texas-and-pennsylvania-study-finds-270735 and Josh Fox's documentary *Gas Lands*.
10 http://www.mintpressnews.com/livestock-falling-ill-in-fracking-regions/211720/
11 http://nysaap.org/update-on-hydrofracking/
12 http://oilprice.com/Energy/Energy-General/The-Facts-about-Fracking-Fluid-and-its-Disposal.html
13 https://stateimpact.npr.org/pennsylvania/tag/deep-injection-well/
14 https://www.newscientist.com/article/dn21120-how-fracking-caused-earthquakes-in-the-uk/
15 http://earthquakes.ok.gov/what-we-know/
16 http://www.resilience.org/stories/2013-01-10/shale-gas-how-often-do-fracked-wells-leak
17 https://www.fractracker.org/
18 http://www.biologicaldiversity.org/campaigns/california_fracking/wildlife.html
19 http://www.frackcheckwv.net/2014/07/22/over-70000-fish-aquatic-creatures-killed-by-pollution-from-ohio-frack-well-fire/
20 http://www.onegreenplanet.org/animalsandnature/no-fraccident-how-animals-are-hurt-by-fracking/
21 Heinberg, 2013. Pg 85.
22 http://www.bloomberg.com/news/articles/2016-04-29/spectra-energy-responding-to-pennsylvania-natural-gas-fire
23 http://www.mcall.com/news/nationworld/pennsylvania/mc-pa-gas-business-decline-20151213-story.html
24 http://www.pennlive.com/news/2016/02/pa_rig_count_lower_than_before.html
25 https://stateimpact.npr.org/pennsylvania/2016/02/17/drilling-downturn-hits-marcellus-shale-industry-hard/
26 http://peakoilbarrel.com/north-dakota-down-over-70000-bpd-in-april/
27 http://www.rigzone.com/news/oil_gas/a/145183/One_Killed_3_Hurt_in_North_Dakota_Well_Explosion_AP
28 https://stateimpact.npr.org/pennsylvania/2016/02/19/worker-dies-in-pipeline-accident-puc-steps-up-calls-for-reform/
29 http://pstrust.org/wp-content/uploads/2014/06/Pete-Chace-Gathering.pdf
30 https://stateimpact.npr.org/pennsylvania/2015/08/04/unmapped-unregulated-maze-of-rural-pipelines-poses-hidden-risks/
31 http://www.wvgazettemail.com/News/201403100090#sthash.g2MSYHU6.dpuf
32 http://www.wsj.com/news/articles/SB10001424052702303754404579310920956322040
33 http://www.huffingtonpost.com/entry/dakota-access-pipeline-protests-water_us_57d85a51e4b0aa4b722d12b1
34 http://www.courier-journal.com/story/tech/science/environment/2015/04/09/new-pipeline-plan-draws-fire-across-kentucky/25532167/

The HIDDEN ONES

fished with the harpoon and the net, and hunted with the bow and arrow, and by setting snares---silent weapons all. They gathered acorns in the autumn, enough if possible to see them through the winter. They ate green clover in April, and brodiaea bulbs in early summer. In midsummer they went to Waganupa, four nights journey, to its cooler air and deeper shade and more abundant game. For the rest, they lived on upper Mill Creek in small houses camouflaged so that from above, the only direction from which they could have been seen, the bent branches which covered them looked like nature's work. Nearby were storage shelters disguised the same way, and containing drying frames, baskets of dried meat and fish and acorns, and utensils, baskets, tools, and hides. They traveled sometimes for long distances leaping from boulder to boulder, their bare feet leaving no print; or they walked up or down stream, making of their creeks a highroad. Each footprint on the ground was covered over with dead leaves, obliterated. Their trails went under the heavy chaparral, not through it, and they traveled them on all fours. A cow could not find such trails; even deer sought more open ones. If a branch was in the way it was gradually bent back farther and farther, and if need be severed by charring and wearing through with a crude tool made from splitting a boulder, a slow but silent process. They never chopped, the sound of chopping being the unmistakable announcement of human presence. They kept their fires small so that the smoke dissipated harmlessly through the brush without rising beacon wise above the bay tree canopy, and they covered the site of a campfire

Ishi: The Hidden Ones

with broken rock as soon as the fire was out. They went up and down the perpendicular cliffs of Mill Creek canyon on ropes of milkweed fiber--a quick and safe way down, since the canyon was well screened by trees that overhung its rim. They could bring up a catch of fish or basket of water, or let themselves down for a swim with far less trouble and time than it took to scramble up and down the little branching trails which led to the water's edge. Also, they preferred to use these trails sparingly so that they would not become too plainly marked but continue to appear no more than the runways of rabbits or weasels. They ground their acorns to flour on smooth stones and made the staple mush, cooking it in baskets. They wore capes of deerskin and wildcat, occasionally of bearskin. And they slept under blankets of rabbit skins. Ethnologists are agreed that they pursued a way of life the most totally aboriginal and primitive of any on the continent, at least after the coming of the white man to America.

From Theodora Kroeber's *Ishi in Two Worlds*.

REVIEWS

Middlecreek. Photo by Yank.

Review: *Becoming Nature: Learning the Language of Wild Animals and Plants.* Tamarack Song. Bear & Co, 2016.

Let me start with a caveat so we can get it out of the way: *Nature*, as a term, up front and center may turn some readers off.

My own thoughts on the term can be read in 'To Speak of Wildness' from *Black and Green Review* no 2, but to sum it up: I'm not a fan when a term like *wildness* could easily suffice. Granted the term is in the title, so maybe there was a bind or something. Either way, wildness by any other name is still wildness.

So, terminology aligned, let's get into it.

Tamarack Song is no stranger to taking on a mentor role to help individuals de-civilize their lives and reawaken our primal hunter-gatherer selves. That's what he does at his Teaching Drum Outdoor School and through his growing number of books and pamphlets. Like the others, that is reflected throughout this book.

Becoming Nature is a combination of exercises and provocation to move beyond our typical rational mind and to learn to trust our own animality to read languages, both verbal and non-verbal, both human and non-human. Tamarack may run a hunter-gatherer based Outdoor School, but his approach is innately different than the many survivalist-based "primitive skills" schools, gurus and the like. His approach is to focus on the mental struggles, to focus on domestication itself: to let the material and physical skillsets come as necessary.

That approach saturates this book and that is what gives it its strength. The focus here is to separate civilization's impact as the domination of the Rational Mind over what Tamarack calls our Animal Mind. How we get stuck in a rut of thinking instead of being. How we come to communicate in verbal communication over all other forms.

He harks upon the immediacy, openness and honesty implicit in the verbal and non-verbal languages of all life, from wolves to elk to trees without getting lost, like other writers have, in the hyperbole of anthropomorphizing the will of trees and rivers. He breaks down the approach that primitive skills and survivalist training instill in terms of tracking as science and identification as memorization.

If we experience the world of wildness as it is, we can forgo the hyper-by-the-book displacement that keeps us in the realm of spectators. He breaks down tracking from moving beyond categories of sign, gait and technicality to encourage closeness, observation and a playful sense of reenactment. It's a method that works.

And it works because of its simplicity.

Your Rational Mind might fear the foolishness of trying to walk through the forest as a deer does, but emulating the movements erupts empathy and understanding not just for how the animal sees the world, but how we view our surroundings. This is how hunter-gatherers teach their children to become master trackers.

This is just one aspect of the book, but it's a strong one. It holds all the nuances of perception that lie at the roots of the domestication process. It also holds all of the language that can make the cynic bat their eyes: to them, this will just be the blathering of back-to-nature hippie preaching an angelic, passive Nature. The language is there for that argument to be made, but it would miss the point entirely.

Fortunately, Tamarack sets out early on to make some of his most important distinctions in print. It's worth quoting here:

> *Some of us believe that animals in the wild dwell in a peaceful state of being and that we need to enter that state in order to find resonance with them. I know people who strive to tune in to the same serene wavelength to which they imagine the animals are attuned. The trouble is that in the natural world peace doesn't exist—it is merely an ideal-based Human construct. A natural-living animal may be relaxed, as mentioned earlier, but he is never at peace. He can't afford to be, as he needs to be ever alert and ready to spring in to action.*
>
> *…*
>
> *On the other side of the wall, natural-living creatures dwell in a state of dynamic tension, where there is neither peace nor war but simply a community of fully present, fully engaged plants and animals immersed in whatever the moment brings. It is this state that we want to enter.* (Pg 23)

Dynamic tension is a concept that makes the book worth reading alone. But there are plenty of other reasons. Depending on your level of engagement, a bit of the book might come across as pedantic, but it's written for anyone who picks it up. And it still has something to offer those of us who have been around.

The stories can become slightly belabored, but the point is there; the process of awakening our intuition becomes needlessly complicated by our Rational Mind interrupting what we feel and know intrinsically.

And there are times where he goes off script a bit from the excellent "dynamic tension" clarification as well. I too cringe over statements like the following that could undermine the clearly articulated earlier passage on "peace":

> *If we were to look at fishing or hunting from the perspective of the animal, we would see that we do not catch the Fish, but rather the Fish chooses the Worm and catches himself. Instead of us trapping an animal, she decides to walk in to the trap.* (Pg 230)

The book ends with a section on counting coup, or how to touch wild animals, either with or without their knowledge. Tamaracks himself speaks openly of his lack of a need or want to do it. But it's something that I've always felt had some unappealing bravado, yet the book doesn't present itself as a textbook.

And for a simple reason, it isn't meant to be one.

There are no mandatory exercises, tests or anything like that. It's a field guide, a book of stories, and a number of reflections on the paths people have taken towards rewilding.

There are caveats throughout that breaking domestication isn't an overnight process nor are there universals in it. None of the minor detractions that I found in the book would have led me to think that they were endemic of innately different approaches to wildness. Instead they bespeak the personal experience of wildness while highlighting the limited and limiting language we have to work with. And, in the end, that's the point: the perfect terminology will be experienced and lived, not spoken.

That's an end that I can aspire to.

Two European Thinkers to the Rescue!

A review of Peter Sloterdijk's *Stress and Freedom* & Alain Badiou's *The Century* by John Zerzan

Once upon a time there were very important contributions to social theory from Europe. Jacques Ellul's *The Technological Society* is invaluable, and the work of Jacques Camatte provided primary insights into domination and civilization. The once-interesting American journal *TELOS*, founded in the 1970s, began largely as a conduit for radical European thought. Detroit's *Fifth Estate* was also very important in this vein.

Today the situation is vastly different, as witness is Peter Sloterdijk's new book, *Stress and Freedom*. This very thin volume by the well-known Sloterdijk, author of *Critique of Cynical Reason* (1983), could hardly be weaker. It's something of a spin-off from his *Rage and Time* (2010).

Early on he remarks on the "maximum improbability" that civilization actually coheres, can continue to hold together. Sloterdijk is evidently unaware of fundamental social institutions such as division of labor and domestication—how their uninterrupted advance forges the grip of civilization, integrating individuals progressively, globally. Only the undoing of these foundational institutions would undo hyper-alienated, suicidal civilization. Sloterdijk is ignorant of the evidence that this is so.

He looks to Rousseau's *Reveries of the Solitary Walker* for his idea of how to contend with society. In the "Fifth Walk", Rousseau floats aimlessly in a small boat on a lake, finding peace in his purposelessness. Sloterdijk approves of this approach because of its inutility for the dominant, unfree order. He condemns Rousseau for later abandoning this "slacker" approach and moving on to his accommodationist Social Contract formulation...
only to abandon it himself and decide on a different solution to what he calls the forced labor camp of society: the power to be found in generosity, nobility of spirit: being Nice! This doesn't begin to describe this absurd little tome.

I was reminded of Alain Badiou's book on the 1900s, *The Century*. The well-known leftist philosopher here provides political and cultural commentary on the last century—without coming to grips with its real context or substance.

In Chapter One Badiou describes the Holocaust as accounting for the century being cursed. "At the heart of the century lies the Crime which provides the paragon for all the others: the destruction of the European Jews." I have no argument with this, but something is missing. Zygmunt Bauman's *Modernity and the Holocaust* provides some necessary depth: namely that there could have been no Holo-

Children of the New World review

caust without industrialism. This Crime is a product of mass society, not a sign of its failure. Not that this exhausts the topic, of course.

Nuclear proliferation in the second half of the century is another topic that Badiou could have explored in an instructive way. Of course it is a political issue, but nuclear proliferation is something more basic. It is a case of the inexorable march of technology itself, the product of a society in which technology is not seen as political. Badiou, who elsewhere mocked Heidegger's misgivings about technology, is blind to its historical pertinence. He would never problematize technology.

These two examples may suffice in exposing *The Century* as weak and largely irrelevant. One who embraces mass society, mass production, and the lethal fullness of civilization could hardly come up with anything qualitatively different.

As the once-Situationist Mustafa Khayati observed, "The university teaches one everything about society, except what it is."

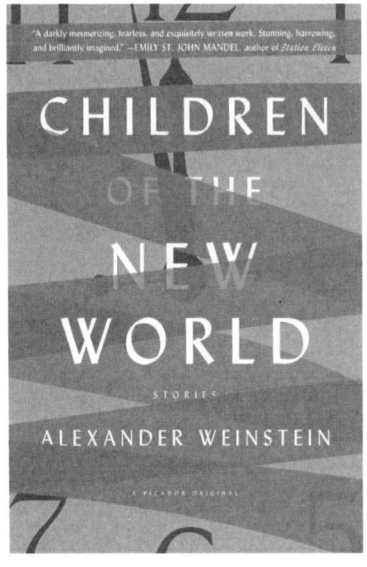

Children of the New World.
Alexander Weinstein.
Picador, 2016.

As the world becomes more literal, as television is based more around the ideal of documenting reality and as reality itself becomes more indecipherable from television and the internet, it becomes increasingly harder to remember the power of fiction as a tool of critique. Satire is increasingly replaced by trolling. Story telling often involves regurgitating old narratives and fantasy rather than hitting closer to the chest.

If there is one stronghold of fiction, it's in critiques of technology. And that is largely in the realm of science fiction. It would seem that yesterday's dystopias offered glimpses of potential technologies. The lessons of those stories were lost on the wide-eyed readers who sought to create the mystical machines from these fictional nightmares.

Children of the New World, a collection of short stories from Alexander Weinstein, joins in a growing expanse of books and TV shows that split fewer hairs than the acculturated dystopian stories. Less like *Terminator*, more like *Her*: these stories largely hit closer to home. Within the realm of probable technologies and our own lifetimes, the realism of this subtler dystopia lies within its familiarity.

These stories aren't reaching into the *Jetsons*. In some ways, they're visions of a near distant future where both the application and dispersion of new technologies are still unevenly handed, the memory of our present still looming. Innovations aren't flawless. But as an extension of the Brave New World programmers have thrust us into: there was no foresight, just technological might and a willing market. Some of the best stories in the book deal with when these advanced machines break down. It's more explorative of the emotional ambiguity of virtual and synthetic lives lost than militaristic cyborgs run amok.

And with references to planned obsolescence and subplots teetering on the edge of ethical and social insecurities surrounding the recently deployed means, the parallels here are hard to overlook.

These stories, by and large, just don't feel all that far-fetched.

As a collection, some stand out more than others. 'Saying Goodbye to Yang,' 'The Cartographers,' 'Children of the New World,' 'Openness,' and, my favorite, 'Migration,' have a number of similar themes. With these stories, it's very easy to see a lot of positive support for this book positioned as a continuation of the excellent British show, *Black Mirror*. The author carries the implicit vision that one of the likely next steps in technological integration moves beyond Google Glasses into a more intrusive kind of contact lens. Something that numerous programmers no doubt lust for and, even in their infancy, it is clear that this is an end goal for image scanning programs.

In that regard, 'Fall Line' feels very close to home and also shows the convergence of near term global warming and realistically looming technologies. 'Ice Age' goes a step beyond, replacing dystopian technology with the unleashed potential of climate instability. 'Moksha' is a good shot at ridiculing the hyper-mediated role of the mystical "Guru" offering electronic Enlightenment.

In short, all of the above stories, to me, feel more palatable as fiction and seem less like science fiction. They aren't unfamiliar plots compared to what Phillip K Dick would wrestle with, but they aren't as far away either. This stories aren't taking place on Mars, even if the Earth sounds a bit like it in 'Heartland.'

A handful of the stories are a little more out there. Perhaps not coincidentally, those are the ones I didn't care for as much. 'Excerpts from *The New World Authorized Dictionary*' fell flat for me. Neither 'The Pyramid and the Ass' nor its back-to-back and very quick 'Rocket Night' felt as organic. I appreciate the idea of 'A Brief History of the Failed Revolution,' another very short piece as a faux-historical essay on the "anti-interface movement." A clear warning shot for when the discussion comes too late, but it pales in comparison to the stories. For the most part, these represent the shortest pieces in the collection and with 13 pieces in total; they're a drop in an otherwise very compelling, engaging and foreboding bucket.

I haven't lost much sleep over the fantasies that programmers like Ray Kurzweil and Kevin Kelly offer over the realities they have helped create through striving towards a world of full technological integration and Artificial Intelligence. As Elon Musk's Space-X explodes and self-driving cars continue colliding, I breathe a sigh of relief. But these stories, matched with the last 10 or 20 years worth of hindsight, are a bit of a frightful reminder that the Brave New World may not be the well-oiled machine that Transhumanists have promised, but some of its worst threats may also not be that far off either.

Black and Green Press was founded in 2000 to spread, promote, and further green anarchist critique, dialog and praxis.

Also available from Black and Green Press:
- *Origins: A John Zerzan Reader - John Zerzan.*
  This reader includes the most fundamental and groundbreaking work from John over the past three decades collected in a single source.
- *For Wildness and Anarchy - Kevin Tucker.*
  This book collects essential essays from anarcho-primitivist Kevin Tucker, originally printed between 2000-2010.
- *Liminal: A Novella - Natasha Alvarez.*
  Liminal grabs you by the heart and brings you down into that uncomfortable space between love, rewilding, and the suffocating despair of a civilization in decline.
- *Black and Green Review 1, 2 & 3.*
  Like what you see here?

To order, check our website: blackandgreenpress.org
Distributed in Europe by Active Distribution.